MORE WORK FOR MOTHER

This is a unique book on a subject that has recently aroused much feminist interest – housework. It is a history of three centuries of household technologies, gracefully and wittily written. While new inventions industrialized the home and freed the man from domestic work, the woman continues to have a full load of chores, working to a higher and higher standard of cleanliness and elegance.

The author analyses the roads not taken – how economic forces led to privatized and individual appliances instead of public ones – communally owned vacuum cleaners, laundries, etc. She also shows how gender influences the conception, design and marketing of domestic technology. The book includes essays on a number of related topics, such as the rise of the consumer, the decline of domestic servants, changes in utilities and transport (preconditions for the freezer and the supermarket) and the lot of the working mother. There are also photo essays on transportation, washday, the rich and poor and the transition from housewifery to housework.

Ruth Schwartz Cowan is Associate Professor of History at the State University of New York, Stony Brook.

MORE WORK FOR MOTHER

The Ironies of Household Technology from the Open Hearth to the Microwave

RUTH SCHWARTZ COWAN

with a new preface

'an association in which the free development of each is
the condition of the free development of all'

Free Association Books / London / 1989

Published 1989 by
Free Association Books
26 Freegrove Road
London N7 9RQ

British Library Cataloguing in Publication Data

Cowan, Ruth Schwartz, *1941–*
More work for mother : the ironies of
household technology from the open hearth to
the microwave.
1. Housework, Sociological perspectives
I. Title
306'.36

ISBN 1–85343–076–5

Printed and bound in Great Britain by
Short Run Press, Exeter

For

Betty Schwartz

and

Louis E. Schwartz

with love

Contents

Contents

Picture Essays

Preface (1989)

A funny thing has happened in the twenty years since I began the research on which this book was based: studying housework has become a respectable pursuit.

When I started on the project that resulted in *More Work for Mother*, my colleagues at the university at which I teach thought that I was crazy. In my absence they probably joked about me in the coffee lounge – 'What could there possibly be to say about the history of such a dumb thing as a washing machine?', 'And even if it turns out to be interesting, how could a young scholar, without tenure, risk her future on such an off-the-wall subject?' Clearly I was 'tetched' (crazed) by feminist enthusiasm; surely I would come back to my senses eventually.

Well, I didn't come back to my senses, and within a few years I had a good deal of company in my apparent insanity. What had started out as a slow trickle in the early 1970s turned into a minor flood by the mid-1980s: economists, sociologists, historians, even a literary critic or two, were all becoming fascinated not only by housework but also by the equipment with which it is done. Papers were being presented at scholarly meetings. Grant proposals got written – and a goodly number (at least in the United States) got funded. Articles began to appear in professional journals. Books were published; within the last twelve months alone I think I have reviewed four of them. Museums that used to concern themselves only with paintings or stuffed animals began mounting exhibits about the evolution of the ordinary kitchen. Several oral history projects were organized to record the experiences (who could have believed it, back in 1970!) of ordinary American housewives.

And it wasn't just Americans who were jumping on the housework bandwagon. When I opened up my file labelled 'new material' in order to start writing this preface, I found, at the top, and in

Preface (1989)

this precise order: a letter from the head of a research team in Sweden; a report on the time expenditures of French housewives; a paper about household technology in Western Australia (based on oral history interviews); a bibliography compiled by a home economist in West Virginia; a paper written by a Canadian, exploring the multiple meanings of such common housework expressions as 'blue Monday'; and a set of cartoons clipped from successive issues of the *Washington Post*.

No one who has been familiar with the history of academe in the last twenty years can have much doubt about why housework has suddenly become a respectable subject for enquiry in disciplines other than home economics. The explanation is composed (proportions may differ in different locales) partly of the growth in the numbers of female scholars; partly of concern about the growing numbers of married women and mothers in the labour force; partly of expanding interest either in women's history or in what is sometimes called the 'new' social history; partly of the growing scholarly reputation of the Annales school; and partly of the popularity of deconstructionist methodology. People who were trained only to examine the abstruse and the esoteric have lately developed an interest in everyday life – and nothing could be more mundane, more thoroughly 'everyday' (as every housewife knows) than housework.

The radical feminists of the 60s and 70s played an important role in calling attention to housework, because it was they who first noticed, and then began loudly to insist, that 'the personal is also political': that public lives were, somehow, inseparable from private lives; indeed, that the conceptual division between 'that which is public' and 'that which is private' had been, and continued to be, one of the convenient ways in which the subservient position of women was repeatedly disguised, hidden from view. What does it mean to organize a political movement, the radical feminists asked, in which all the women type and stuff envelopes and all the men give speeches? What does it mean, their descendants have learned to ask, to campaign in favour of 'family values' when your grown children do not speak to you? And what precisely does it mean to be in favour of women's liberation while refusing to change the baby's nappies?

One of the most hostile reviewers of *More Work for Mother* complained bitterly that my argument is conservative because I suggest that women's liberation begins (and ought to begin) at home, that feminists ought to get their act together over the nappies and the laundry before taking on the legislatures and the corporations. This does not seem to me to be a conservative notion at all, but one which derives directly from the lesson the radical feminists were trying to teach. The notion that 'the personal is political' is one of the major contributions that radical feminism has made, not only to scholarship, but also to the campaign for equality, and I take it to apply to political action as well as to scholarship. If it is true (and I think it is) that we cannot understand modern (public) history without knowing what was also happening in people's (private) lives, then it is also true that we cannot (and ought not to) devise a progressive policy for women without knowing and assessing what is going on around the kitchen table and in the extramarital bed. Here lies another part of the reason why so many people, most especially feminists, have been turning their attention to housework in the past decade.

Apparently, in the United States, there are a few signs that patterns of housework behaviour have also been changing. Several recent statistical studies of housework have indicated not only that women are doing somewhat less of it, but also that men are doing somewhat more. John P. Robinson (now of the University of Maryland, formerly of the University of Michigan) has systematically studied daily time use in the United States over the past twenty years. He concludes that there was a six-to-one ratio between women's and men's share of housework in 1965; this had changed to three-to-one ten years later and to two-to-one by 1985. * Sex segregation continues to exist in the American household workforce (men do most of the odd jobs and home repairs; women most of the cooking, cleaning, laundry and infant care), but men have increased the time that they spend in certain gender-neutral chores (such as bill paying, gardening, transporting and shopping)

---

* John P. Robinson, 1988, 'Who's doing the housework?', *American Demographics*, December: 25–8, 63–4. Robinson's figures, however, do not consider childcare as part of housework.

Preface (1989)

while women have been spending less time overall – thus accounting for the changing ratios. If prospects for completely equal and completely gender-blind division of household work don't look bright for the immediate future, those of us who have been writing about (and fighting about) housework in the last twenty years can at least be cheered by the current US statistics, while those who would like to make the study of housework a continuing, vital enterprise will still know that there is yet more work to be done.

What remains to be done? Quite a lot. First, most of what we now know about housework in the developed economies concerns mainstream households. In the United States, for example, we know very little about patterns of housework amongst minority groups, especially those (such as the blacks and the native Americans) whose history has been, economically, very different from that of most other Americans. Second, we know less than we ought to know about the interaction between patterns of household labour and patterns of workforce participation. Some scholars have argued that women earn less than men because of the particular pattern into which household labour is divided; since women bear most of the responsibility for the work that is essential to the maintenance and sustenance of people's health (especially cooking and home nursing), this argument runs, they cannot really act as free agents in the labour market. Other scholars see this approach as putting the cart before the horse; they argue, in reverse, that the household division of labour is a direct function of the low status that women occupy in the labour market. One telling piece of information in this connection concerns the behaviour of homosexual couples (both male and female); apparently, in such couples, it is frequently the case that the person who is paid the least is the person who does most of the housework.* If such studies were followed up, and if, in general, we had more systematic efforts to sort out the varied relations between the work that people do when they are being paid and the work that they do for free, then not only might scholarly differences of opinion be resolved, but more useful, and more truly progressive, political programmes might be devised.

* Philip Blumstein and Pepper Schwartz, 1983, *American Couples: Money, Work and Sex.* New York: Morrow, pp. 148–51.

We ought also to know more about houseworkers – the people who do housework for pay – than we do. In every country about which I have immediate knowledge, they remain underpaid, underorganized – and also under-studied. Similarly we don't know as much as we ought to know about the gender division of labour in housework. How far back in Western history does it run? Do other cultures divide the same work differently, define it differently? Why, in the West, are certain aspects of housework so laden with emotion. So tied to concepts of masculinity and femininity, that few women will unambivalently give up control over the work, and few men unambivalently do it? This last is one of the questions I would most like to have attended to when writing *More Work for Mother*, but I felt unable, both because of lack of time and lack of training, to take it on.

There are a few other things that I wish, now, that I had had the patience or the foresight to have investigated when I was doing the research on which this book was based. Two important technological systems (the communication system and the health-care system) were virtually neglected: the former because I simply did not have the energy to do the research; the latter because I did not fully understand its significance until later. Both would make wonderful subjects for yet another book, and each will be difficult to unravel historically.

The telephone is now central to the functioning of most households (as we all discover when ours go on the blink), but it will not be easy to discover when this came to be the case and what precisely its impact, both on work processes and on attitudes, has been. The history of the household health-care system is an even more complex topic, but one which may very well hold a most crucial key to understanding not only the history of housework, but also the history of married women's workforce participation. In the pre-industrial world housewives were nurses; they cared for people who were sick and (in any given community or even any given household) someone was likely to be sick a good deal of the time. In the first stages of industrialization nurses could not be spared from the home without threatening the health of everyone else who lived there, which may be why infant mortality rates were highest and life expectancy lowest amongst the working poor.

Preface (1989)

But in the twentieth century medical technologies of various sorts (ranging from vitamin supplemented wheat, to pasteurized milk, to polio vaccines and antibiotics) have eliminated some of the need for long-term household nursing, and technologies of other sorts (X-ray machines, anaesthetics, intravenous feeding devices) have drawn some sick people out of their homes and into hospitals. When it comes to nursing, there really does appear to be less work for mother to do at home and (this is also important) less need for her to be held at home in reserve for emergencies. If my hypothesis is correct, then there really is a technological system which has shortened the time required to do housework and freed women to enter the workforce; it just isn't the system I (or most other people) would have initially looked at. I hope someone will take up this health-care hypothesis and see if it can be made to hold water. The detective work involved will be fascinating – and the pay-off at the end may well be the set of crucial insights that will finally make coherent sense out of the history of housework.

Finally, if I had the energy to write *More Work for Mother* over again, I would emphasize the central cultural importance of housework. All of the developed economies of the world depend on the unpaid work of housewives: *all* of them, whether they are capitalist, socialist or mixed economies. At various times and in various places experiments in eliminating (by communalizing) housework have occurred but none (repeat, *none*) have lasted for very long or spread very far. We can argue endlessly (and scholars have) about why this should be so: in Chapter five I suggest (although the suggestion is not very well developed) an ideological explanation, that Judaeo–Christian–Islamic cultures place a high premium on privacy. Other scholars believe that the cultural supremacy of the private family household results from the constraints of capitalism, while others argue that the cause lies in patriarchy; still others that it lies in biology. Yet the fact is undeniable: the private dwelling, cared for by those who live in it, is the bedrock on which all the developed economies have been built. This means that in the recorded past as well as in the foreseeable future our cultures have depended and will continue to depend on the unpaid work that housewives do.

Many people seem to have read *More Work for Mother* as if it denigrates the role and minimizes the importance of housewives. Nothing could have been farther from my intention. I do a lot of housework myself (as do the other members of my household) and I have nothing but admiration for those who devote themselves to it and/or do it well. I wish I fully understood why so many people either hate the work or, in their hate, can barely see that it exists. There are scholars who study housework whose idea of utopia would be the elimination of the work they study; I am not one of them. My idea of utopia would be a world in which houseworkers and teachers would be paid as well (and trained as well) as programmers and physicians; in which housework had so much status that men, women and children would do it happily and unambivalently; and in which employers and governments would be so convinced of the importance of housework that they would construct their enterprises to conform with its constraints (developing job sharing plans, providing benefits for part-time workers, establishing on-site daycare centres – to suggest just a few possibilities) instead of the other way around.

Although this book focuses on household technology, I hope that you will come to understand, as you read it, that the vision which informed it was social, not technological. Years ago many people believed that utopias could be achieved through invention (if not through the design of an improved dishwasher, then certainly by the creation of a perfect robot). In the course of writing *More Work for Mother* I became convinced not only that this was unlikely (since it certainly hadn't happened in the past), but also that it was impossible. Real social change can only occur when people's attitudes and behaviour change. Technologies can affect our attitudes and our behaviour of course, but their effects are neither instigating, controlling nor determinate. People are still in control, not machines, which means that ultimately we cannot blame what we do not like (nor commend what we do) on the objects with which we have surrounded ourselves.

GLEN COVE, NEW YORK
January 1989

Acknowledgments

I have always been puzzled by the convention that suggests that authors should leave their most heartfelt acknowledgment for last. Mine will come first, because that is where it belongs. During the past fifteen years, my husband, Neil M. Cowan, has treated my research and writing as if they were welcome and honored third and fourth parties to our marriage. He is the dictionary definition incarnate of the word *helpmate,* and I wish that I had words sufficient for thanks.

All scholars hope to leave a legacy for the future; the ultimate inspiration for this book has been the three people who are my personal legacy to the future: Jennifer Rose, May Deborah, and Sarah Kiva Cowan. I would not have persisted as long as I have with the effort that this book required had I not been blessed with three marvelous daughters. I hope that, when they reach an age to make sense of such things, they will understand that my love for them inspired every page.

Financial support from three different institutions freed me from my teaching obligations during a number of semesters, allowed me to employ research assistants, and paid for some of the expenses normally encountered in historical research. The National Science Foundation (under grants SOC–7602424A02 and SOC–7912968), the Research Foundation of the State University of New York (under its program of summer research grants to faculty members), and the American Council of Learned Societies have all underwritten this endeavor, and I am grateful for their support. Ronald Overmann, program officer for the history and philosophy of science at the National Science Foundation, was especially helpful over several years, and I hope that he understands how much not only I but all historians and philosophers of science owe to him.

Acknowledgments

My résumé is dotted with governmental acronyms because I have been supported, at least in part, with public funds from the time that I graduated from high school until the present. When I was only sixteen years old, I held a New York State Regents Scholarship; this was followed a few years later by an NSF Undergraduate Summer Fellowship, and then by National Defense Education Act graduate fellowships, by various grants and fellowships from other federal agencies, and by fifteen years of employment at a tax-supported university. I must, therefore, acknowledge that all the tax-paying citizens of the United States, and most especially those who also pay taxes in New York State, have—however unwittingly—made it possible for me to write this book. I hope that at least a few of them will decide that the investment paid off.

My academic training was in the discipline called the "history of science." When I began this project I knew almost nothing about the history of technology, social history, women's history, or, for that matter, American history. As a consequence I have depended, repeatedly, on the encouragement, support, advice, and good counsel that I received from practitioners of these latter disciplines whom I am pleased now to count among my colleagues and friends. For countless conversations, critical readings, gentle nudgings, research clues, relevant citations, and supportive letters, my thanks go to: Riva Berleant-Schiller, Rose Coser, Eugene Ferguson, Dolores Hayden, Thomas Parke Hughes, Melvin Kranzberg, Eric Lampard, Ned Landsman, Gene Lebovics, Gloria Main, Carroll Pursell, Mark Rose, Joel Rosenthal, Naomi Rosenthal, Fred Weinstein, George Wise and Bob Young. I fear that some of the people on this list may be angered by some of the views that I express in this book, and may wish that they had never proffered their assistance, but I am grateful for it nonetheless and hopeful that we will remain friends and colleagues however the historiographic chips may fall.

Similarly, I knew almost nothing about what is involved in publishing a book when I began converting my research into a manuscript, but the good offices of Alice Fahs made it possible for me to meet Jane Isay, whose enthusiasm encouraged me to finish

Acknowledgments

the manuscript, and Phoebe Hoss, whose critical acumen saved me from more embarrassments than I care to recall.

Many current and former graduate students in the History Department of the State University of New York at Stony Brook have worked with me on this project. In some instances, their contributions are acknowledged in the text; but in other instances, I could not do so without awkwardness because the material that they located, or the data that they accumulated, or the books that they summarized, were never specifically cited. Hence I want to take this opportunity to tell each of them that, even if the projects on which they worked so assiduously do not emerge clearly on these pages, my understanding of what I was doing would have been profoundly constricted without their help. With apologies for my more than occasional incoherence and disorganization, I extend my thanks to: Dominick Cavallo, Evelyn Foundos, David McDonald, Nancy Marr, Valerie Parks, Timothy Patterson, David Schmitz, Susan Strasser, and, most especially, to Virginia Quiroga whose enthusiasm and patience made the last two hectic years so pleasurable. In addition, I want to pay special tribute to Richard Grant, who, as an undergraduate at Stony Brook, helped me for more than a year, without compensation, simply for the joy of doing research.

Between 1978 and 1980, I had the good fortune to participate in an unusual educational experiment: The Federated Learning Communities Program on Technology, Values and Society. The Federated Learning Communities was the brainchild of Patrick Hill, then a faculty member at the State University of New York at Stony Brook; and the Program on Technology, Values and Society, which he directed, encouraged eight members of the faculty to share their views on those subjects through interdisciplinary teaching and weekly seminars. Every chapter of this book benefited, in some way, from the insights that I acquired during those years, and I am pleased to acknowledge my debt to the seven people who struggled through them with me: Ted Goldfarb, Don Ihde, Jack Ludwig, Juliet Papadakos, Chick Perrow, Marshall Spector, and John Truxal.

Every scholarly work depends upon the goodwill and the la-

Acknowledgments

bors of people who either remain anonymous or are too numerous to mention: those who type successive drafts of a manuscript, who assemble and catalogue archives, who supervise reference desks and interlibrary loan services, who prepare indexes or index abstracts. Thus, I cannot let pass the opportunity to thank all those others who have been of such help to me. In closing, I want them to know that, were it within my power, I would see to doubling (nay, trebling!) their salaries immediately.

Glen Cove, New York
April 1983

More Work for Mother

Chapter 1

An Introduction:
Housework and Its Tools

INDUSTRIALIZATION transformed every American household sometime between 1860 and 1960. For some families, this transition occurred very slowly: each generation lived in homes that were just a bit "more modern" than the generation immediately before it, and the working lives of the members of each adjacent generation were not so profoundly different as to leave unbridgeable communication gaps between them. For other families, the transition was more rapid; in these families, as the result of immigration or urbanization or sudden affluence, one generation of people may have been living and working in conditions that would have been familiar in the Middle Ages, and the very next generation may have been completely modernized—inhabitants, as it were, of a totally different world. Yet despite these differences in pacing, if we consider the broad spectrum of American households, from rich to poor, from the most urban to the most rural, a simple generalization can describe what happened in the century that was ushered in by the Civil War: before 1860 almost all families did their household work in a manner that their forebears could have imitated—to wit, in a pre-industrial mode; after 1960 there were just a few families (and those either because they were very poor or very isolated or ideologically committed to agrarianism) who were not living in industrialized homes and pursuing industrialized forms of labor within them.

Now usually, when we think of the word *industrialization,* we think in terms not of homes but of factories and assembly lines and railroads and smokestacks. In our textbooks of history and economics and sociology, the terms *industrialization* and *home* are usually connected by the word *impact,* and we are usually asked to consider what happened when one term (industrialization) caused some significant economic process (productive work or the manufacture of goods for sale in the marketplace) to be removed from the domain of the other term (home). Implicitly (and sometimes explicitly) we are given the impression that industrialization occurred *outside* the four walls of home. The popular imagination goes one step farther; industrialization is conceived as being not just *outside* the home but virtually in *opposition* to it. Homes are idealized as the places to which we would like to retreat when the world of industrialization becomes too grim to bear; home is where the "heart" is; industry is where "dogs are eating dogs" and "only money counts."

Under the sway of such ideas, we have had some difficulty in acknowledging that industrialization has occurred just as rapidly within our homes as outside them. We resolutely polish the Early American cabinets that hide the advanced electronic machines in our kitchens and resolutely believe that we will escape the horrors of modernity as soon as we step under the lintels of our front doors. We are thus victims of a form of cultural obfuscation, for in reality kitchens are as much a locus for industrialized work as factories and coal mines are, and washing machines and microwave ovens are as much a product of industrialization as are automobiles and pocket calculators. A woman who is placing a frozen prepared dinner into a microwave oven is involved in a work process that is as different from her grandmother's methods of cooking as building a carriage from scratch differs from turning bolts on an automobile assembly line; an electric range is as different from a hearth as a pneumatic drill is from a pick and shovel. As industrialization took some forms of productive work out of our homes, it left other forms of work behind. That work, which we now call "housework" (see page 17), has been transformed in the preceding hundred years, and so have the implements with which it is done; this is the process that I have chosen to call the "industrialization of the home."

Households did not become industrialized in the same way that other workplaces did; there are striking differences between housework and other forms of industrialized labor. Most of the people who do housework do not get paid for it, despite the fact that it is, for many of them, a full-time job. They do not have job descriptions or time clocks or contractual arrangements; indeed, they cannot fairly be said even to have employers. Most of their work is performed in isolation, whereas most of their contemporaries work in the company of hundreds, perhaps even thousands of other adults. Over the years, market labor has become increasingly specialized, and the division of labor has become increasingly more minute; but housework has not been affected by this process. The housewife is the last jane-of-all trades in a world from which the jacks-of-all trades have more or less disappeared; she is expected to perform work that ranges from the most menial physical labor to the most abstract of mental manipulations and to do it all without any specialized training. These various characteristics of household work have led some analysts to suggest that housework (or the household economy) is the last dying gasp of feudalism, a remnant of precapitalist conditions somehow (miraculously) vaulting the centuries unimpaired, the last surviving indicator of what the Western world was like before the market economy reared its ugly head.*

Perhaps this is true, but there are other sides to the coin; indus-

---

*This is one of the many interesting insights about housework which can be derived from reading the Marxist debate about the relations between household and market labor.[1]

trialized housework resembles industrialized market labor in significant ways. Modern housework depends upon nonhuman energy sources, just as advanced industrialized manufacturing systems do. Those of us who regularly perform household chores
may regard this as an erroneous, or at least an ironic, statement,
but it is nonetheless true. The computer programmer turns an
electric switch in order to power the tool that makes his or her
labor possible—and so does the houseworker; we are all equally
dependent upon the supply lines that keep these energy sources
flowing to us. We may be thoroughly exhausted by our labors at
the end of a day of housework, but without electricity or the
combustion of certain organic compounds (like natural gas or
liquid petroleum or gasoline), our work could not be performed
at all. None of us relies any longer solely on animal or human
energy to do our work.

Thus, even if the household is an isolated work environment,
it is also part of a larger economic and social system; and if it did
not constantly interact with this system, it could not function at
all—making it no different from the manufacturing plant outside
the city or the supermarket down the street. The pre-industrial
household could, if necessary, function without a supportive
community—as is demonstrated, most clearly, in the settlement
pattern of our frontiers. Individual families were capable, when
need arose, of supplying themselves with their own subsistence
and protective needs, year in and year out. Very few families are
capable of doing that any longer. Very few of us, for example,
would know how to make our own bread, even if our lives (quite
literally) depended upon it; if we could find and follow a recipe
for making the bread, it is highly unlikely that we could (1) grow
the wheat, (2) prepare it properly for use in bread, (3) obtain and
keep the yeast alive, or (4) build and maintain a suitable fixture
for baking it. We live in isolated households and do our marketing for the tiniest of consumption units; but, to get our bread to
the table, we still need bakers, agribusiness, utility companies,
and stove manufacturers. This is the second significant sense in
which household work and market work have come to resemble
one another.

Finally, both household labor and market labor are today performed with tools that can be neither manufactured nor understood by the workers who use them. Industrialized households contain vastly more implements than pre-industrial ones did, and those implements are much more likely to have been made by persons and in locales that are totally foreign to their eventual users. Pre-industrial households purchased some of their tools (especially those made of pottery, glass, or metal), but today we buy almost everything we use—from forks to microwave ovens. As a result, despite the diversity of what is available for purchase, almost nothing that we buy has been made "for us," to fit special needs that we may have. In addition, the implements that we have today are more complicated than the implements with which our foreparents worked—so much more complicated that most of us either cannot or will not repair them ourselves. If a brick fell out of an eighteenth-century fireplace, someone in the household would probably have known how to make and apply the mortar with which to replace the brick. If, on the other hand, a resistance coil comes loose on a twentieth-century electric oven, no one in the household is likely either to know what to do or to have the appropriate tools at hand. In these senses houseworkers are as alienated from the tools with which they labor as assembly-line people and blast furnace operators.

In sum, we can say that there are three significant senses in which housework differs from market work (in being—most commonly—unpaid labor, performed in isolated workplaces, by unspecialized workers) and three significant senses in which the two forms of work resemble each other (in utilizing nonhuman —or non-animal—energy sources, which create dependency on a network of social and economic institutions and are accompanied by alienation* from the tools that make the labor possible). If we take all six of these criteria and group them together, we will have a good definition of industrialization. Then we might be able to see that, in the West over the last two hundred years, women's work has been differentiated from men's by being incompletely industrialized or by being industrialized in a somewhat different manner.

---

*I am using the term *alienation* here in the psychosocial sense of "strangeness."

How—and why—this situation came to pass is one of the great unresolved puzzles of Western history. Although the social arrangements to which we have become accustomed seem sometimes to have a rationale and a life of their own, there really is no *a priori* reason why things should have worked out in quite the way they did. Even if we assume, as the anthropologists tell us we should, that every society will construct some sexual division of labor for itself, there is no apparent reason why, for example, men's work could not have been incompletely industrialized instead of women's. We might then have had communal kitchens, to which we would repair for all of our food needs, but household metal goods that we forged in smithies in our own backyards; or perhaps electronic looms in every kitchen and communal nurseries in which children of our female physicians could be cared for and reared. Clearly we have the technological and the economic capacity to have constructed our society this way, but for some complex of reasons we did not do so.

This book is an attempt to discover some of those reasons and to describe the historical path that led us from one particular pattern of work to another. We all know that work is one of the activities through which we define ourselves as we mature; by analogy we might say that a society does the same thing, defining itself through the work that it does as it matures. Social scientists know that the industrialization of work has been one of the most traumatic processes of recent Western history, and yet work has not been a particularly popular focus for historical attention—and housework even less so. I regard this omission as unfortunate, even tragic. In the last decade or two, some historians have attempted to repair the damage and to write the history of work as it has altered for different classes of people in the last few centuries; but, as admirable as these studies have been, they have focused almost exclusively on market labor—work that is done in order to produce products or services to be sold.[2] Yet in many ways housework is more characteristic of our society than market work is. It is the first form of work that we experience as infants, the form of work that the largest proportion of us (to wit, almost all women) identify as the work that will be the principal definition of our adulthood.

An Introduction: Housework and Its Tools

It is also the form of work that each of us—male and female, adult and child—pursues for at least some part of every week; and it is the occupational category that encompasses the single largest fraction of our population—to wit, full-time house-wives. The absolute number of full-time housewives may be decreasing with every passing year, but more people spend their days in this "peculiar" form of labor than in either of the two more "standard" forms—blue-collar or white-collar work. If work shapes individual lives and social forms, and if industriali-zation has reshaped work in the past two centuries, then to fail to understand the history of housework is to fail to understand ourselves. If housework is a dominant social activity, and if it has been only incompletely industrialized, then, as a society, we may not be as industrialized as we think we are, or as "modern" as our pundits would have us believe.

In truth, however, this book has a dual focus. As its title is meant to suggest, it is a history not just of housework but also of the tools with which that work is done: household technology. Human beings are tool-using animals; indeed, some anthropolo-gists believe that, along with speech, the ability to use and to refine our tools is precisely what sets us apart from other species of primates. One of the few generalizations that can be made about people living under vastly different social conditions is that they all use tools to do their work. Because of our peculiar set of cultural blinders, we do not ordinarily associate "tools" with "women's work"—but household tools there nonetheless are and always have been.

Tools are not passive instruments, confined to doing our bid-ding, but have a life of their own. Tools set limits on our work; we can use them in many different ways, but not in an infinite number of ways. We try to obtain the tools that will do the jobs that we want done; but, once obtained, the tools organize our work for us in ways that we may not have anticipated. People use tools to do work, but tools also define and constrain the ways in which it is possible and likely that people will behave. Here is a simple example. In my house, we recently installed standard wall cabinets with doors above the counters in our kitchen; these cabinets are tools that we intended to use as containers for other tools (mostly notably our dishes), with the specific intention that they would make those other tools easy to locate when needed and would keep them clean between washings. Before we had the cabinets we kept our dishes on a remodeled floor-to-ceiling bookcase that did not have cabinet doors; we thought our new cabinets would make our housework easier to perform. Before we installed our new cabinets, the process of having our table set for dinner involved: (1) an adult's decision that it was time to have the table set; (2) the communication of that decision to children—which communication needed to be repeated more than once and in increasingly insistent tones; (3) the removal of the dishes by the children and their placement, in appropriate order, on the table. The adults in the family functioned as managers and decision makers; the children, as workers—often workers under duress. Our new cabinets have changed all of our behavior patterns. Since the children are too small to reach the shelves on which the dishes are now placed, the adults must become involved in the work process. Not only must my husband and I make the decision that it is time to set the table, but we must also do part of the physical labor; we have ceased to be the managers of the work and have been forced to become unwilling participants in it. In addition, if we have erred in our labor ("But, Mommy, you didn't *give* me the water pitcher!"), then we must be responsible for correcting our errors. The acquisition of this one new tool has temporarily (at least until the children grow taller) altered our domestic work process as well as the set of emotional entanglements that that work process entailed. At the very least, the acquisition of that new tool will now require us to acquire yet another tool (a stool) in order to return to the *status quo ante*—a behavioral alteration that was also unintended.

Multiply this small example millions of times, and you will have some sense of what it means to say that tools are not entirely passive instruments. This is precisely the lesson that the sorcerer was trying to teach his apprentice in the famous fable. Our tools are not always at our beck and call. The less we know about them, the more likely it is that they will command us, rather than the other way round.

An Introduction: Housework and Its Tools

Thus the history of housework cannot properly be understood without the history (which is separate) of the implements with which it is done—and vice versa. The relation is reciprocal, perhaps even dialectic. Tools have set limits on what could be done in households, but inventors have repeatedly broken through those limits by fashioning new tools. The tools have reorganized the work process, creating new needs, for which some people have attempted to provide new tools—and so on. What makes the history of household technology separate and distinguishable from the history of housework is the existence of social institutions that mediate the availability of tools to households. In times past, these mediators were institutions such as blacksmith shops and blacksmith guilds, peddlers, and international trade arrangements. As industrialization has progressed, the nature of the institutions has changed—we now have manufacturing firms and advertising agencies and market researchers; but the impact of the institutions remains structurally the same. They mediate the availability of tools by keeping some tools off the market and promoting others, or by organizing the pricing and distribution of tools. Just as the history of industrialization cannot properly be written without the history of housework, so the history of household technology cannot be written without the history of the social and economic institutions that have affected the character and the availability of the tools with which housework is done.

In order to make the complex task of writing this multifocused history less daunting, I have made use of two organizing concepts: *work process* and *technological system.* Both awkward phrases need to be explained before I proceed farther. The phrase *work process* is used instead of the simpler term *work* in order to highlight the fact that no single part of housework is a simple, homogenous activity. One might be tempted to say that housework can be divided into a series of separable tasks—cooking, cleaning, laundering, child care, et cetera. This analysis does not go far enough, however, because each of these tasks is linked to others that it does not resemble. Cooking, for example, involves the treatment of raw or semi-raw foodstuffs so that they can, or will, be consumed; that much is obvious. Perhaps not so obviously, cooking also involves the procurement of those foodstuffs (by buying them or raising them), and their storage and prior preparation (by canning, salting, freezing, refrigerating, et cetera), the maintenance of the energy source (stoking the hearth, damping the stove, adding the coal) that is used to do the cooking, the maintenance and cleaning of the tools that are used to do the cooking, and the disposal of the waste that results from the process. Similarly, laundering is a matter not just of washing clothes but of moving them from place to place, of drying them, perhaps ironing them and putting them away, as well as acquiring the chemical agents—most notably soap and water—that will assist in the process. The concept of work process reminds us that housework (indeed, all work) is a series not simply of definable tasks but of definable tasks that are necessarily linked to one another: you cannot cook without an energy source, and you cannot launder without water. This concept also becomes important when we try to discover whether industrialization has made housework easier. We must ask not only whether one activity has been altered, but also whether the chain in which that activity is a link has been transformed. If, for example, we view cleaning rugs as work, then we might reasonably argue that this work can be done faster and with less expenditure of human energy with a vacuum cleaner instead of a broom. If, on the other hand, we view cleaning rugs as a work process, then we might see that it is composed of several activities (moving the instrument, moving the rugs, removing the accumulated dust, and so on), and that at least one of these (moving the instrument) is much harder to do with the vacuum cleaner than with the broom. In addition, if it is more likely that the presence of the vacuum cleaner will increase the frequency with which the work is done (once a week instead of once a season or once a year), or will involve fewer people in the work (for example, by releasing the stronger members of the household from the obligation to move the rugs outside, or the younger members from the obligation of beating them), then the question of whether cleaning a rug has been made easier or faster by the advent of vacuum cleaners becomes considerably more difficult to answer. Easier for whom? Faster for whom? Under what conditions? The history of housework studied in the light of the concept of work process, turns up some surprises, and some of these surprises will be central to my analysis.

Just as the activities of which housework is composed are complex, linked, and heterogeneous, so are the implements with which it is done—a situation that justifies my using the second of those awkward phrases, *technological system.* Each implement used in the home is part of a sequence of implements—a system—in which each must be linked to others in order to function appropriately. To put it bluntly: an electric range will not be much good if electric current is missing, and a washing machine cannot function in the absence of running water and grated soap. I have often thought that if the concept of a technological system were more generally understood, no one would have poked fun at the inhabitants of Appalachia who were reported (perhaps apocryphally) to have put coal in the bathtubs that were given them through federal largesse during the Depression. If you were obliged to haul your bathwater from stream or pump to stove and tub, what would you want with a four-footed, enamel-over-cast-iron bathtub on your porch? A stream, a pond, a lake, or a lightweight zinc tub would be infinitely preferable. Heavy bathtubs (indeed, recessed unmovable bathtubs) are part of a technological system that contains (among other things) municipal reservoirs, underground pipelines, hot water heaters, not to speak of soap-manufacturing plants and textile mills (would you bathe very often if you had no towels?). Some of those items could be dropped from the system without entirely altering it (one could make one's own soap if it came to that), but others (the drainpipes, for example) are absolutely essential.

The concept of a technological system becomes important in understanding the processes by which the American home became industrialized. On a superficial level, the industrialization of the home appears to have been composed of millions of individual decisions freely made by householders: the Jones's down the block decided to junk their washtub and buy a washing machine, and the Smiths around the corner fired the maid and bought a vacuum cleaner. On this level, industrialization of the home seems to have been the product of the perpetually rising expectations of American consumers—expectations that had been rising from at least the 1830s, when de Tocqueville toured the country, if not before. But the matter is not as simple as that. The Jones's washing machine would not have done them a bit of good if the town fathers had not decided to create a municipal water system several years earlier, and if the local gas and electric company had not gotten around to running wires and pipes into the neighborhood. Similarly, the Smiths' new vacuum cleaner might have cost a good deal more than it did (and might have thus forestalled the Smiths' decision to replace a maid with it) if the managers of the company that made it had not earlier decided to shift to assembly-line modes of production. To put the case more generally: the industrialization of the home was determined partly by the decisions of individual householders but also partly by social processes over which the householders can be said to have had no control at all, or certainly very little control. Householders did their share in determining that their homes would be transformed (indeed, we have very few records of any who actively *resisted* the process), but so did politicians, landlords, industrialists, and managers of utilities.

These two concepts, the work process and the technological system, are the warp and the woof with which I hope to weave a description of the changes that occurred in the work that was done in American homes in the last one hundred years. The phrases are awkward, but the concepts that they denote are important. On one level, they seem to introduce complications that may be annoying; but on another level, they simplify descriptions and analyses so that certain essential features can emerge more clearly—to put it another way, they help us to see the forest through the trees. Housework is as difficult to study as it is to do. The student, like the houseworker, is hard pressed to decide where the activity begins and where it ends, what is essential and what is unessential, what is necessary and what is compulsive. If you are doing a time study of housewives, are you supposed to define the time they spend watching their children play in the park as leisure or as work? If you are trying to keep house yourself, is it really necessary to remove the chocolate stains from the front of a toddler's playsuit? The two problems have many conceptual similarities. I have found that the dual notions of a work process and a technological system have helped me to deal effectively with the scholarly problem of thinking and writing about the history of housework. The postscript contains, among other things, my insights about what might happen if these notions are also generally applied to the practical and emotional problems of doing the work itself.

Chapter 2

Housewifery: Household Work and Household Tools under Pre-Industrial Conditions

E TYMOLOGY can illuminate some of the murkier realms of social history. *Housewifery* has had a long history; in English the word can be traced back as far as the thirteenth century. Women have always cooked, laundered, sewed, and nursed children; but it was not until the thirteenth century, when the feudal period was ending and the capitalist organization of society just beginning, that some of the women who did these chores were given the name, and the very special social status,

Household Work under Pre-Industrial Conditions

of "housewives."* Housewives were the spouses of "husbands"; and husbands, as the compound character of the name implies, were people whose work was also focused on the house (hus is the older spelling of our house) to which they were "bonded"—houses that they either rented or owned houses that were, in some socially identifiable sense, their own. Thus husbands and housewives both derived their status from the existence of their house and its associated land—the man because he had some title to it, and the woman because she was married to him. Husbands and housewives were not aristocrats and did not govern large households that employed and gave shelter to dozens, even hundreds, of people; neither were they transient laborers residing, if they resided at all, under roofs that belonged to other people. Housewives and husbands were among the first occupants of that singular social niche—the middle class. They worked the land (hence the term *husbandry* for what we would now call *farming*), and they made independent decisions about the disposition of livestock and tools that were in their possession. Any economic security they had they achieved by working together and *husbanding* their resources. The success of these early independent agricultural families, the yeomanry, depended on the hard labor of both men and women, as this bit of doggerel from the introduction to a popular sixteenth-century domestic manual makes clear:

> In jest and in earnest, here argued ye finde,
> That husband and huswife together must dwell,
> And thereto the judgement of wedded mans mind,
> That husbandrie otherwise speedeth not well:
> So somewhat more now I intende for to tell,
> Of huswiferie like as of husbandrie told,
> How huswifelie huswife helps bring in the golde. [1]

The labor that was called "housewiferie" from the thirteenth to the eighteenth centuries acquired a new name, "housework,"

*This analysis is based upon the entries for *housewife* and *husband* in *The Oxford English Dictionary* (Oxford, England, 1933). The earliest date given for *housewife* is 1225 and for *husband*—in the sense of a spouse to a housewife—1290.

in the nineteenth; the *Oxford English Dictionary* gives 1841 for the earliest date of its appearance in England and 1871 for the United States.* The nineteenth century was the period when industrialization began in England and the United States. Prior to industrialization the word *housework* would probably have been nonsensical since—with the exception of seamen, miners, soldiers, and peddlers—almost all people worked in or on the grounds of a house, their own, or someone else's. One of the most profound effects of industrialization was, and is, the separation of "work places" from "home places"—and the attendant designation of the former as the "place" for men and the latter as the "domain" of women—the set of ideas and behavior which was called, in the nineteenth century, the doctrine of "separate spheres."† This physical and ideological separation of men from women created novel conditions for the performance of women's traditional work, and a new word was coined as testimony to the change. *Housewifery* was too firmly rooted in the older, more rural world, peopled by families of yeoman farmers, artisans, and merchants. *Housework* belongs to the nineteenth and, later, the twentieth centuries—the world of workers, managers, and "sales personnel."

Housewifery and the Doctrine of Separate Spheres

Social and intellectual historians have described with considerable skill the nineteenth-century transition from pre- to post-industrial conditions. They have shown us precisely when the doctrine of separate spheres developed, and have also identified the behavioral, moral, emotional, and political consequences of the doctrine that justify calling it not just a doctrine but an ideology. The physical artifact "home" came to be associated

*See the entry under *housework* in *A Supplement to the Oxford English Dictionary* (Oxford, England, 1976). Significantly, the earlier volumes of the dictionary do not contain an entry for this word, presumably because the etymological research for those volumes was undertaken during the nineteenth century at a time when the word had not yet passed into frequent use.

†Many social historians have commented on the origin and impact of this doctrine.[2]

with a particular sex, "women"; with a particular emotional tone, "warmth"; with a particular public stance, "morality"; and with a particular form of behavior, "passivity"; while at the very same time, "work" became associated with "men," "hardheartedness," "excitement," "aggression" and "immorality." Some historians have also suggested that these new sets of social definitions served the interests of certain powerful segments of society: manufacturers who needed markets for the goods they were producing, mill owners who needed tractable workers for their factories, ministers who needed audiences for their sermons, political leaders who needed to stabilize their electorates, and the newly rich men who needed to be able to cement their status with the mortar of elaborate hospitality that only homebound wives could provide.

The traditional methods of social and intellectual history, based as they are on surviving written texts, published and unpublished, can provide us only with a circumstantial connection between a set of ideas and a set of social conditions, between the attitudes and the needs of interest groups. We can assert that a given set of ideas were held in common by a given set of people, and we can try to reconstruct the ways in which those ideas served to control their behavior so as to satisfy their needs; but since any single individual or social group usually has many different needs, some of which are contradictory, and since all individuals in a group will differ from each other in some ways, the connections that historians want to make will frequently appear dubious, based on the shifting sands of conjecture, assumption, interpretation, and insufficient evidence, rather than on the firm ground of empirical fact.

The history of technology offers a partial solution to this difficulty by allowing us to examine not the ideas and the attitudes but the physical constraints under which people lived their lives. In the present instance I hope to show that an examination of the tools with which housework was done in eighteenth- and early nineteenth century America can teach us a great deal about why the doctrine of separate spheres both suited the needs and encouraged the development of the emerging industrial order.

Household Tools and Household Work

Any effort to describe the technological systems of cooking, cleaning, and laundering in the eighteenth and nineteenth centuries is fraught with difficulty. At different times and in different places women labored under widely variant conditions. Some were rich, and others were poor; some lived in times of turmoil, and others in times of peace. Some had easy access to markets, and others were isolated on unpopulated frontiers; some had many children, others few; some were lazy, and others compulsive—the list could go on endlessly. Technological and supply systems differed from place to place; some economies were based on corn; others on wheat, tobacco, cotton, or mineral goods. Some households burned wood; some, coal; some, peat; some, dried sod; some, dried dung. Some people hauled their water from running brooks; some collected it in rain barrels; some pumped it from wells; and some purchased it from peddlers. Some people kept cows and were thereby able to make their own butter and cheese; some purchased theirs from neighbors or shopkeepers. Some women baked their own bread, others made their dough and brought it to a neighbor's oven for baking; some brought it to a bakeshop, others purchased theirs readymade. It is not easy to generalize about what it was like to be engaged in cooking, cleaning, and laundering under such vastly different conditions.

One way would be to work backward from some sample end product and to describe the technological systems and the work processes that would have been necessary to produce it under various sets of conditions; for this purpose it is essential to choose some end product that is both common to people living under variant conditions and central to their lives. Most travelers' accounts of the meals eaten by Americans in those centuries mention the ubiquity of some kind of "stew"—meat and vegetables cooked, for a long time, in a liquid. Here, for example, is a traveler's account of the daily diet of prosperous Dutch families living in Albany, New York, in the 1750s, but it is fairly representative (give or take a different beverage, a different grain, or a different kind of meat and vegetables) of what one can read about people living a century before or a century after in places as diverse as Maine, Maryland, and Michigan:

> Their breakfast here in the country was as follows: they drank tea ... and with the tea they ate bread and butter and radishes.... They sometimes had small round cheeses (not especially fine tasting) on the table, which they cut into thin slices and spread upon the buttered bread.... At noon they had a regular meal, meat served with turnips and cabbage. In the evening they made a porridge of corn, poured it as customary into a dish, made a large hole in the center into which they poured fresh milk. . . . This was their supper nearly every evening. After that they would eat some meat left over from the noonday meal, or bread and butter with cheese. If any of the porridge remained from the evening, it was boiled with buttermilk in the morning . . . and to this they added either syrup or sugar.[3]

Before the twentieth century, most people ate an extraordinarily unvaried diet; conditions of weather, crop cycles, and transportation were such that, day in and day out, only a very few foods were available, although what was available might change with the season. The lengthy menus and eight-paragraph recipes that are sometimes trotted out as exemplars of cooking in the "good old days," are actually derived from documents left by people who were exceedingly rich, or they represent the stuff from which great feasts and celebrations were made. Ordinary people ate bread, cheese, butter, porridges, eggs, raw fruits and vegetables in season, preserved fruits and vegetables out of season (in the form, for example, of applesauce, jams, relishes, and pickles), all of it washed down by beer, cider, milk, tea, or coffee (rarely water as that was often undrinkable). When fresh meats were available, they were frequently roasted; otherwise, pork, lamb, and beef were either fried (as with bacon) or cooked for a long time in a liquid (in part to lessen the effects of whatever preservation process had been used). Conditions of household routine were such that the simplest and least exerting forms of cooking had to be utilized most frequently; hence the ubiquity and centrality of those classic "one-pot" dishes, soup and stew.

Pre-twentieth-century cookbooks do not describe the process

is great detail, perhaps because it was regarded as too familiar to warrant description; but here is one of the few exceptions:

> It resteth now that we speak of boild meats and broths . . . that can feed the poore as [well as] the rich. We will first beginne with those ordinary wholsome boiled meats, which are of use in every good mans house: therefore to make the best ordinary pottage: you shall take a racke of mutton cut into peeces, or a legge of mutton cut in peeces: for this meat and those joints are the best. Although any other joint, or any fresh beefe will likewise make good pottage: And having washt your meat well, put it into a cleane pot with faire water, and set it on the fire: then take violet leaves, endive, succory, strawberie leaves, spinage, langdebeefe, marygold flowers, scallions and a little parsley, and chop them very small together, then take halfe so much oatmeale well beaten as there is herbs, and mix it with the herbes, and chop all very wel together: then when the pot is ready to boile, skumme it very wel, and then put in your herbes: And so let it boile with a quicke fire, stirring the meat oft in the pot, till the meat be boild enough, and that the herbes and water are mixt together without any separation, which will be after the consumption of more then a third part: Then season them with salt, and serve them up with the meate.[4]

With variations this dish could have been cooked and served anywhere in the colonies, states, or frontiers, any time between the earliest days of settlement and the end of the nineteenth century; indeed, it remains pretty much the standard technique to this very day. In the South and in the West, pork might have more characteristically replaced the lamb and beef mentioned in the recipe; and in winter months, onions, potatoes, cabbages, or turnips would have replaced the spring greens prescribed. Similarly, corn would have served as the likely thickener in the seventeenth and eighteenth centuries, while wheat flour would have replaced it in the nineteenth. Whatever the ingredients, the technique remains essentially the same, and so this dish can serve as the focus for our investigation of the tools with which it would have been done—and the work processes dictated by them—at various periods of time.

Let us begin by imagining that this particular pottage was being prepared in the home of a young childless couple living on a small farm in Connecticut in the middle of the eighteenth century, a farm that was as yet too small to require hired help in the fields or in the house, but was large enough to supply the basic needs of wife and husband. To butcher the animal from which the meat was to come, the husband would have used a set of knives made of wood and iron. This being Connecticut, the water to be used in preparation and cleaning would likely have come from a nearby stream and would have been carried to the house in a bucket made of wood, although the staves might have been gir- dled in iron or leather. The housewife would have put the meat and water into a large iron kettle, and this kettle would have been suspended over the fireplace on an iron lugpole (fifty years earlier it might have been made of green wood) inserted into the mortar of the chimney (lacking a lugpole, the housewive could have used a trammel or a crane made of iron, standing on the floor of the hearth). The fuel for the fire would be hardwood logs, cut, hauled, chopped, and stacked by her husband. The fuel would sit on iron or brass andirons in a fireplace constructed either of bricks or local fieldstones; as masons were not then common (or inex- pensive), the likelihood is that her husband had constructed the fireplace himself. If the housewife had been following standard practice on these matters, the herbs and vegetables that were added to the stew would have come from a kitchen garden that she had planted and tended herself (although, when plowing in the spring, her husband might have turned over the soil if it was particularly wet and heavy). The grain that went into the stew for thickening might have been corn or wheat—and, unlike the herbs and vegetables, would have been the product of male, rather than female, labor. The husband would have superintended the grow- ing of it as well as its subsequent processing; had it been corn, he would have husked it and scraped the kernels from the ear; if wheat, he would have supervised the cutting, threshing, and winnowing, although the housewife might have helped. If they had a hand mill (made of stone) for either form of grain, he would have pushed it or managed the draft animals doing the pushing; and if the grain was to be taken to a local water mill to be ground (which would have been the most likely choice in Connecticut in this period), he would have hauled it in a cart drawn by the same draft animals. Skimming and stirring were tasks that the housewife performed with wooden spoons; the spoons themselves had most likely been whittled by the husband during the previous winter when there was little work to be done in the fields. The salt (and other spices, had she had them) would have to have been purchased, as they could not have been made from locally available materials. Once made, the stew would have been served up in wooden trenchers (also whittled by hand), which then would have been wiped clean with a rag (which, at this date, would most likely have come from cloth imported from England, but which could also have been American homespun, although not of this particular housewife's manufacture, since the couple were too early in their life cycle to be able to afford either a loom or the time required for weaving). The last task remaining to the housewife would have been the cleaning of the kettle, accomplished with some water, perhaps some sand, a rag, and a brush that she had made herself, as its name implies, from branches and twigs.

This brief scenario illustrates two important points. First, under the conditions that prevailed in the American colonies during the eighteenth century, the work processes of cooking required the labor of people of both sexes; cooking itself may have been defined as women's work (which it was), but cooking could not be done without prior preparation of tools and foodstuffs, and a good deal of that prior preparation was, as it happens, defined as men's work. Second, acquisition of a technological system of cooking (the fireplace, andirons, pots, and accessory implements) required that there be some contact between the household and the market economy in which it was embedded. Even as simple a household as this one could not have been entirely self-sufficient, for it needed some surplus of cash or goods with which to purchase tools or raw materials that were essential for subsistence. To put this latter point in its baldest form, you cannot cook without a pot, and pots have to be purchased because only skilled artisans have the requisites for making them.

Had I focused on any other meal of the day or on any of the other tasks included in the standard definitions of housewifery —cleaning, laundering, care of infants, care of the ill, manufacture of clothing—these two points would have remained valid generalizations. Buttermaking required that someone had cared for the cows (and, at least among several of the ethnic groups that first settled these shores, this was customarily men's work), and that someone had either made or purchased a churn. Breadmaking required that someone had cared for the wheat (men's work) as well as the barley (men's work) that was one of the ingredients of the beer (women's work) that yielded the yeast that caused the bread to rise. Men grew the flax that women eventually spun into linen, and also had to "brake" it (crushing the fibers in a special, exceedingly heavy instrument) before it could be spun. Women nursed and coddled infants; but men made the cradles and mowed the hay that, as straw, filled and refilled the tickings that the infants lay on. Women scrubbed floors, but men made the lye with which they did it. If the tools used in any of these tasks had been purchased, the household would have had to have some surplus product to exchange for them; if not then the tools would have been made at home by men (with the possible exception of brooms used for sweeping and brushes for scrubbing), since working in wood and leather and metal was defined as men's work. If an eighteenth-century woman had attempted housekeeping without the assistance of a man (or of a good deal of cash with which to purchase the services of men), she would most likely have had markedly to lower her standard of living, to undertake tasks for which she had little training, and to work herself into a state of utter exhaustion—all of which conditions would have seriously endangered her health and probably her life. A similar fate would have befallen a man under the same circumstances had he tried to farm without the help of a woman. Small wonder that most people married and, once widowed, married again. Under the technological and economic conditions that prevailed before industrialization, survival at even a minimally comfortable standard of living required that each household contain adults (or at least grown children) of both sexes, and that each household have some minimal ability to participate in the market economy, at the very least so as to be able to acquire and maintain its tools.

The Household Division of Labor

The division of labor by sex in household work seems to have no rhyme or reason to it, but it was unquestionably a real fact of social existence before industrialization, just as it is today. Men made cider and mead (a drink made from fermented honey); women made beer, ale, and wine (except among the French, where the men made wine). Women mended clothing that was made out of cloth, but men mended clothing—particularly shoes, breeches, and jackets—that was made out of leather. Women had some tasks with which they filled the interstices of their days (sewing, spinning), but so did men (chopping wood and whittling). Men had some tasks that were thought to require brute strength (pounding corn, hauling wood), but so did women (doing the wash or making soap from tallow and lye). A few tasks appear to have been sexually neutral: weaving, milking cows, carrying water, and paring apples or potatoes were chores that, according to the available records, both men and women regularly undertook as the need arose.

Under duress, of course, people were capable of breaking out of their stereotypical roles. If a man was ill or disabled or away from home, a woman could go out to cut down the wheat or feed the cows; similarly, if a woman was unable to work at butchering time, a man could salt the beef or prepare the fat for tallow. But men and women were not well trained to undertake the tasks assigned to members of the opposite sex and consequently could not perform them expertly. The tasks may seem simple when viewed by people, like us, who do not have to perform them; but they were far from simple to the people whose sustenance depended on them; a winter of starvation could result from one small mistake.

An experience of this sort was related by Rebecca Burlend, a Yorkshire peasant woman, who immigrated to Illinois with her husband in 1831 and consequently experienced a kind of trip backward in time, from farming in a locale that was just experiencing the changes wrought by industrialization to farming under conditions that were essentially pre-industrial. The Burlends came to this country with few possessions and little money; they lacked almost all the tools they needed for farming. As there were sugar maples on the property on which they settled, they learned to tap the trees for sap and sold the resultant syrup to a local merchant in exchange for a few hoes and an axe. With the hoes (and the loan of one day's plowing from a neighbor with a plow and a team) they planted wheat their first spring. When the crop was ready for harvesting, they visited another neighbor and borrowed two sickles from him; but on the trip home Mr. Burlend fell on one of the sickles and so badly wounded his leg that he was in danger of dying for several days. When this danger was past, it was clear that he would not be able to stand for several weeks and consequently could not bring in the crop:

> Our wheat was quite ripe, indeed almost ready to shake, and if not cut soon, would be lost. We had no means of hiring reapers, and my husband could not stir out. I was therefore obliged to begin myself. . . . I worked as hard as my strength would allow . . . and in little more than a week had it all cut down. . . . But the wheat was still unhoused, and exposed to the rays of the burning sun, by which it was in danger of being dried so as to waste on the slightest movement. Having neither horses nor waggon, we here encountered another difficulty. The work however could not be postponed. . . . My partner had by this time so far recovered as to be able to move about . . . *and thus he came to the door to shew me how to place the sheaves in forming the stack.* [5] [Italics mine]

Although she had lived and worked on farms for her entire life, Rebecca Burlend did not know how to perform the final stages of reaping wheat; had her husband had not been there to advise her, she was certain that the entire crop would have been lost. People had to be under considerable duress, however, to step out of their accustomed sex roles, as Rebecca Burlend did. As her own testimony, and other first-hand accounts of such situations attest ("we had no means of hiring reapers"), the more usual solution to such a dilemma would have been to hire someone of the appropriate sex to perform the task in the absence of a partner: a "hired girl" to mind the children while a mother was ill or if she had died; a "hired man" to do the butchering or the plowing or the repair of fences if a man was disabled or away from home.

Young men and young women received from parents, relatives, and employers the training that they needed to perform their adult work. Children learned their work-related sex roles by becoming assistants to their parents and by being sent to the homes of relatives when need or circumstance made such an arrangement desirable. A young boy might be "given" to his grandparents if they needed help, or a young girl "lent" to neighbors with many small children to care for; a country niece might be boarded with a city uncle so that she could go to school and help her aunt, or a young city cousin invited to visit in the country to help bring in the harvest.

From the earliest days of settlement, people had complained about the "servant problem" in this country, but not because servants did not exist. In the seventeenth century, young people regularly came to these shores as indentured servants; and in the eighteenth and nineteenth centuries, girls routinely worked as servants in the other people's homes before they married, and boys either served as apprentices or hired themselves out as day laborers in order to accumulate the cash that they needed to start off on their own.[6] The servant problem arose, as most people who attended carefully to the situation could attest, because the easy availability of land meant that the class of people who, in any of the countries of Western Europe, might spend a lifetime (or at least many years) in service did not have to do so here. Even if indentured servants could not buy out their periods of service early, they rarely stayed beyond the period for which they had contracted. In prosperous communities, young people married early and thus stayed in service for only a short time. Adolescents in straightened circumstances could always marry and "head west"—as many of them did. Thus the servant problem arose from a shortage not of help but of "good help"—by which the complainer almost always meant someone who was (1) beyond adolescence, (2) experienced and skillful, and (3) subservient. Despite this shortage, most adults, no matter how poor, had assistance with their work at some time in their lives. This assistance came from their own children, from the children of relatives, from the relatives themselves, from neighbors, or from people hired on a casual or transient basis when other expedients failed. This help may not have been long-term, and it may not have been particularly skilled, but it was there. I have read dozens of diaries and hundreds of letters written by people who lived in this country between 1660 and 1860, and have yet to encounter a single instance of a household that did not, at some point in its lifespan, employ "hired" (that is, paid a wage) or "boarded" (that is, living and working under the same roof as though they were members of the family) help; even the Burlends were able to employ hired hands by the time three years had passed.[7] These assistants—men and women, boys and girls—helped to lighten the burden of toil for husbands and housewives (and to provide company for people who lived in isolated situations), but they also served (and this is the more crucial point here) to keep the sexual division of labor intact by filling in with the skills appropriate to their sex when the occasion warranted. Thus they helped to ensure that the mutual dependence of one sex on the other would be perpetuated into the next generation.

Where children or servants were enlisted or employed and the elders were not disabled, a hierarchy of tasks existed which distinguished the young from the old, the skilled from the unskilled, the employer from the employee; this hierarchy seems to have existed even when, as frequently happened, the senior and junior workers in the enterprise were working side by side. Only those who were extraordinarily rich could afford to divorce themselves entirely from the day-to-day operations of their households; other people established status for themselves by differentiating their work from the work of those who were subordinate to them. It is difficult to be precise about these hierarchies because each household represented a unique combination of factors (age and number of children, size and location of the house, number of people to be fed, et cetera), and because the relevant factors might change from season to season and year to year. Roughly speaking, the chores that required the least skill or organizational ability went to children (carrying water, milking cows, simple mending); those that were most arduous went to servants (scrubbing floors, doing laundry, minding small children, pounding corn); but those that either required fine judgment (churning butter) or some creativity (fine sewing) or much experience (making clothes) or considerable organization skill (cooking meals) remained with the housewife herself.

The experiences of Elizabeth Koren, a young Norwegian woman who immigrated to Iowa with her husband, a minister, in the 1850s, provide examples of these hierarchies and of how they were likely to change over the course of just one person's life.[8] The Korens were childless when they arrived in Iowa, and they lived with another family for several months while waiting for their house to be built. Elizabeth had almost nothing to do during the time; her hostess, on the other hand, had two small children, all the household work, and some farm chores to perform (the host was a farmer and carpenter who spent a few days out of most weeks at work "in town"). Elizabeth was an exceedingly kind woman, anxious to be of help to her hostess, but status considerations were such that she neither could nor would share any of the cooking, laundering (which was done once a week), or floor scrubbing; her hostess was, after all, "a peasant," and she, Elizabeth, was "an educated woman." On the other hand, she was willing to make clothes for the family, a chore for which her hostess had little time. A few months later when the pregnancy of the hostess had made it impossible for her to carry the extra burden of guests, the Korens moved into a small cabin of their own, their house being not yet completed. Here Elizabeth did her own cooking (at which she was clearly skilled), but she brought her laundry to another woman, a "peasant," and hired a teen-age girl to scrub the floor and do other chores. Later on that year, when the house was finally inhabitable and Elizabeth herself pregnant, she had two helpers: the same young girl, upon whose shoulders the ironing, but not the cooking, now devolved; and a young boy who carried water, ran errands, and helped with the butchering and salting down of beef and pork. These two young people continued to live in the homes of their parents. After her child was born, Elizabeth hired a young woman to live with her and take over the cooking; but later on, when her teenage helpers had departed for better opportunities, Elizabeth returned to cooking and sewing, leaving all the other tasks to her now-unassisted live-in servant. At this juncture, ironically, the diary breaks off, as Elizabeth found that she was too engrossed in the upkeep of her household to continue it. The point that we can draw from this example, however, is that social arrangements in a household were such that certain tasks carried with them certain implied statuses: cooking, fine sewing, care of infants, ironing, and care of the sick were fairly high on the status hierarchy; laundry, cleaning, hauling, and minding small children were fairly low. These latter tasks were displaced onto servants or children whenever possible.

The Household and the Market Economy

Much has been written about the self-sufficiency of pre-industrial households, most particularly in the American colonies and later on the frontier. Evidence abounds that American households of all classes were capable of manufacturing many essential items required for basic subsistence, and that they were more likely to do this than were European households of the same social class. In this country economic and demographic conditions during the first two hundred years of settlement dictated that self-sufficiency was often either simply necessary or politically expedient; patterns of trading and of manufacturing in the colonies were neither as well developed nor as well differentiated as in the older countries of Western Europe. There, butchers and bakers and candlestick makers were specialized artisans; here, they tended to be the householders themselves, jacks- and janes-of-all-trades. This situation continued, especially on the frontiers, well into the nineteenth century. In 1831, Rebecca Burlend noted, for example, that in rural Yorkshire, from which she had come, farmers regularly purchased soap and butcher's meat; whereas in rural Illinois, to which she was immigrating, farm families manufactured these items for their own consumption.[9]

Yet this self-sufficiency was not absolute. Even during the earliest days of settlement or on the very edges of frontiers, there were some essential raw materials that people could not supply for themselves (salt, for example, or lime), some essential manufactured goods (particularly those made of metal) that they could not make for themselves, and some essential services (especially masonry) that they were not particularly skilled at performing. For these goods and services people were dependent, in one form or another, on the market economy; they had to purchase tools that had either been imported from abroad or been made by an artisan in the colonies.

The important point about this dependency is not that it existed, but that it related to goods that were absolutely essential to the survival of individuals and communities: guns for obtaining fresh meat, salt for preserving the meat of domesticated animals, plows for breaking the soil, pots and pans for cooking, axes for felling trees. Without these tools (and replacements for them when they wore out or were damaged), the colonists could not initially feed, clothe, and shelter themselves and certainly could not subsequently improve living conditions. Some of the early immigrants brought these tools with them, but it was not long before the colonists endeavored to create indigenous sources of supply: ironworks were established, for example, in Virginia in 1622, in Massachusetts in 1643, and in Connecticut in 1657.[10]

In the pre-industrial economy the relationship between tools and productivity was straightforward: the more tools people had, the more they were able to wrench from the land. They could break the soil without a plow, a team, and a yoke—but not as effectively as they could do it with these. They could make maple sugar with wooden taps, buckets, and a large kettle, but with wooden or metal troughs they could collect more sap with the same expenditure of labor. The fur trade was enhanced by better traps and guns; potasheries, by larger kettles; fishing, by more effective nets and larger boats. The productivity of domestic chores was also dependent on the availability of tools. A man or a woman could obtain milk from a cow with just a pair of hands, but possession of a pail meant that more milk would be collected at one time, and of a stool that the work could be done in a more comfortable position. Addition of a sieve, a press, and a churn meant that cheese and butter could be made; of boxes and baskets and tubs and salt, that the cheese and butter, once made, could be preserved for a longer period of time. Bread can be baked without an oven (the standard way to do this was to put the dough in a covered pot and place it in the ashes of a fireplace), but an oven allows many more loaves to be baked at one time. Every domestic chore required a set of tools, a technological system of tools linked in series. Cooking required axes, knives, andirons, lugpoles, as well as pots and pans—and all of these were made of metal. Clothmaking required shears, and cards and wheels and reels and bobbins and looms and vats (for dying, bleaching, fulling)—and many of these could be produced only by appropriate craftsmen: wheelwrights, carpenters, joiners, coopers, tanners, blacksmiths, foundrymen.

Whether imported or of domestic manufacture, goods manufactured by artisans were not inexpensive; and householders frequently had to bear the additional cost of transporting them (or the raw materials out of which they were to be made) over long distances. Purchase of a loom or a plow could be a major investment for a household, as could construction of a brick fireplace or a baking oven. In Maryland at the turn of the eighteenth century, for example, the materials for building a simple wooden house cost about four to five pounds and a bed about one quarter of that amount, or about one pound; but two simple iron pots cost about as much as a bed. A printed Bible could cost from six pence to six shillings, but a simple stone hand mill for grinding corn cost almost one pound, or the equivalent of forty inexpensive Bibles.[11] In Illinois one hundred years later, the Burlends found that the entire spring crop from their stand of four hundred sugar maples amounted to about three hundred pounds of maple sugar, which they were able to trade for some Indian corn for seed, some meal for household use, some coffee, three hoes, and an axe. As they got about eight cents a pound for the sugar, this whole purchase came to about twenty-four dollars, which is twice what they had paid a month before for a cow and a calf, and about half of what they had paid for their eighty acres of partially cleared land with a small cabin on it.[12] Bowls, kettles, knives, and plates were not incidental purchases either. These simple material goods seem to twentieth-century eyes to be so disposable as to be almost beneath notice. To seventeenth- and eighteenth-century eyes they were sufficiently valuable to require itemized treatment in wills and probate accounts; indeed, inheritance of a set of farming or housekeeping tools in itself represented a sufficient economic base from which young people could start housekeeping on their own.

Logic suggests, and the available evidence confirms, that the rich would, in general, possess more tools than the poor.[13] Since the tools I am referring to are those needed to provide basic subsistence, it follows that, possessing more tools and being able to purchase the labor of more people to operate the tools, rich householders could be more productive than poor ones. As a consequence, the rich would be likely to have greater flexibility in the face of changing market conditions. If, for example, tobacco seemed more likely than corn to yield a profit, a rich householder could plant all his available land in tobacco and buy whatever corn his household required in a given year; but if the price of tobacco was down, he could—since he already possessed the tools to do it—grow and grind corn and sell the resultant meal to those of his neighbors not as fortunate as he. This flexibility, made possible by the possession of surplus tools, served to increase the likelihood that the rich would remain rich or become even richer.

This point can be made somewhat clearer by comparing the household contents of those who were poor and those who were rich; probate records, in which court officials list a dead person's possessions for the evaluation of his or her estate, are a useful source of such information.[14] For example, a poor widow named Elizabeth Davis died in Brookhaven township on Long Island in 1825.[15] Although she owned a house and some land, at the time of her death her debts far exceeded the value of her property, and she was clearly living in reduced circumstances. According to the probate records of her estate, she possessed the bare minimum number of tools that were necessary to maintain a fire and cook on it: one axe ($1.25); one pair of andirons and dogs ($2.00); a crane, a shovel and tongs set, one frying pan, one tea kettle, and two pots ($5.00). She also had a water pail, a small stove, and two pots to go on it ($1.00), which suggest that she did her own laundry (such a stove was commonly used for heating water for this purpose). The rest of her furnishings consisted of two bedsteads, two featherbeds, two tables, three chairs, four trunks, some bowls, plates and tableware. At the time of her death, she had one half barrel of wheat flour ($2.50), twenty pounds of salt beef ($1.00), and four rods of firewood ($2.50). Thus, the only technological systems in which Elizabeth Davis participated were those of the fireplace and the laundry. She could cook and serve simple meals and wash her own clothing, but she would have had to purchase almost all of the raw material for her meals (she had no gardening implements, no agricultural tools, no butchering knives) and a host of other essential commodities (soap, for example, or cloth). She lacked the tools necessary to produce anything that could have been sold for cash or traded for other goods, —a lack that may have been part of the reason she had so many debts.

Others of her neighbors lived in better circumstances. Another widow, Ruth Mulford, who died just two years later, had much the same kitchen equipment as Elizabeth Davis but, in addition, owned a piggin (a milk pail), sieves, stone jugs, and a churn ($1.00), which suggest that she kept a cow and made her own butter and cheese; a large keg with soap grease in it ($.25), which suggests that she made her own soap; cards, a spinning wheel, a reel, and some woolen rolls ($2.25), which suggest that she spun wool; a bake pan and four large wooden bowls, which suggest that she regularly made bread; and a coffee mill ($.50), which suggests that she bought green beans and roasted and ground them herself.[16] Her estate also contained twenty-three sheets, eleven tablecloths, twenty-four pillowcases, twelve towels, and six bed quilts—quantities so out of line with her other possessions (she had only two bedsteads) as to suggest that she had either purchased linen or cotton fabric for finishing or made these articles at some time in the past (when, presumably, she had owned the appropriate tools) and was holding them for sale in the future. Thus, Ruth Mulford was capable of producing some daily staples for her table—milk, butter, cheese, bread (which Elizabeth Davis would have been forced to purchase)—and had the tools necessary to produce certain important commodities (soap and woolen knit goods in particular) from raw materials that were easy to obtain. Furthermore, she had the wherewithal to obtain cash when she needed it—a potentiality that probably explains why, unlike Elizabeth Davis, she was not in debt when she died. Because she had more tools she could have been more flexible in her economic behavior and would have found it somewhat easier to adjust her expenditures of money or labor to accord with changes in market conditions.

The household of General John Smith who died, a widower, in 1817, illustrates an even more comfortable—and more flexible— standard of living. General Smith was probably the richest man in Brookhaven at the time of his demise, and his household could have been likened to a small manufacturing establishment.[17] In addition to the tools necessary for cooking, dairying, laundry, and wool spinning, General Smith owned those for processing and storing meats (butchering knives, sausage guns, empty kegs and barrels), preparing linen cloth (quills, creels, brakes, wheels, and looms), manufacturing soap and candles (tallow barrels, vats, molds), weaving woolen cloth (woolen looms, spare gears), preparing vinegar, cider, beer, or other liquors (jugs, funnels, presses), and ironing (irons and an ironing table). Like Ruth Mulford, General Smith was in the business of producing cloth goods, but on a much grander scale; at the time of his death he had on hand 37 tablecloths, 17 woolen blankets, 9 pounds of woolen yarn, 2 1/2 pounds of silk thread, 18 yards of toweling, 32 yards of sheeting, 28 pairs of pillowcases, 359 pounds of sheared wool, 62 towels, 33 1/2 pairs of finished sheets, and 10 pounds of linen yarn. For cooking and dairying General Smith owned more abundant tools than had either Mrs. Davis or Mrs. Mulford (he had a cheese press, for example), and his were frequently either larger or made of better materials: steel instead of iron knives, earthenware instead of wooden bowls, brass and copper instead of iron pots. The Smith table could have been set with serving pieces of pewter, silver, and porcelain, with tableware of china and glass, with brass-handled knives and silver forks. Guests at dinner parties in the Smith home were no doubt served by one or several of the eight household assistants (three indentured servants, five slaves—five women and three men) who are also listed in the inventory. Indeed, the Smith household contained the parts of a technological system that was scarcely in evidence in the Davis and Mulford homes—the tools for entertaining, for manufacturing hospitality. Hospitality was then, as it is now, a significant economic commodity; by solidifying business relationships, a properly managed dinner party, for example, could bring far more wealth into a household than it cost to produce.

General Smith's household represents, for its time, the ultimate level of economic flexibility and self-sufficiency. If conditions had required the general to do so, he could have supplied his household with almost everything that was needed for a fairly comfortable level of sustenance without recourse to the marketplace. He could also, as occasion demanded, alter the output of his household so as to take advantage of fluctuations in market prices: if apples were scarce in any given year, for example, he could have sold his household stores of cider at fairly high prices and subsisted on beer or coffee or tea until the next crop was in; if sheets and pillowcases were in demand, he could set his household to producing them; but if the price fell, he could withhold from the market, awaiting more favorable conditions. As a rich man, General Smith had acquired many tools and many hands to run them; he could adjust the productivity and the consumption of his household as the vagaries of trade and prices required without endangering his health or that of the people who worked for him. As the richest man in town, he could behave most flexibly in the market, but he could also be most independent of the market when he wished to be. Lacking tools, Mrs. Mulford and Mrs. Davis lived more straitened lives, in greater jeopardy of being injured by the vagaries of the market.

Conclusion

I seem to have come far afield from the simple meal with which this discussion began; but—by way of conclusion and reiteration —let me return to it and to the young couple preparing it on their hearth in Connecticut. That meal, the stew, symbolizes the very simple standard of living that most Americans (and, indeed, most Europeans) maintained in the centuries prior to industrialization. Everyday meals were uncomplicated and monotonous; much of the food that people ate was served without preparatory effort or with minimal cooking. Diets lacked variety, and standards of cleanliness were not what they are today. Houses were much smaller, and so were wardrobes; most people lived in one, two, or at most three rooms and wore the same articles of clothing day in and day out. There were, of course, a few people who knew what it was to sleep each night on clean sheets, or lean against a mantel that was not covered with ash, or eat a meal that consisted of more than one course; but there were very, very few such people, and they were all very rich. The poor, and even the middling comfortable, could not aspire to such creature comforts —not even those among them who were economically secure enough to own a small parcel of land and to hire one or two servants. Cleanliness of body and variety of foodstuffs were perquisites only of the very rich in ages past.

The young couple, similarly, reminds us that although housework was socially defined as "women's work," in reality the daily exigencies of agrarian life meant that men and women had to work in tandem in order to undertake any single life-sustaining chore. The relations between the sexes were reciprocal: women assisted men in the fields, and men assisted women in the house. Women were responsible for cooking, cleaning, laundry, and infant care, just as men were responsible for plowing, sowing, mowing and horse (or oxen, or cow, or pig) care; and all of these chores were essential.

Finally, the tools with which the chores were done—the hoes and axes and pails and pots—seem to us simple devices, but they actually involved a household in complex relations with the market economy in which it was embedded. As self-sufficient as people may have been, they could not cut themselves off entirely from the artisans who made and repaired metal products or from the merchants who transported salt and lime and other household staples over long distances.

In addition, and somewhat ironically, the poorer people were, the fewer the tools they had; and the fewer the tools they had, the more likely they were to be dependent upon the vagaries of the market to provide them with the commodities—food, clothing, and shelter—that were needed for basic subsistence. Thus, our imaginary young couple in Connecticut, if they had wanted to improve their standard of living, would have been well advised to work hard, sustain each other, and take good care of their tools. Their grandchildren, or perhaps their great grandchildren, having passed over the great divide of industrialization would require different advice—as we shall see.

Chapter 3

The Invention of Housework: The Early Stages of Industrialization

DURING the nineteenth century the United States became an industrialized country—indeed, probably the most industrialized of all countries in the world. The process took a long time and, for the country as a whole, had many facets. For international merchants it meant a shift from dealing in raw materials to dealing in manufactured goods. For landless laborers it meant a shift from the farm to the factory as the locus for their work. For politicians it meant having to cope with complex questions of finance and corporate structure for which there were few legal precedents. For bankers it meant modifications of routine practices so as to satisfy the needs of capitalists who wished to invest —not in land but in machinery. For poor young men who had big plans for themselves, it meant casting those plans in terms of new businesses, new inventions, and technical training rather than in terms of one of the professions or progressive farming. For local merchants, proprietors of general stores, and rural peddlers, it meant learning to insist on payments in cash rather than in kind. For farmers it also meant learning to deal in cash and to acquire cash, for the new implements that could increase yields and re-place farm laborers—the harvesters and combines, the nursery-men's seeds and chemists' fertilizers—could be paid for only in cash. Industrialization brought with it new forms of transport (the canal and the railroad), new forms of communication (the telegraph, the telephone, the typewriter, the daily newspaper), and new kinds of goods that would alter social relations of all kinds: ready-made cloth, which might eliminate home spinning and weaving; ready-made clothing, which might eliminate home sewing or jobs for seamstresses; canned milk to substitute for the fresh and perishable kind; iceboxes, which required the invention of a new social role, the iceman; and so on.

The household was affected by and implicated in this process, just as much as were the law courts, the countinghouses, the workplaces, and the general stores. For it was from the households of the countryside and the cities that young people and adults went out to work in the factories, and it was to those households that their wages were returned, providing the cash that was traded for goods. Furthermore, it was the demand for those goods that continued to fuel the economy being formed by those who were organizing the manufacture of the goods. During the nineteenth century, households ceased to manufacture cloth and began to buy it; they similarly ceased to manufacture candles and, instead, purchased kerosene; they ceased to chop wood and, instead, began to purchase coal; they ceased to butcher their own meat and, instead, began to purchase the products of the meat packers in Chicago. There were a variety of reasons for these changes. Some once-rural, now-urban households found that many of these activities were not possible in an urban setting. Other households ceased carrying them on out of economic con-siderations, since the wages of the young or of parents were able to buy more goods or a higher standard of goods than any of these individuals could have produced by themselves. Other people were forced to give up these activities, having lost whatever stake they had had in the land and its products upon voyaging from the Old World to the New. For whatever reasons, and there were many more reasons than those I have alluded to, the relationship between the household and the economy in which it was placed was profoundly—and irreversibly—altered by the process of industrialization. Whatever disadvantages some of us may now see in the alteration of this relationship, the fact remains that some of the people who made decisions about the conduct of life in their own households in the nineteenth century wanted those changes to occur and acted on that impulse: buying manufactured goods, willingly selling their labor in return for cash, bringing up their children so as to be socialized appropriately for the role of employee rather than of owner, or, alternatively, by bringing up their children to expect the perquisites of being owners. Some people were dragged unwillingly into the industrialized world; but others, for their own good reasons, greeted it with open arms. The latter group appear to have been in the majority or, at the very least, in the places of power.

It has proved difficult, however, to assess the relationship between the work that women did in their homes—"housework," as it came to be called in this century—and the process of industrialization. Many historians have concluded that the substitution of manufactured goods for homemade goods eased the burden of women's work: for example, it is surely easier to buy kerosene than to make candles; to purchase cotton cloth than to comb, card, spin, and weave it; to buy milk from a vendor than to tend to the milking and management of a cow. Furthermore, since the process of industrialization involved a growth in the size both of the urban population and of the middle classes, it is easy to argue, on structural grounds alone, that in the nineteenth century fewer women had to work their fingers to the bone in order to maintain the health and security of their families than in any previous century. Surely it must be easier to do housework under urban conditions and with the assistance of servants (the possession of which was, in that century, virtually the only sure way of defining who was a member of the middle classes). This argument becomes even more persuasive when we remember that it was during the nineteenth century that, by whatever mechanism, white American families succeeded in limiting their fertility; the total fertility rate (the average number of children borne by a woman) fell from 7.04 in 1800 to 3.56 in 1900; fewer children, almost by necessity, must have meant fewer women with broken health (and broken backs!). It seems easy to conclude that, during the nineteenth century, the many facets of industrialization conspired together to make life easier for the average American woman.[1]

Unfortunately contemporary documents tell a different tale: from the beginning of the century until its end, from one coast to the other, American women seem to have been exhausted a lot of the time. "A woman's work is never done, and happy she whose strength holds out to the end of the [sun's] rays," wrote Martha Moore Ballard in her diary in 1795, after she had spent a full day preparing wool for spinning.[2] Her sentiments were echoed almost a century later in a letter written by Mary Hallock Foote: "I am daily dropped in little pieces and passed around and devoured and expected to be whole again next day and all days and I am never *alone* for a single minute."[3] Famous women, even when they had several servants, were not immune to pressure either. "The arranging of the whole house . . . the cleaning . . . the children's clothes and the baby have seemed to press on my mind all at once. Sometimes it seems as if anxious thought has become a disease with me from which I could not be free," wrote Harriet Beecher Stowe to her husband, Calvin, in 1844.[4] Observers of the American scene frequently commented on the ill health of American married women. In 1832, Frances Trollope attributed their waxen complexions, stooped shoulders, and careworn faces to the burdens of their domestic work.[5] Twenty years later Gro Svendsen, a young Norwegian immigrant, made a similar observation in a letter to her parents:

We are told that the women of America have much leisure time but I haven't yet met any woman who thought so! Here the mistress of the house must do all the work that the cook, the maid and the housekeeper would do in an upper class family at home. Moreover she must do her work as well as these three together do it in Norway.[6]

Catherine Beecher, an early disciple of what later came to be called "home economics," waged many a long campaign against what she regarded as the widespread ill health of American married women, and also laid a good part of the blame on the nature of the work that they did:

> There is nothing which so demands system and regularity as the affairs of a housekeeper . . . and yet the perpetually fluctuating state of society seems forever to bar any such system and regularity. The anxieties, vexations, perplexities and even hard labor that come upon American women . . . are endless; and many a woman has, in consequence, been disheartened, discouraged and ruined in health.[7]

Census statistics, articles in women's magazines, economic histories, genre paintings, patent records, and the extant artifacts themselves all converge to tell us that hundreds of household conveniences were invented and diffused during the nineteenth century. There were hand-driven washing machines and taps for indoor cisterns, eggbeaters and pulley-driven butter churns, tinned milk and store-bought flour, porcelainized cookware, airtight heating stoves, and a multitude of additional small gadgets and large utilities, from apple parers to piped coal gas, that were intended to make housework easier.[8] Yet, when discussed by the people who actually did housework, or by the people who watched the people who were actually doing it, it seems not to have become one whit more convenient—or less tiring—during the whole of the century. What a strange paradox that in the face of so many labor-saving devices, little labor appears to have been saved!

One is tempted to resolve the paradox by assuming that the commentators were, in some ways, biased: that, as housewives, Mary Hallock Foote and Harriet Beecher Stowe were either a bit paranoid, or a bit spoiled, or particularly poor organizers, or perhaps that they were trying, as some housewives always have, to "do too much." Similarly, we might want to argue that, as observers, Frances Trollope, Gro Svendsen, and Catherine Beecher were either misguided, or observing the wrong housewives, or grinding some other, unstated, historical axe. The paradox can be resolved, however, without impugning either the reputations or the motives of these, and many other, participants in and observers of the patterns of daily life in nineteenth-century America. Labor-saving devices were invented and diffused throughout the country during those hundred years that witnessed the first stages of industrialization, but they reorganized the work processes of housework in ways that did not save the labor of the average housewife.

This point can best be dramatized if we analyze the work processes and the technological systems involved in preparing a beef stew in 1850. Meat was still a dominant constituent of the average American diet, and stewing was still (as it is today) a standard form of preparation. Let us imagine what it might have been like for the grandchildren, or perhaps the great-grandchildren, of the young Connecticut couple who appeared in the last chapter, to be preparing the same dish a century later, some place in Connecticut, perhaps in a farm town in the Connecticut River valley which was just beginning to feel the impact of industrialization.

The stew would require, then as it does now, roughly the same ingredients: meat, vegetables, salt and other spices, water to do the stewing, fuel to heat the water, and grain to thicken the resultant liquid so that it could be served effectively as sauce. In a farm household in rural Connecticut in 1850, these ingredients would have been obtained in much the same fashion as was common one hundred years earlier—with one exception. The meat would have come from an animal that was owned by the family and butchered at home, and the vegetables from a garden that was likely to have been tended by the wife; the fuel to have been cut by the husband and his assistant on their own woodlot; the salt and some of the spices obtained by trade (either in cash or in kind); and the water carried, by hand, from their own well or from a nearby spring. The single exception would have been the grain—the thickening agent for the stewing juices; and thereby hangs a significant point about the ways in which household labor changed in the early years of industrialization.

Milling Flour and Making Bread

In the first half of the nineteenth century, the product of the merchant flour mills of Rochester, Buffalo, Baltimore, and Pittsburgh began to replace the product of local grist mills on the tables of ordinary families living both in urban and in rural circumstances in New England and the Middle Atlantic states. Despite the fact that textiles and armaments have received more attention from economic and technological historians, it was actually the flour business that first underwent industrialization in this country.[9] Sometime early in the decade of the 1780s, Oliver Evans, a young wheelwright from Newport, Delaware, designed an automatic flour mill which was driven by water power and used a series of pulley-driven conveyer belts to carry the grain from one part of the mill to another, thus eliminating work that had previously been done by laborers. Evans also designed a "hopper boy"—the name is significant—which automatically sorted the various grades of meal and flour after the grinding, thus eliminating work that had previously been done by one worker, often a boy. Just after the close of the Revolutionary War, Evans and two of his brothers invested in the construction of a mill after this design; and not long after that, other mill owners, principally the Ellicott family of Baltimore, began to incorporate aspects of the design in their own newly constructed mills. In 1795, Evans and Thomas Ellicott published a complete set of instructions and designs for such a mill; thereafter, not surprisingly, Evans found it difficult to protect what he regarded as his right to licensing fees from people who adopted his designs —and he died poor and extremely embittered.[10]

The Evans mill required approximately half the standard number of workers; in addition, modifications that Evans made to the operation of the grinding stones themselves resulted in the production of more fine (white) flour from each bushel of wheat. The Ellicotts estimated that, by thus producing more of the highest priced flour, they had increased the profits of their mill by $32,-500 in the first year of operation and had, at the same time,

(1) One of the sketches in Lewis Miller, "Sketches and Chronicles," 1800.
Historical Society of York County, Pennsylvania.

From Housewifery to Housework

If you had been a housewife living before 1800, you would have cooked and baked aplenty (1), but your husband would have done much of the preparation —such as chopping wood (2), shelling corn (3), and pounding grain into meal (4); and your children would have helped as well, helping with such seasonal tasks as making sausages (5). But with the coming of industrialization, your life and theirs would have changed radically. The cast-iron cooking stove (seen here [6] in one of its earliest incarnations), the automatic flour mill (this is an early drawing of its innards [7]), and factory-produced food and clothing ($4.50 was close to the weekly wage of an unskilled worker when these outfits were advertised in 1897 [8]) meant that you bore the whole burden of housework. For your husband and your children, the house became a place of leisure (9). The kitchen became a place in which men had no useful role to play (10), and the shop became a place in which men were more comfortable behind, rather than in front, of the counter (11).

(2) Detail from "Winter Scene in Brooklyn"
by Francis Guy, 1817–2
Museum of the City of New Yor

(3) "Corn Shelling," by Eastman Johnson, 1864.
The Toledo Museum of Art,
gift of Florence Scott Libbey.

(4) "Pounding Meal on the Frontier,"
by an unknown artist, c. 1845.

(5) "Making Sausage in the Old Manner,"
by Henry Barott.
From H. L. Fischer, S alt Marik-Haus
in D'r Schtadt un Die Alt Zeite, Ein
Centennial Poem in Pennsylfanish Deutsch, 1879.
Historical Society of York County, Pennsylvania.

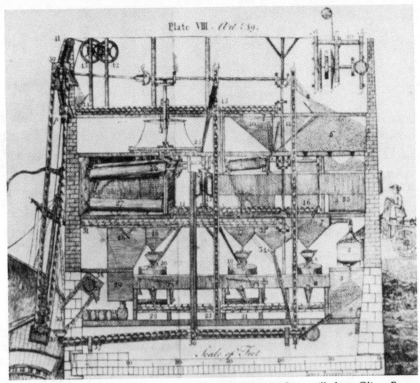

(7) Diagram of an automatic flour mill, from Oliver Evans, *The Young Mill Wright and Miller's Guide*, 1795.

) An early box-type heating stove, with a small baking oven cut into its side, made in Pennsylvania in 1767.

(8) Courtesy of Chelsea House Publishers, New York, publishers of 1897 *Sears Roebuck Catalogue*, 1968.

(9) Detail from "Birth and Baptismal Certificate
of Margaret Munch," by Carl E. Munch, 1826.
National Gallery of Art, gift of
Edgar William and Bernice Chrysler Garbisch.

(10) Stove advertisement, c. 1870. Landauer Collecti
New-York Historical Socie

(11) Grocery store, Hempstead, New York, c.1895, by an unknown photographer.
Long Island Picture Collection, Hempstead Public Library.

reduced the wages they had to pay out.[11] Merchant flour milling was a booming business in the latter years of the eighteenth century; flour, biscuit, and meal had been the second most important American export product since the middle of the century (second only to tobacco), and the devastation wrought in Europe by the French Revolution and subsequently by the Napoleonic Wars made the people of that continent even more dependent upon American grains than formerly—and the American business that much more prosperous. In this period, almost all of the product of the merchant mills was intended for export; and it was principally the superfine flour—the white flour that had been deprived of germ and bran—that was so used, since it did not deteriorate. Residents of American cities purchased some of this merchant flour; but, by and large, Americans continued to grow their own grain and mill it at home or at a local grist mill, and thus cornmeal and whole flours (rye, but sometimes wheat) continued to be staples of their diets.

This situation began to change during the 1820s. With the cessation of European hostilities, the export market for wheat products collapsed, and American merchant millers, who had expanded their operations in the previous two decades, found themselves with surplus goods and surplus manufacturing capacity; they quite naturally attempted various techniques for expanding domestic sales of their goods. At the same time, canals were opened in upper New York State, New England, Pennsylvania, and Ohio, which greatly facilitated the transport of wheat products, thus lowering their price to consumers. Carriage between Buffalo and New York cost 19.12¢ per ton mile in 1817 (before the Erie Canal opened) and 1.68¢ in 1840 (after it had been in operation for about fifteen years).[12] The advent of the canals encouraged the growth of settlement and wheat production in the Middle Western states. Thus, at the very same time that it became easier and cheaper for ordinary households to obtain "mass-produced" grain, it also became less profitable for farmers in New England and the Middle Atlantic to grow wheat, rye, and corn for market. The end result of this dual economic process (as an early health-food advocate noted[13]) was the disappearance of home-grown and locally ground grains on the tables of ordinary families—urban and rural—in many settled parts of the country by the outbreak of the Civil War.

Unfortunately neither the government nor anyone else was in the habit of gathering data on household consumption during this period, so that we have no handy guide to the overall displacement of one form of flour by the other. Manufacturing and trade statistics can, however, provide a rough sense of the profound expansion in commercial flour milling during the first half of the nineteenth century. In 1835, 268,000 barrels of flour were shipped on the Erie Canal; this figure rose to 1,000,000 barrels just five years later and had quadrupled to 4,344,000 barrels by the time another decade had passed.[14] The average wholesale price of 100 pounds of flour was $8.48 from 1801 to 1805, and $5.36 (a fall of about one third in price) from 1855 to 1860; the largest drop in the price occurred during the five-year period from 1820 to 1825.[15] In 1808, Evans designed a mill powered by a steam engine (also of his own design) rather than a water wheel. The development of this type of mill, which was prevalent by 1860, meant that milling could be conducted almost anywhere.[16] By 1860 flour milling was the leading American industry; the value of its product was $249 million, more than twice the value of the product of the cotton industry ($107 million) and three times that of iron and steel ($73 million).[17]

Thus it seems likely that our imaginary rural couple, living in Connecticut in 1850, would have switched from the home-grown wheat, rye, and cornmeal, with which their ancestors had been familiar, to the fine and superfine wheat flours that were being produced not at local grist mills but at large automated flour mills scattered throughout the eastern half of the country. They would thus have made, in one, not insignificant aspect of their lives, the crucial transition from being producers to being consumers, from being involved with the product (grain) at almost all stages of its preparation to encountering it only at the very last stage—and acquiring it only through trade. They would have, in short, begun the first stages of the industrialization of their household.

The impact of this transition would have been different on each member of the family. Hand grinding of corn or wheat had traditionally been part of the male (both adults and children) contribution to household work: "Pounding hominy was an evening job. If the men were notified that some was needed, they would on one evening select and shell half a bushel or a bushel of corn, and the next evening carry it to the mortar and pound it. We never took daylight to do it in."[18] The chore of hauling grain to the mill for grinding in those communities where such a facility was available also fell to men. "Today we all eat a dinner of pork, potatoes, and cucumbers without any bread," one young woman wrote in her diary in 1805. "Father went to mill yesterday and expected to come home the same day but was hindered."[19] These grain-related chores were fairly burdensome. Rye, wheat and corn will keep indefinitely once they have been harvested and dried; but as soon as they have been ground into meal or flour, they begin to deteriorate fairly quickly. Thus large quantities could not be ground at one time, even where there was a mill large enough to do the chore. Trips to the mill (or hand milling itself) had to be undertaken at fairly regular intervals throughout the year. The trip to the mill and back might occupy a whole day, or even more (if the mill was faraway), and had to be made (depending on the size of the family or the season of the year) as frequently as once a week but rarely less than once a month. Hand grinding at home had to be done once every several days. Fine white flour does not deteriorate as quickly, but it could not be produced by a home mill; and even in a grist mill, little of it could be produced from a given quantity of grain. So white flour was expensive, and few families used much of it. Thus, in most families, processing of grain was a frequent and sometimes a tiresome chore. The switch from home-grown to "store-bought" grains relieved men and boys of one of the most time-consuming of the household chores for which they had been responsible.

At the very same time, the switch may well have increased the time and energy that women had to spend in their tasks, particularly cooking and baking. Before the early nineteenth century corn was the dominant grain on American tables in every settled section of the country; it was the easiest to grow, the easiest to harvest, and the easiest to cook with once it had been made into meal. Baking with cornmeal was a fairly straightforward process; liquid and leavening were added to meal, after which it was either fried or baked; neither yeast nor kneading was required or recommended. The process is simplicity itself; witness these descriptions of two basic techniques commonly used in the hills of Kentucky at a time when the way of life there was still unaffected by industrialization:

> She mixed a little cornmeal with a pinch of salt and soda, and mixed it with a little water, making a very thick paste. Then she took a board from behind the wood pile stacked in the corner of the room. This board was about three feet long, eight inches wide, and one inch thick. One side of it had been made very smooth. She placed this board at a forty-degree angle before the fire, propping it up by placing a smaller one behind it. She divided the cornmeal dough into two patties and placed them on the hot board. . . . Soon the cabin was filled with the smell of food.

> The bread [could be baked] under the grate in the hot cinders. . . . You add a little soda and salt to cornmeal and just enough water to make a thick paste. The skillet must be preheated and the inside covered with a small layer of lard or grease. . . . the fire must not be too hot. The cinders under the grate are hollowed out to form a place for the skilletful of dough. Some folks put a lid over the skillet and then knocked more hot coals on top.[20]

Similarly, the coarse flours that were produced by hand grinding or grist milling of wheat and rye were prepared into "quickbreads," porridges, and griddle cakes, none of which required complex or laborious preparations. One quick bread was called "salt rising":

> To one quart of water, [add] one teaspoon salt, [and then] thicken with flour until a stiff batter. I then set the little bucket containing this yeast into the . . . kettle (covering it tightly to keep out the dust) and letting it remain in the . . . sun to keep it warm. [When it has risen, after occasional stirring] pour it into the bread pan adding as much more water and thickened flour; when it becomes again light, knead it into a large loaf and bake.[21]

The leavening for this bread was apparently accomplished by the interaction between the salt and certain components of the whole grain flour (the dough will not rise if made with white flour). Those who were rich and blessed with many servants may have regarded corn and whole grains as coarse fare; but whatever their failings may have been, they were the staff of life to those who depended upon them.

What caused them to pass from the scene was the introduction of fine wheat flour at reasonable prices—the product of the merchant flour mills. This flour is a profoundly different material from the product of the hand or the local grist mill, as it is composed of very small particles of the endosperm of the grain, and lacks the germ and the bran. Prior to industrialization, this flour was used only by the rich, by city dwellers, by people who were going on long voyages—or for the preparation of special treats. "White flour was used at my grandfather's," wrote one woman, recalling the middle-class household in which she was raised at the beginning of the nineteenth century, "only to make pie crust, cake and such delicacies. It was bought only in quantities of seven pounds at a time. Rye flour and Indian cornmeal were used to make the bread which was ordinarily eaten."[22] As the years wore on, however, and white flour became cheaper and easier to obtain, yeast breads began to replace quickbreads on American tables. Yeast breads, when prepared by the standard technique of the time, required hard labor (in the kneading) and considerable attention to details (particularly in maintaining yeast cultures). The conversion from meal to flour and from quickbreads to time-consuming breads indicated that the household could afford both the cash that was necessary for the purchase of the flour and the housewifely (or servantly) time that was required for its preparation. Thus, white bread became one of the first symbols of status in the industrial period.

> Bread: What ought it to be? It should be light, sweet, and tender. This matter of lightness is the distinctive line between savage and civilized bread. The savage mixes simple flour and water into balls of paste, which he throws into boiling water . . . of which his common saying is "Man eat dis, he no die." . . . So far as we know there are four practicable methods of aerating bread [and of the four] the oldest and most time-honored is by fermentation. The only requisites for success in it are, first, good materials and second, great care in small things. . . .

The true housewife makes her bread the sovereign of her kitchen—
its behests must be attended to in all critical points and moments, no
matter what else must be postponed. Some persons prepare bread for
the oven by simply mixing it in the mass, without kneading, pouring
it into pans and suffering it to rise there. The air-cells in bread thus
prepared are coarse and uneven: the bread is as inferior in delicacy
and nicety to that which is well kneaded as a raw servant to a perfectly educated and refined lady.[23]

Quickbreads were, in short, thought to be fit only for Negroes,
Indians, and the Irish; the maintenance of status (as well, it was
thought, as the maintenance of good digestion) required the
whitest breads, prepared in a manner that was both time and
energy consuming.

What was true of bread was also true of cakes. Meals and
whole flours do not lend themselves to cake making; only fine
flours can be used successfully in pastries, cakes, and other con-
fections. Eighteenth-century travelers rarely reported that cakes
constituted an important part of the American diet, but the situation had clearly changed one hundred years later. Charles Latrobe, a Frenchman who toured the United States in 1836, was
just one of many foreign visitors who noticed this phenomenon:

Nowhere is the stomach of the traveller or visitor put in such constant
peril as among the cake-inventive housewives and daughters of New
England. Such is the universal attention paid to this particular branch
of epicurism in these states that I greatly suspect that some of the
Pilgrim fathers must have come over to the country with the Cookery
book under one arm and the Bible under the other.[24]

Under the conditions that prevailed in nineteenth-century kitchens, cake baking required a great deal of hard work and a considerable amount of time. Since sugar was sold in loaves, it had to
be beaten before it could be combined with other ingredients;
eggs and butter had to be worked by hand or with a spoon until
they had reached the necessary state of aeration. Even the most
energetic of cooks could well have been exhausted after making,
for example, this simple cake:

Take eight eggs, yolks and whites, beat and strain them and put to
them a pound of sugar beaten and sifted; *beat it three quarters of an hour*

together, then put in three quarters of a pound of flour well dried and two ounces of carraway seeds; beat it all well together and bake it in an oven in broad tin pans. [Italics mine][25]

The eggbeater, which was invented and marketed during the middle decades of the century, may have eased the burden of this work somewhat; but unfortunately the popularity of the beater was accompanied by the popularity of angel food cakes, in which eggs are the only leavening, and yolks and whites are beaten separately—thus doubling the work.[26]

In short, whether it was bread or cakes that she was routinely preparing, the nineteenth-century housewife whose household (like that of our imaginary couple in Connecticut in 1850) had converted from the product of the local grist mill to the product of the far-off flour factory, would have found, for a variety of reasons, that she was spending considerably more time working with that flour than her grandmother had—and her husband considerably less than his grandfather. The advent of industrialized flour brought with it a profound shift in the responsibilities and time allocations of the two sexes vis à vis their work in their own homes: men's share in domestic activity began to disappear, while women's share increased. Thus, housework was becoming truly "women's work"—and not an obligation shared by both sexes.

The Evolution of the Stove

The imaginary nineteenth-century stew with which I started—the one containing fine white flour instead of coarse brown meal—would have been prepared with tools that were also slightly, but significantly, different from its eighteenth-century predecessor. The knives, spoons, pots, and brushes that the Connecticut couple used to do their work in 1850 would have been more or less similar to the ones their grandparents had used a century earlier; but the open hearth—with its andirons, bellows, cranes, and trammels—would have disappeared, to be replaced by that marvelous product of American ingenuity, the gargantuan cooking stove. The cast-iron cooking stove could well serve as the single most important domestic symbol of the nineteenth century; kitchens are almost invariably represented with open hearths in the early years of the century and with stoves later on. Cookbooks published during the century track the transformation. In 1841, Catherine Beecher's chapter "On the Construction of Houses" contained a long section on fireplaces; twenty-eight years later, when she and her sister published *The American Woman's Home,* this chapter had been replaced by an entirely new one, "On Stoves, Furnaces and Chimneys."[27]

The evolution of the stove is difficult to trace because it was an implement that changed profoundly in a short time.[28] The changes were wrought by hundreds of independent manufacturers, scattered throughout the country, some of whom patented their designs, some of whom did not. Benjamin Franklin's stove, which he invented during the 1740s, was intended for room heating, not for cooking, and it was not enclosed; the original Franklin stove had an open hearth, with channels through which the warm combustion gases could pass (so as to provide additional heat) before being vented out the chimney. Enclosed stoves developed from simple plate or box stoves that were made by German or Scandinavian ironworkers, this form of stove having been common in their countries of origin. When the idea of controlling the passage of the combustion gases so as to provide heat for other functions was combined with the design of the European box stove, the American cooking stove was born. Benjamin Thompson (Count Rumford) advocated the use of such stoves in several works that he published toward the end of the eighteenth century, but the earliest cooking stoves are so different in design from the ones that Rumford advocated that it is hard to know precisely what impact his ideas actually had.[29] Most likely some enterprising, and now anonymous, foundryman discovered that a door could be made in one of the plates of a heating stove, and that a box created inside this door could serve as a baking or warming oven.

The Invention of Housework: Industrialization

Someone else may have noticed that if a circular hole were cut in the top of a stove, directly over the firebox, the heat was sufficient to allow water to boil in a pot placed over the hole.

Within very few years the simple small stoves, which were little more than enclosed heating stoves with a few minor modifications, had been elaborated into the monster American cooking stove with four to eight cooking holes on its top surface (or surfaces, since some of the early stoves were "stepped"), two or three ovens for warming and baking (the heat being controlled by proximity to the firebox and by dampers), and attached reservoirs dispensing hot water. By the 1830s the cookstove had come into its own, and the heating stove had begun to evolve on a separate path. As cookstoves got bigger, heating stoves got smaller, culminating in the very efficient "base burner" (which had the fire at its base and a magazine for maintaining a continuous supply of fresh coal above) that became popular toward the end of the century. The poor, or those for whom portability was a prime consideration (especially westward pioneers), used stoves that could, as the open hearth once did, serve as both heaters and cookers; the middling classes and the rich used separate instruments. In some middle- and upper-class households, individual room heating stoves were even being replaced by central-heating furnaces as early as 1860.

The enclosed stove, whether for cooking or for heating, was not greeted with complete enthusiasm, at least by some segments of the population, when it first came on the market. The hearth, with its blazing fire, had long been a potent symbol of home to people of English descent. The roasted joint cooked in front of that fire (when we make a roast beef today we are actually baking, not roasting, it) had also been a symbol of prosperity, particularly in England's American colonies, where meat had been abundant. Albert Bolles, an early historian of the stove industry, was probably expressing the sentiments of the dominant English part of the population (and consequently ignoring the attitudes of the people of German or Scandinavian descent) when he wrote:

> The old-fashioned fireplace will never cease to be loved for the beau-
> tiful atmosphere it imparts to a room, and the snug and cheerful effect
> of an open wood-fire. When stoves were first introduced, a feeling of
> unutterable repugnance was felt by all classes toward adopting them
> and they were used for a generation chiefly in school houses, court-
> rooms, bar-rooms, shops and other public and rough places. For the
> home, nothing except the fireplace would do. The open fire was the
> true centre of home-life, and it seemed perfectly impossible to every-
> body to bring up a family around a stove.[30]

As late as 1869, when the stove revolution had been under way
for almost forty years, the Beecher sisters—themselves members
of the old English élite—still railed against the caprices of the
newfangled invention; in classic English fashion, they expressed
their objections in the quasi-scientific/quasi-religious vocabulary
of natural theology. "Warming by an open fire," they wrote, "is
nearest to the natural mode of the Creator, who heats the earth
and its furniture by the great central fire of heaven, and sends
cool breezes to our lungs."[31]

Ethnicity, symbolism, status, and tradition aside, cooking and
heating stoves had replaced the open hearth in most American
homes by the close of the Civil War for reasons that lie partly on
the demand side of the situation and partly on the supply side.
People wanted stoves in their homes because stoves were economical, portable, and efficient; stovemaking, on the other hand,
began to flourish in the 1830s because of internal changes in the
iron and steel industry itself. The demand for stoves and the
ability to meet that demand were—fortunately for the prosperity
of the stove industry—contemporaneous social developments.

Stoves were economical for two reasons: first, because they
required less fuel than fireplaces; and, second, because they were
cheaper to install. In a stove the flow of air to the fire is restricted
and controlled, thus slowing combustion and extending the useful life of the fuel. We cannot be certain precisely how much fuel
was saved by converting from fireplace to stove because the
amount would vary considerably, depending upon the nature of
the fuel itself (whether hard wood or soft, for example), upon the
functions to which fireplaces or stoves were being put, and the
peculiarities of their construction. Promoters of stoves estimated

savings ranging from 50 percent to 90 percent; and even if we take their lowest estimate as the one closest to reality, there must have been considerable savings—either in time or in money—for people who made the transition. The price of wood increased steadily during the early decades of the century in the eastern parts of the country because land clearing had slowed (most agricultural land having been cleared in the preceding century) and urbanization had accelerated (creating a large class of people who were forced to purchase fuel). As coal began to replace wood (a transition that began in the eastern cities early in the century and spread west with the advent of the railroad), stoves found even greater favor, because they could burn the cheaper fuel more effectively, foul air and filthy walls being a constant threat when coal is burned in a fireplace. In the unsettled portions of the country, where wood was abundant, stoves were still an economical choice because they could be installed without the services of skilled masons and without the use of brick—both of which were scarce, and consequently expensive, on the frontier. Small wonder, as a traveler reported after visiting Wisconsin in 1855, that "few houses in this part of the country have fire-places, the stove having almost banished them altogether."[32]

Many people preferred stoves to fireplaces (at least for heating) because stoves were more efficient, providing more comfort for a given quantity of fuel. Since a stove could be placed more centrally in a room, the heat that it provided could warm a greater portion of the area where people actually spent their time. Large portions of the heat did not escape up the chimney flue (as was the case with open fireplaces). The room with a stove seemed warmer, even when one was at some distance from the source of heat; with a fireplace "one could see one's breath upon the air while sitting at the fireplace and find apples frozen upon the table in the centre of the room when the family were roasting in the blaze of the log fire."[33] Some people thought that the excess heat, coupled with dry air and poor ventilation, was actually ruinous to the health; but others were willing to suffer with any of the complaints so engendered rather than return to the frigid conditions that had formerly prevailed, as Edward Everett Hale recalled:

Sometimes, in later years, when we children were sounding the praise of wood fires . . . my mother would dash cold water on our enthusiasms by telling us of her experiences with them in the early days of her married life. . . . [S]he would tell of the long cold winter days she had passed in piling ineffectual logs in the huge fireplaces in a fruitless endeavor to make some impression upon the freezing atmosphere of the rooms where the side of the unhappy fire-tender which was next to the fire would be scorched by the blaze which roared up the chimney, while the side towards the room would be shivering. She used to say: "You may take the poetry of an open wood fire of the present day, but to me in those early days it was only dismal prose, and I am grateful to have lived in the time of anthracite coal . . .".[34]

When this kind of efficiency was combined with economy (and, for westward migrants, with portability as well), the stove was hard to beat, the Beecher sisters and old English tradition notwithstanding.

As I have said, the demand for stoves that was generated by their economy and efficiency coincided with developments in the iron industry which made it possible for stoves to become readily available at reasonable prices. During the middle years of the eighteenth century, several innovations in iron production were introduced in Great Britain; for a variety of reasons, these innovations were slow to diffuse across the Atlantic until after the Revolution, but they began to have an impact on the character of the American iron industry in the early decades of the nineteenth century. The traditional technique for refining iron ore had been to reduce the ore (which is mainly iron oxide) through direct contact with a fuel (usually charcoal) in a blast furnace. Charcoal was the preferred fuel because it was not contaminated with other minerals (particularly sulphur) that would endanger the quality of the resultant metal. Once refined, the molten iron was tapped off and cast directly into end-product molds (such as those for gun barrels, kettles, or stove plates) or into all-purpose molds (called "pigs"), so that the resultant product (called "pig iron") could be stored or transported somewhere else, for subsequent remelting and recasting, or for refining (by heating and hammering) into wrought-iron products. In the traditional form of the industry, furnaces (for the melting), foundries (for casting and finishing), and forges (for the treatment of wrought iron) were frequently parts of the same business establishment, which might also include ovens for preparing the charcoal and even mines for harvesting the ore.[35]

Briefly described, the innovations that were introduced in Britain made it possible both to substitute coke and coal for charcoal as fuels in the refining of iron ore, and also to produce wrought iron directly from molten ore without passing through the pig-iron stage (by the techniques known as "puddling" and "rolling"). These innovations were significant in several ways: they allowed the substitution of a cheaper fuel and reduced the amount of labor required to produce wrought iron, and thus cut costs. As the innovations were capital-intensive (requiring the construction of entirely new furnaces), they produced differentation in the industry: producers of cast iron became different organizations from producers of wrought iron, and both separated from producers of the fuel. The innovations also altered the nature of the product itself; cast iron refined with coal is a different kind of material from cast iron refined with charcoal, and wrought iron made by puddling and rolling can be handled in ways that wrought iron made from pig cannot.

All of these changes were important factors in the growth of the large-scale industrial economy. The iron industry was one of the leading, and determinant, sectors of that economy; the rate of the production of steam engines and railroad tracks and manufacturing machinery (all of them necessary for industrialization) was dependent upon the rate of production of iron. These same changes were also of great significance in the industrialization of the home, because the production of such humble implements as stoves and kettles—the implements on which household economy depends—were also affected.

Prior to the 1830s stoveplates had been produced directly from molten ore; foundrymen believed that stoves made from remelted pig iron would crack under the heat generated by domestic fires. Some foundries cast the plates and assembled the stoves themselves, selling directly to local customers; other foundries sold the plates to "stovemakers" who assembled the stoves (using bolts and rods from other sources) and sold them at retail. Stovemaking seems to have been a relatively prosperous business in the early decades of the century: several foundrymen and stovemakers patented new designs, both for heating and for cooking stoves; and some of those designs appear to have sold fairly well, if one can judge from the longevity of the companies that made them. The business entered a boom phase early in the 1830s, however, when a New Yorker named Jordan Mott discovered that pig iron that had been made with coke or coal could be successfully remelted into stove plates.[36]

Mott was born in New York in 1798; in 1819 he invented a stove that would burn small pieces of anthracite coal (known as "nut coal") for which, until then, no function had been found. Anthracite coal burned cleaner than bituminous coal but did not ignite easily and so was difficult to use in homes; Mott's design solved this problem. Mott went into business as a stovemaker and had plates made to his order by foundries in Pennsylvania and New Jersey. During the 1820s, he found it increasingly difficult to obtain plates made according to his specifications at prices that he found reasonable, so he decided to try making the castings himself. With a small capital outlay he built a cupola furnace (for remelting pig iron) and soon discovered that he could make perfectly suitable stove plates, just as long as he used pig iron that had been smelted with coal. Mott was thus the first stovemaker who actually "made" stoves (rather than simply assembling them); and his innovation spread rapidly to other firms, since it was profitable and did not require an enormous investment. "Mott's operation gained the attention of iron men, and before the close of the year [1835] cupola furnaces began to be erected, and soon spread over the cities and villages of the Union."[37] The boom period for manufacturers of stoves had begun. Fully one third of all the cast-iron products reported in the 1860 *Census of Manufactures* were stoves; and most of those had been made, not at traditional multipurpose foundries, but by single-product stove manufacturers. Of such establishments, 220 were reported in the census, which was the first to enumerate stove manufacturing as a branch of business separate from general iron founding.[38] Mott's innovation was thus part of the gradual process of differentiation in the iron industry; a group of businesses was created that specialized in manufacturing one product and in serving only one kind of customer, the householder.

The cast-iron stove was, consequently, the first product to deserve the appellation "consumer durable." It was fairly expensive, but still not out of the reach of ordinary people. Through the middle decades of the century stoves ranged in price from five to twenty-five dollars, at a time when the standard pay for common laborers was one dollar a day, and a barrel of flour, enough to last a family of five for eight weeks, cost between five and six dollars.* Most people, except the very poorest, could probably have afforded to install some kind of stove in their living quarters. Not surprisingly Jordan Mott, who had been innovative in the production of stoves, was also innovative in marketing them. He purchased refuse heaps of nut coal and sold it, along with his stoves, to his customers. Other manufacturers soon followed suit with similar innovations, and it was not long before stoves were being marketed with all the hoopla that we have come to expect in the sale of consumer durables: large illustrated advertisements in newspapers and magazines, extravagant claims, competitions at county fairs, installment-buying plans, attractive give-aways (such as extra kettles and frying pans), licensed traveling salesmen, and "free" donations to prominent citizens.[40]

The impact of those stoves on the houses in which they were installed is not difficult to discern: stoves were labor-saving devices, but the labor that they saved was male. The important activity that was radically altered by the presence of a stove was fuel gathering; if a stove halved the amount of fuel that a household required, it thus halved the amount of work that men had to do to in cutting, hauling, and splitting wood. The labor involved in cooking, which was the female share of the work, seems barely to have been affected at all; the process of frying bacon on a stove is little different from the process of frying bacon over a hearth. Hearth fires were difficult to maintain at constant or specialized temperatures—but stove fires were not easy either. "Had an offal [sic] time to get breakfast,

*Stove prices have been garnered from household account books such as those of Phebe Hagner (1840–45) and Frederick E. Westbrook (1840–43). Mrs. Hagner paid $11.69 for her stove (including the pipe, elbows, sheet iron—for the floor—and installation; Mr. Westbrook paid $20.00 for his, and it came equipped with a set of pots and pans.[39]

the fire would not burn. Did not get to school in time for prayers," confided one young woman in her diary in 1868—and her sentiments were echoed in the pages of domestic manuals that advised women on how to manage the cantankerous grates and dampers of their stoves.[41] Pots and pans and kettles continued to be exceedingly heavy (as they continued to be made from cast iron for most of the century); and although the advent of the stove may have somewhat reduced the amount of stooping that had to be done to tend those implements, the stove did not eliminate the need to move thirty- and forty-pound burdens awkwardly back and forth.

As with the conversion from meal to flour, the conversion from hearth to stove may well have augured more work for mother, rather than less. One of the advantages of the stove—according to contemporary cookbooks—was that different kinds of cooking (say, fast boiling, slow simmering, and baking) could be accomplished with the same fire; the skilled cook needed to know how to regulate the dampers of her stove and how to move her pots various distances from the firebox; but once she had conquered this art, it was possible for her to boil potatoes, simmer a soup, and bake an apple pie for dinner all at the same time; this combination would have been near to impossible on a hearth. The stove, in short, augured the death of one-pot cooking or, rather, of one-dish meals—and, in so doing, probably increased the amount of time that women spent in preparing foodstuffs for cooking. The diet of average Americans may well have become more varied during the nineteenth century, but in the process women's activities became less varied as their cooking chores became more complex.[42]

Furthermore, a stove had to be cleaned. As stoves were made from cast iron, they would rust if left dirty (or undried) for any length of time; once a stove started to rust, it would, if left unattended, eventually wear thin and crack. Thus stoves, unlike fireplaces, had to be cleaned at the end of each day, and stove polish (a black, waxy material) applied fairly regularly, in order to ward off the danger of rust. This work was done by women, since cleaning, like cooking, was one of the jobs that was stereotypically allocated to women, and to women alone.

The Invention of Housework: Industrialization

More Chores for Women, Fewer for Men

If we imagine our Connecticut family making the transition, over several generations, from a wood-burning fireplace (with fuel supplied by the husband from his own woodlot) to a wood-burning stove (with some of the wood purchased in any given year) to a coal-burning stove (when local supplies of wood had given out, and the railroad had made it possible to bring in coal), we can understand precisely why men were more likely to enter the labor force than were women, and why, eventually, these rural Connecticut families became dependent upon the cash that wage labor supplied. The stove reduced the amount of labor that a man had to do in order to maintain the standard of comfort to which his family was accustomed; with his time thus freed, he could look for seasonal or part-time work that might bring in cash with which to purchase luxuries or necessities. When coal was substituted for wood, cash became itself such a necessity; coal could rarely be obtained by barter or by trade in kind, since the people who sold coal had to purchase it from the people who had transported it (as well as from other "middle" men); and this series of transactions required cash. As each generation of fathers ceased to cut, haul, and split wood, each generation of sons knew less and less about how it should be done—and more and more about how to find and to keep a job that paid wages. Each generation of mothers, on the other hand, would have found the burden of their domestic chores more or less the same—perhaps even heavier—and thus would have been less likely to look outside their homes for employment, unless dire necessity intervened. Each generation of young girls, consequently, continued to be trained in the pursuits of domesticity—despite the fact that their brothers had gone on to other sorts of enterprise.

And what was true of cooking was true of other household chores as well. As the nineteenth century wore on, in almost every aspect of household work, industrialization served to eliminate the work that men (and children) had once been assigned to do, while at the same time leaving the work of women either untouched or even augmented. Factories made boots and shoes (this was one of the ten leading industries in the United States in 1860), so men no longer had to work in leather at home. Factories also made pottery and tin ware, so men no longer had to whittle. Piped household water (which was introduced in several eastern cities even before the Civil War and was fairly common in middle-class homes throughout the country by the end of the century) meant that children no longer had to be burdened with perpetual bucket carrying. The growth of the meat-packing industry, coupled with the introduction of refrigerated transport in the 1870s and 1880s, meant that men no longer spent much time in butchering. Virtually all of the stereotypically male household occupations were eliminated by technological and economic innovations during the nineteenth century, and many of those that had previously been allotted to children were gone as well.

But not so with the occupations of women. If the advent of manufactured cloth eliminated the need for women to spin (as well as for men to weave and children to card), it did not in the least affect the need for them to sew—and sewing was the part of clothing preparation which had always been exclusively female. Indeed, the advent of manufactured cloth seems to have been accompanied by an increase in the amount of clothing that people expected to own—and since ready-made clothing had not yet appeared on the scene, there was a radical increase in the amount of sewing that had to be done. The diaries and letters of women who lived during the middle decades of the nineteenth century are filled with comments about the pervasiveness and tediousness of sewing. Here is a representative sample, from a letter written by Ellen Birdseye Wheaton, a middle-class housewife living in Syracuse, New York, in April of 1850:

> Since the second week, in March, I have been preparing garments, for children's summer wear, having shirts altered and made, for Charles [her husband], and having dresses made, and fixed till I am at times, almost bewildered. I began this work earlier than usual, this season, hoping much to get the main part of my sewing done, before the extreme heat of summer, but oh! it seems at times as tho' it could never be done.[43]

The Invention of Housework: Industrialization

Like many of her contemporaries, Mrs. Wheaton hired seamstresses to come into her home to help during these sewing seasons (another occurred during the early fall, when cold-weather clothing was prepared), but the seamstresses assisted and did not replace her labor: they might work on the girls' dresses, while she worked on the boys pants; or she might cut out fabrics, while they did the plain stitching. According to letters and diaries of women living later in the century, the advent of the sewing machine eliminated the need to hire seamstresses but not the hours spent by the housewife herself.

Manufactured cloth also served to augment women's work by increasing the amount of household laundry that had to be done, laundry—like sewing—having been one of those tasks that had long been exclusively female. Prior to industrialization, much of the clothing that people wore was virtually unwashable: the woven woolen goods, the alpacas and felts and leathers of which outer clothing was made, were cleaned by brushing; and the linen or knitted wools of which underclothing was composed, although potentially washable, were in fact rarely laundered. When cotton replaced linen and wool as the most frequently utilized fabric, laundering increased; indeed, one of cotton's attractions as a fabric was that it could be washed fairly easily. This development was no doubt viewed as an improvement by many people, but there is no question that it altered the pattern of women's household labor for the worse. In the diaries and letters of nineteenth-century women, laundering appears, for the first time, as a weekly—and a dreaded—chore. Since it was exceedingly hard work (what with the rubbing, wringing, toting, and ironing), children rarely became involved in it. Whether done by a female servant or by the housewife herself, laundry was a major component of women's work in the nineteenth century—and arduous work at that.

Like clothmaking, some female chores disappeared during the century, but almost every one was replaced by other chores, equally time and energy consuming. Candlemaking became a lost art. In its place there were the glass globes of oil and the gas lamps from which soot had to be removed almost every day—a chore that housewives were advised not to assign either to children or to servants, since the globes could not survive rough handling. Waste-water systems (commonly known as "water closets") eliminated the chore of collecting "slops" but added the chore of cleaning toilets. Furthermore, in those cities in which the cleaning of outhouses and cesspools had been a commercial enterprise undertaken by men, the water closet privatized this work—and shifted it to women. Home canning equipment made it possible to preserve more fruits and vegetables for consumption during the winter but vastly increased the amount of work that women were expected to do when the season was "on."

Small wonder, then, that so many people commented on the exhaustion and ill health of American women during the nineteenth century. Industrialization had introduced many novelties to their homes and probably had, overall, improved their standard of living—but they still had a great deal of hard work to do. With the exception of the very poorest women, or those who were dwelling on the most primitive frontiers, American women living toward the end of the century probably ate a more varied diet, suffered less from the cold, enjoyed more space and more luxuries in their homes, and kept their bodies and their clothes cleaner than their mothers and grandmothers who had lived earlier. These improvements had not, however, lifted the burden of women's domestic cares, in spite of radical changes in the patterns of daily work at home. The processes of housework had changed in such a way that adult males and small children of both sexes were no longer needed to do domestic labor: wood did not have to be chopped, nor water carried, nor grain hauled to the mill. Men and children could be spared, to the schools, to the factories, to the offices of the burgeoning industrial economy. Adult women and their grown daughters, on the other hand, could not be spared: meals still had to be cooked; sick children had to be tended; infants to be nursed; clothes to be made, mended, and laundered—and industrialization had done nothing at all to ease the burden of those particular chores.

Industrialization, at least in these its earliest phases, had in fact created the material conditions under which the doctrine of sepa-

The Invention of Housework: Industrialization

rate spheres—could take root and flourish. Merchant flour, cast-iron stoves, municipal water, and manufactured boots had made it possible for men to work at wage labor without endangering (indeed, with some chance of improving) the standard of living of their families. As time wore on, the need to pay cash for flour, or for coal, or for any of the other commodities that were so swiftly appearing on the market, ensured that, once having entered the market for wage labor, men would stay there. Once that had happened, they ceased to train their sons in the multitudinous crafts that had been the heritage of men's work at home—preparing fuel, mending ironware, working in leather, building fireplaces, making cider, butchering pigs—and then the process was complete. A new generation of men came into adulthood having learned the skills needed to work for wages, not the skills needed to work at home. For these men the doctrine of separate spheres served to make sense of the new patterns by which they were living, and it was this new pattern of living and thinking that they taught to their sons.

For women the transition to the industrial order was different. Merchant flour, cast-iron stoves, municipal water, and manufactured boots did not free them from their labors. Insofar as these commodities allowed men and boys to leave their homes, and insofar as these commodities also created new jobs that only women could perform, women were tied even more strongly than they had been before to their cast-iron hearths. Angel food cakes, strawberry preserves, clean clothes, ironed ruffles, and leavened bread may have made life easier and pleasanter for their families, but they also kept women working at home. The factories and the schoolrooms may have sung a siren call to some women, but most of these were either unmarried or in dire distress. For the rest, the material conditions of domestic life during the first phases of industrialization required women to stay at home so as to protect (and even to enhance) the standard of living of their families: when women were absent, meals were irregular, infant mortality was higher, clothes were dirtier, and houses poorly maintained. Grown daughters were needed at home as well (at least until they married) because, in the absence of servants, who was left to help? Girls learned the crafts that their mothers practiced; boys did not. In this way the obverse side of the doctrine of separate spheres, the side that identified women with home and with homely virtues, was sealed in the best social cement of all: the patterns of daily life and the relations between parents and children.

Chapter 4

Twentieth-Century Changes in Household Technology

I N the first phase of industrialization, changes in household technology altered the work processes of housework so that "separate spheres" for men and women became, from the point of view of the household, not only possible but also desirable. In the second phase, the phase that is more or less congruent with the twentieth century, inventors and entrepreneurs and advertising copywriters and consumers themselves simply assumed that the separation of spheres was a normal arrangement, and they continued to build, to refine, and to accept the technological systems of housework accordingly. Eventually, however, the increased productivity that became possible with these new technological systems would serve to undermine the very ideology that lay at their base. In order to understand this dialectical process, we must first understand the nature of the changes that occurred in household technology during the twentieth century;

and in order to understand them, we must first disabuse ourselves of a set of commonly received notions.

Conventional wisdom has been telling us—for many decades now—that twentieth-century technology has radically transformed the American household, by turning it from a unit of production to a unit of consumption. Put into plain English, this means that the food and clothing that people once made in their homes is now produced in factories, and that what we do in our homes (eat the food, get dressed in the clothes, occasionally launder them) actually has little economic significance.

Now this particular piece of conventional wisdom (which, ironically enough, seems to be subscribed to by people as diverse as sociology professors and newspaper editors, political conservatives and Marxists) is a cultural artifact of vast importance, because it has two corollaries that guide people in the conduct of their daily lives: first, that as American families passed from being units of production to being units of consumption, the economic ties that once bound family members so tightly to each other came undone; and, second, that as factory production replaced home production, nothing was left for adult women to do at home.[1] Many Americans believe that these corollaries are true, and they act on this belief in various ways: some hope to reestablish family solidarity by relearning lost productive crafts such as baking bread or tending a vegetable garden; others dismiss the women's liberation movement as "simply a bunch of affluent housewives who have nothing better to do with their time"; husbands complain that their wives spend too much time doing inconsequential work ("What *do* you do all day, dear?"); and housewives can find no reasonable explanation for why they are perpetually exhausted.

The conventional wisdom was once not so conventional; it has its roots in the painstaking sociological observations and patient economic research undertaken by the pioneer social scientists who did their most important empirical and theoretical work in the years from 1890 to 1930.[2] All of them were, in one way or another, keen and disciplined observers of the world in which they lived. They witnessed monumental technological changes in their own lifetimes (from the steam engine to the electric motor, from the horse to the automobile, from handmade to factory-made clothing, from gas lamps to electric lights), and they were not unreasonably impressed with the impact that those changes were having on the daily life—and on the communal life—of their contemporaries. Unfortunately the conclusions that these social scientists reached may not be as fine a guide to our past (and to our present) as we have let ourselves believe.[3]

Twentieth-century household technology consists of not one, but of eight, interlocking technological systems: the systems that supply us with food, clothing, health care, transportation, water, gas, electricity, and petroleum products. Some of these systems have followed the conventional model—moving production out of the home and into the factories; but (and this is the crucial point) some of them have not. Indeed, some of the systems cannot even be made to fit this model at all. A brief historical sketch of the development of these eight systems, tracing them back, in some cases, to their nineteenth-century origins, should reveal, rather quickly, why the conventional model is, at best, incomplete and, at worst, grossly misleading.

The Shift from Production to Consumption

The food, clothing, and health-care systems are the ones the early social scientists examined in greatest detail—and they are the ones, not surprisingly, that fit the "production to consumption" model most precisely.

THE FOOD SYSTEM

Flour milling, as we have seen, had become an industrial enterprise fairly early in the nineteenth century; and by the latter decades of the century, the local grist mill had become a vestigial institution in most American communities. People were buying the flour that they needed (it was now more likely to be wheat flour than corn, oats, or rye; fine flour rather than meal or any of the coarser grinds; and "white" rather than "whole") in barrels and in sacks rather than producing it themselves or carrying it themselves to the mill to be ground. The only significant change that occurred during the twentieth century was a shift from wood and cloth containers to paper ones, a decrease in the standard size of the package, and a decrease in the average household consumption of plain flour itself (a decrease that is coincidental with an increase in the use of factory-, or bakery-, made breads, biscuits, and cakes.)[4]

Butchering also became a lost household art during the second half of the nineteenth century as the technology for canning meats was perfected (beginning about 1870) and the technology for refrigeration developed to the point where it became possible to keep large quantities of meat at low temperatures in packing plants and then ship it in ice-cooled (later machine-cooled) railroad cars to refrigerated warehouses in other cities. Even before the twentieth century, Americans were becoming unaccustomed to the sight of herds of cattle being driven through city streets to slaughterhouses, and few families (except in some rural areas) were eating meat that had been killed at the hand of some family member and preserved by the hand of another. The most significant change in this domain of food supply in the twentieth century was the introduction of the mass-produced (hence neither raised nor slaughtered at home) chicken in the years after the Second World War.[5]

Like milling and butchering, canning had become a big business during the last decades of the nineteenth century. A French inventor, Nicholas Appert, took out the first patents on the process before 1810: raw foodstuffs were placed in glass containers and cooked in water baths (container and all) for a long time. At first the food produced in this way was unpalatable and fairly likely to spoil—hence, early in the nineteenth century canned food was produced mostly under contract to national governments, who supplied it to soldiers and sailors on campaign. As the decades wore on, however, improvements in the technique (such as the introduction of vacuum cookers and tin, rather than glass, containers) increased the attractiveness of the food—at the same time rendering it sterile and thus longer lasting.[6] During the

1820s, William Underwood went into the business of selling various meat products put up in bottles. Gail Borden patented a technique for condensing skimmed milk and preserving it with sugar in 1856; within a decade, his product had spread to all the national (and even some international) markets. During the Civil War years and immediately thereafter, businesses that specialized in canning such fruits and vegetables as cherries, tomatoes, peas, and corn flourished. H. J. Heinz began selling crocked pickles, horseradish, and sauerkraut in the 1870s. By the time another decade had passed, he had added cooked macaroni products to his line of goods, had entered all the major national markets, and had begun the practice of buying up whole crops of fruits and vegetables even before they were planted. The Franco-American Company was selling canned meals late in the 1880s—and in 1897, Dr. John Dorrance invented the process by which soup could be condensed, thus ensuring the continuing good fortune of the firm (Campbell's) that then employed him.[7] The total national output of canned goods was only about five million cans in 1860 but, by 1870, was up to thirty million and, by 1880, had increased fourfold.[8] By the turn of the century, canned goods were a standard feature of the American diet: women's magazines contained advertisements for them on nearly every page, standard recipes routinely called for them, and the weekly food expenditures of even the poorest urban families regularly included them. Indeed, by the end of the century, processed foods of all kinds—packaged dry cereals, pancake mixes, crackers and cookies machine-wrapped in paper containers, canned hams, and bottled corned beef—were part of the staple output of some of the largest, and most monopolistically organized, business enterprises in the nation. Not surprisingly, the meat-packing companies, the manufacturers of tin cans, and the biscuit makers were among the first groups of "trusts" to feel the impact of the government's "busting" activities.[9]

THE CLOTHING SYSTEM

By 1900 the manufacture and sale of ready-made clothing was also a booming enterprise in the United States: the total output of men's, women's, and children's clothing intended for domestic consumption in that year was estimated at $817 million.[10] The clothing trades, like the food trades, had begun to develop early in the nineteenth century. In cities such as New York, Philadelphia, and Boston, some tailoring shops expanded in the early decades of the century and adopted the practice of cutting and preparing fairly large batches of clothing to be sold "ready-made," rather than made up to individual order.[11] In the early years, ready-made clothing was intended for men, and poor men at that; it was made up in fairly coarse cloth and in the fairly loose-fitting styles that characterized the attire of laborers, sailors, farmers, and slaves. The invention of the sewing machine early in the 1850s greatly expanded the volume of ready-made clothes that could be produced by the enterprises then in existence (since the use of even the earliest sewing machines made it possible for each tailor or seamstress to increase production ten to fifteen times); and the development, during the 1860s, of better techniques for cutting clothes to fit (based in part upon statistical data about men's body sizes accumulated by the United States Army during the Civil War) made it possible for manufacturers to begin marketing ready-made clothing of higher quality. By 1879 an economist surveying the men's clothing business adjudged that it had become possible for any man or boy, from any walk of life, to obtain, at a reasonable cost, a well-fitting suit of clothes. By 1875 the Montgomery Ward Company (as well as other mail-order firms) was making it possible even for those men who did not live within easy access of clothing stores to dispense with their wives' handiwork.[12]

Women's clothing was industrialized somewhat later. Before the Civil War, there were a few manufacturers who specialized in producing ready-made cloaks, shawls, and mantuas—items of outer clothing that were difficult for women to work up at home and that, because of their loose fit, were suitable for manufacture; crinolines and hoopskirts followed, for much the same reasons. The Census Bureau did not begin enumerating manufacturers of women's clothing until 1860; but by that time, there were already ninety-six businesses engaged in this trade in cities up and down the Eastern coast. By 1870 the number had doubled; and by 1900, as Eastern European immigrants were being attracted into this branch of industry, it had multiplied tenfold.[13] During the 1870s and 1880s a few daring entrepreneurs attempted ready-made women's suits (actually they were what we would call two-piece dresses), but they were sold (by some of the early department stores such as Lord and Taylor's and B. Altman's) with the caveat that they would have to be altered by a seamstress in order to fit properly.[14] Later in the century, especially after the advent of the "Gibson girl" style (which consisted of a blouse, called a shirt-waist, and a skirt which were purchased separately), the problem of fit became somewhat easier to solve—and at that juncture, the industry began to expand even more rapidly. By 1910, by which date sewing, cutting, and pressing machines had all been elec-trified, another economist, surveying women's ready-made clothing this time, adjudged that every article of women's cloth-ing could be had ready-made, in styles and prices suitable for everyone from the poorest farm girl to the richest society matron. Contemporary documents tend to bear out this judgment: the Sears Roebuck catalogue, for example, did not contain a single item of women's clothing in 1894; but by 1920 it had ninety illustrated pages of female attire. In ensuing decades of the twen-tieth century, fashions and fabrics changed, and the industry continued to expand—but the nation had made the conversion from home-made to factory-made clothing before the outbreak of the First World War.[15]

THE HEALTH-CARE SYSTEM

The health-care system developed its modern form somewhat later than the food and clothing systems, but was also in the throes of moving out of the household and into centralized insti-tutions by the end of the nineteenth century. Manufacturers of patent medicines were the first to take over some of the work that had earlier been done by housewives. Early in the nineteenth century most cookbooks or advice manuals had contained lengthy chapters devoted to the preparation of medicines and foods for the sick.[16] By midcentury a few entrepreneurs had begun manufacturing these "home" remedies in bulk and marketing them by mail order, by peddlers, or in retail establish-ments; Lydia Pinkham's Potions and Carter's Little Pills (for-merly, "Little Liver Pills") are just two, still famous examples of this popular type of medication.[17] By the end of the century, the patent drug business was so active, and so many varieties of remedies were available, that pages upon pages of advertisements in women's magazines were devoted to them—and cookbooks had stopped giving recipes for preparing them at home.*

At the same time, various forms of health care which had once been proffered by housewives increasingly became the responsi-bility of specially trained workers. Nursing began to profession-alize in the latter years of the century. The first schools for nurses were founded in New York, Philadelphia, and Boston between 1859 and 1862; by 1900 there were 432 schools that had produced 3,456 graduates, and a professional association of such graduates (the American Nurse's Association) had been formed.[19] Nurses were employed in hospitals (by 1900 there were roughly 4,000 such institutions throughout the country with almost 400,000 beds), in sanitariums for the tubercular and the mentally unsta-ble, in settlement houses, in schools, and in home-nursing as-sociations—and every hour of care that they offered to their patients was an hour that would earlier, and under other circum-stances, have been offered by a housewife.[20] By 1900 there were also 16,000 funeral directors and embalmers abroad in the land; and every dead body that they prepared for burial, and every wake that they supervised on their premises, represented that much less burdensome and grievous work that women had earlier performed.[21]

During most of the nineteenth century, hospitals had been institutions devoted to the care of the urban indigent, precisely those people who could not be cared for adequately in their own homes, if they had them. Mortality rates in hospitals were high, and the care offered was essentially primitive and custodial; peo-ple of any means whatsoever avoided them and physicians used them, not to care for private patients in distress, but to learn their

*For example, *The Boston Cooking School Cookbook,* one of the most popular cookbooks of its day, contained no special section on "household remedies" and only a few recipes for special foods for the sick.[18]

trade and give vent, for a few hours a month, to their charitable inclinations.[22]

This situation began to change in the 1890s, however, as the principles of what was then called "scientific medicine" began to spread from Germany and France, where they had first developed, into the United States—and as physicians and hospital boards of trustees became increasingly aware that middle-class patients would be willing to pay for suitable hospital care.[23] Scientific medicine meant, among other things, that surgery could and should be performed under sterile conditions with the aid of anesthesia, and that wounds should be dressed with sterile bandages so as to lessen the danger of infection; clearly, these were tasks that could be performed better in hospitals than in homes and better by trained personnel than by amateurs. Increasingly, middle-class people, who could not care for the sick at home according to the standards that were becoming acceptable, were willing to pay for the service; at the same time, hospitals found the provision of private rooms a particularly easy way to offset their chronic shortages of funds. Physicians were, apparently, more than happy to go along with the trend, since the hospitalization of their patients meant less time and trouble spent in travel —and probably better care for their patients. The transition to hospitalization—even for pregnant women—was fairly rapid, as such social transitions go: between 1900 and 1920 the number of hospital beds doubled; it did not double again for another fifty years.[24] By 1930, when the first nationwide survey of such matters was undertaken, out of every one thousand people surveyed, seven hundred days were recorded as having been spent in the hospital in the previous year—and each of those days meant, from the point of view of the adult women who might otherwise have had to care for those patients in their own homes, a significant shift from the net production to the net consumption of health-care services.[25]

CONCLUSION

Thus, in all three of these technological systems (for food, clothing, and health care) the shift from production to consumption occurred slowly, over a long period—but with increasing momentum as the twentieth century approached. Butchering, milling, textile making, and leatherwork had departed from many homes by 1860. Sewing of men's clothing was gone, roughly speaking, by 1880, of women's and children's outerwear by 1900, and finally of almost all items of clothing for all members of the family by 1920. Preservation of some foodstuffs—most notably peas, corn, tomatoes, and peaches—had been industrialized by 1900; the preparation of dairy products such as butter and cheese had become a lost art, even in rural districts, by about the same date. Factory-made biscuits and quick cereals were appearing on many American kitchen tables by 1910, and factory-made bread had become commonplace by 1930. The preparation of drugs and medications had been turned over to factories or to professional pharmacists by 1900, and a good many other aspects of long-term medical care had been institutionalized in hospitals and sanitariums thirty years later. Individual families no doubt differed in the particular times and particular patterns by which they made (or underwent) this transition. Those who lived in urban areas probably had shifted from the production to the consumption of most goods earlier than those who lived in rural districts, and those who were economically comfortable before those who were economically deprived—but there were significant variations in these overall patterns. The urban poor received hospital care long before the urban rich, and some of the rural poor were probably wearing ready-made clothes decades before the urban rich (or even the urban middle classes) had made the same transition. Personal idiosyncracies also make generalizations difficult because there were surely people who—for reasons of pride in skills well learned, or reverence for traditions, or religious scruple, or aesthetic judgment, or pure intransigence—refused to give up brewing their own beer when everyone else was buying theirs in bottles, or continued to make strawberry jam when everyone else was settling for store-bought, or continued to construct hand-made clothes when everyone else was getting theirs from the catalogues or the department stores.

Twentieth-Century Changes in Household Technology

A Shift in the Other Direction: Transportation

Yet whatever variations of social station or personal inclination there may have been, the general pattern that most American families would adhere to in most of the arrangements for providing food, clothing, and health care had been settled, at the very latest, by 1930. This, of course, is the social trend that the earliest social scientists so correctly observed. What they did not observe —perhaps because the Depression and the Second World War gave them other problems to worry about, or perhaps because the postwar years found them either in retirement or in pursuit of other realms of investigation—was the impact that developments in the fourth of the household technological systems—the transportation system—would have on the work processes of housework and on the time allocations of housewives. As most modern housewives know far too well, you cannot consume frozen T.V. dinners or acrylic knit sweaters or aspirin or a pediatrician's services unless you can get to them, or unless someone is willing to deliver them to your door. In either case you, or someone else, is dependent upon whatever means of transportation is most convenient. Consequently, in order to understand why housework did not magically disappear when twentieth-century factories, pharmacies, and hospitals took over the work that nineteenth-century women once had done, the history of urban and rural transportation must also be considered.

The household transportation system has developed in a pattern that is precisely the opposite of the food, clothing, and health-care systems: households have moved from the net consumption to the net production of transportation services—and housewives have moved from being the receivers of purchased goods to being the transporters of them.[26] During the nineteenth century, many household goods and services were delivered virtually to the doorsteps of the people who had purchased them— and many others were offered for sale in retail establishments located a short walk from the houses in which people lived. Peddlers carried pots and pans, linens, and medicines to farm-

houses and to the halls and stairways of urban tenements. Seamstresses almost always came to the homes of the women and
children for whom they were fashioning clothing; and tailors
occasionally provided the same service for men. Milk, ice, and
coal were regularly delivered directly to the kitchens and basements of middle-class urban dwellers and not infrequently also
into the homes (or at least to the curbsides) of those who were
poor. Butchers, greengrocers, coffee merchants, and bakers employed delivery boys to take orders from and then carry purchases back to the homes of their more prosperous customers.
Smoked, dried, and pickled fish, fruits and vegetables, second-
hand clothing, and linens were routinely sold from pushcarts that
lined the curbs and traveled the back alleys of poor neighborhoods. Knife sharpeners traveled the streets with flintstones and
grindstones on their backs or in their carts, and frequently so did
the men who repaired shoes and other leathergoods. Bakeries and
grocery stores were located in every city neighborhood, so that
housewives, children, and servants could "run out" for extra
supplies whenever they were needed. Even doctors made house
calls. Under ordinary circumstances the individual urban
householder, whether rich or poor, rarely had to travel far from
his or her own doorstep in order to have access to the goods and
services required for sustenance. For rural householders such
convenience was not feasible; what shopping there was to be
done in rural areas usually waited for the weekly, monthly, or
even, in some cases, the annual trip into town or arrival of the
peddler.

In the latter decades of the nineteenth century, this pattern of
shopping began to change. In urban areas department stores
flourished: Marshall Field went into business in Chicago in 1852;
Stewart's opened in New York in 1861; and Wanamaker's, in
Philadelphia one year later.[27] At first these stores (which, by
definition, sold more than one category of goods) were patronized
only by the "carriage trade"—people who could afford to keep a
horse and carriage and hence could travel to such a store to do
their shopping; but later in the century, the range of their business expanded somewhat as horse-drawn omnibuses and trolley
and subway cars made it possible for people of lesser means to

travel. Even after the turn of the century, however, the department stores still did not appeal to the poor, and their total sales represented only a fraction of the retail sales in most urban areas. Most people living in cities, especially those who were in less comfortable economic circumstances, still acquired most of the goods that they needed, day in and day out, without having to spend much time either getting to the places where goods were offered for sale, or in getting their purchases home.

In rural areas, toward the end of the century, the total time spent in shopping for and transporting goods was additionally decreased by the widespread popularity of mail-order catalogues. A good part of the business done by urban department stores had always been either by mail (or, later, by telephone) ordering; in the last decades of the nineteenth century, this service became available to rural Americans as well. Montgomery Ward and Sears Roebuck (as well as hundreds of smaller enterprises) had entered the mail-order business during the 1870s; and by the time twenty years had passed, there was virtually nothing—from soup to nuts, from underwear to outerwear, from nails and screws to plows and buggies—that rural residents could not order from a catalogue.[28] And clearly they did: the mail-order companies were among the country's leading business enterprises by the turn of the century—and continued to flourish for decades afterward. The creation of rural free-delivery services, which were begun on an experimental basis in the 1890s and extended to most parts of the country before the First World War, further increased the accessibility of this service. Rural women, like their urban counterparts, simply did not have to spend much time either in shopping or in transporting the goods they were buying—even though, as the decades passed, they were buying more than their mothers and grandmothers ever had.

Prior to the advent of the motorcar, many transportation services were provided—when they were provided by the household at all—by men or by servants.[29] Stereotypically, it was the man of the family who hitched the horse to the buggy and went into town to get the mail and buy the flour and the cloth or whatever else it was that his family required. Similarly, in urban middle-class families it was the servant who fetched the doctor, or went to market in search of fresh meat or vegetables, or drove the family carriage through the streets. Among some immigrant groups men were responsible for handling the family's money and hence for making the family's purchases in the marketplace —carrying over into the New World traditions of the Old; and in these families, at least in the first generation of immigration, women were not regular participants in shopping expeditions or decisions. Needless to say, in actual practice stereotypic conditions did not always prevail. There must have been many occasions when, for one reason or another, mother rather than father made the trip into town, or a middle-class urban housewife chose to do her marketing herself; and there were certainly immigrant groups (for example, the Jews) among whom the standard of sex-role behavior dictated that purchases of food and clothing were made by women rather than by men. Yet even when these exceptions are included, it seems a fair generalization to say that in the years before (roughly) 1920 what shopping and transporting there was took little time, and that a large part of that time was spent by men and servants.

In the years just before and after the First World War, all this began to change—and the agent of change was, of course, the motor car.[30] "Why on earth do you need to study what's changing this country," one person asked Helen and Robert Lynd during 1925, when they were studying social conditions in Muncie, Indiana. "I can tell you what's happening in just four letters: A–U–T–O."[31] The speed with which the automobile became an integral part of daily life in America was, in historical terms, astounding. In 1890, for all intents and purposes, the automobile simply did not exist, except in the dreams of a few willful inventors. A decade later, there were already several dozen American entrepreneurs in the business of manufacturing automobiles, but their products were extremely expensive and intended for the delight of only the wealthiest segment of the population. By 1910, Henry Ford was already manufacturing the Model T, in a determined effort to lower the cost and thus increase the diffusion rate of the motor car to all classes of the population—and twenty years afterward, just at the onset of the Depression, he had virtually succeeded.[32] In 1921, President Harding told the Congress

(1) "The Yankee Pedlar," artist unknown, 1840–45.
Collection of the IBM Corporation.

The Transportation System

In times gone by, all kinds of goods and services came right to your door. Peddlers visited farmhouses (1), horsedrawn wagons delivered groceries (2) or trundled vegetables (3) or pots and pans (4) up and down city streets, pushcarts brought all kinds of goods right to the curb (5), laundry could be picked up and delivered (6), and even doctors made house calls (7). Although you might have used your first automobile just for fun (8), before many years had passed you would have been using it every day for domestic chores (9). As the years passed and suburbia spread, delivery services disappeared, and you would have hardly been able to run a household without a car, performing services that retailers had once offered (10) and chores—such as picking children up at school (11)—that had never existed before.

(2) Old Westbury, New York,
photographer unknown, *c.* 1905.
Velsor Collection,
Nassau County Museum.

(3) Homestead, Pennsylvania,
Lewis Hine, *c.* 1910.
Courtesy of the
Russel Sage Foundation.

(4) Travelling Tin Shop,
Brooklyn, New York,
Berenice Abbott,
22 May 1936.
Abbott Collection,
Museum of the City
of New York.

(5) Street Vendors, Hester Street, New York City, photograph by Byron, 1898. The Byron Collection, Museum of the City of New York.

(6) Probably Oakland, California, by an unknown photographer, *c.* 1939.

(7) Scott County, Missouri, John Vachon, 1942. Library of Congress.

(8) Illustration from Robert S. Crandall,
Around the World in an Auto, 1907.

(9) Bellerose Village, New Yor
photographer unknow
c. 1907. Nassau County Museu

(10) Supermarket parking lot, Glen Cove, New York, Ruth Schwartz Cowan, 1983.

(11) Picking-up children, Cherrywood School, Levittown, New York,
photographer unknown, c. 1968. Levittown Public Library.

that "the motorcar has become an indispensible instrument in our political, social and industrial life."[33] By 1930, just as bad times were beginning, there were roughly thirty million households in the United States—and twenty-six million registered automobiles.[34] Allowing for some households that had two automobiles (not yet a common practice, even in the upper middle classes) and for some automobiles that were used only for business purposes, it still seems reasonable to conclude that the daily lives of at least half the people then living in the United States had been touched by this newfangled mode of transportation before the advent of the Depression. When horse transport had been the rule, a private carriage was beyond the means of all but the very rich; everyone else depended upon his or her feet, on public transport, and—in rural areas—on saddled horses or open carts. The automobile brought the advantage not just of speed in transport but also of privacy to more Americans than had ever before had this privilege. The Lynds estimated that, in Muncie in the 1890s, only 125 families owned a horse and buggy—and they were all members of the élite; by 1923, there were 6,222 passenger cars in the city, "roughly one for every 6.1 persons, or, two for every three families."[35] And what was happening in Muncie was apparently happening nationwide (with the possible exception of the older Eastern cities which were well supplied with public transportation systems): people of many social classes were finding that it was possible for them to get where they wanted to go faster, over longer distances, according to their own schedules—and with carrying capacity attached.

Interestingly enough, when the automobile began to replace feet and horses as the prime mode of transportation, women began to replace men as household suppliers of the service. For reasons that may be clear only to anthropologists and psychologists, automobile driving was not stereotypically limited to men. This situation may have arisen because advertisers of automobiles made a special effort to attract the interest of women, or because the advent of the automobile coincided with the advent of what was then called the "new girl"—more athletic, better educated, less circumscribed by traditional behavior patterns—or for a host of other reasons presently beyond our ken, but it unquestionably happened. The woman who could drive even became something of an ideal for a time:

> Like the breeze in its flight, or the passage of light,
> Or swift as the fall of a star.
> She comes and she goes in a nimbus of dust
> A goddess enthroned on a car.
> The maid of the motor, behold her erect
> With muscles as steady as steel.
> Her hand on the lever and always in front
> The girl in the automobile.[36]

The girl who drove an automobile in 1907 (when this jingle was published) was a middle-aged matron by 1930—and then what she was driving to was not the moon but the grocery store. As the nation shifted from an economy dominated by the horse to an economy dominated by the automobile—and as the Depression created stiff competition among retailers for shares of a declining market—delivery services of all kinds began to disappear. The owners of grocery shops and butcher's markets began to fire their delivery boys in an effort to lower prices and thus more effectively to compete with the chain stores and supermarkets which were cropping up throughout the land.[37] Some of the chain stores began to eliminate these services as the Depression deepened. The supermarkets (self-service markets with many departments) almost by definition had never had them. After the Second World War, mail-order companies such as Sears Roebuck and Montgomery Ward discovered that they could compete effectively with department stores by opening retail outlets of their own, thus converting their mail-order customers into shoppers. Department stores discovered that many of their customers had moved out of the central city neighborhoods and so opened suburban branches—which were accessible only by car. Physicians discovered that they could stop making house calls and require that all ambulatory patients (in itself an ironic euphemism) be brought to their offices—without losing a significant number of patients. Indeed, a survey of private practitioners in Philadelphia in 1929 revealed that physicians were spending roughly six hours a week making house calls during an average working week of fifty hours; the rest of the time they were in offices, hospitals, or clinics.[38] Medical care, in general, became more dependent upon the availability of complex and expensive equipment (X-ray machines, iron lungs, intravenous feedings, anesthetics), so that visiting nurses were less able to cope, and hospital visits (which required transporting the patient back and forth, rather than waiting at home for the nurse to arrive) became more frequent.

These various individual and corporate decisions were spread out over two decades, but they all conspired in the same direction —to shift the burden of providing transportation services from the seller to the buyer. By the end of the 1930s, the general notion that businesses could offer lower prices by cutting back on services to customers was ingrained in the pattern of business relations. The growth of suburban communities in the postwar years did little to alter that pattern: as more and more businesses converted to the "self-service" concept, more and more households became dependent upon "herself" to provide the service.

By midcentury the time that housewives had once spent in preserving strawberries and stitching petticoats was being spent in driving to stores, shopping, and waiting in lines; and the energy that had once gone into bedside care of the sick was now diverted into driving a feverish child to the doctor, or racing to the railroad station to pick up a relative, or taking the baseball team to the next town for a game. The automobile had become, to the American housewife of the middle classes, what the cast-iron stove in the kitchen would have been to her counterpart of 1850—the vehicle through which she did much of her most significant work, and the work locale where she could most often be found.

The Household Utility Systems: Water

The historical development of four household utility systems —those that supply us with water, gas, electricity, and petroleum products—reveals other deficiencies in the "production to consumption" model; and thus their history is appropriately considered separately. The ways in which water and energy are supplied to households are important determinants of the work processes of housework, yet the details of these systems have rarely been considered by those who are convinced that women's work has been markedly lightened in the last one hundred years.

Water supply is probably the oldest of these systems.[39] Even before the outbreak of the Civil War, most major American cities had established municipal water systems: reservoirs of fairly pure water, pipelines, and aqueducts to bring the water into various parts of the city; and pumping stations, equipped with large steam engines, to carry the water along. Before 1860 some of these cities had also begun to build sewer lines for the disposal of waste and storm waters; and in the latter years of the century, more cities followed suit as the public health consequences of stagnant and fouled water became increasingly clear. The earliest supply and sewerage systems were intended not for domestic, but rather for industrial, customers; but in the latter decades of the century—especially when water closets became popular—more and more middle- and upper-class home owners began to pay for the privilege of connecting their residences to the municipal water pipes and sewers, and new houses began regularly to be provided with these conveniences. By the end of the century, "running water" was a standard convenience in urban households, even those of the very poor—whose tenements might have been provided with a water tap in the courtyard or a water closet at the end of the communal hall, although rarely in the individual apartments.

Rural residents were not so lucky; lacking municipal corporations that could finance and organize water-supply and sewerage projects, they had to provide individual solutions to the problem of obtaining water. In rural areas for most of the nineteenth century, "advanced conveniences" meant a hand-powered pump beside the kitchen sink. Otherwise, farm people carried water, as their forebears had done, from outdoor pump or from a nearby well, brook, stream, or lake. Water closets were virtually unknown in nineteenth-century rural America, as most households lacked pumps that could sustain sufficient water pressure to make one operable; outhouses, privies, or open pits were the most common toileting facilities.

In any event, tap water and water closets are only small parts of what we now consider the total water system. The full system contains pipes to conduct water into more than one room of a house, devices for heating some of the water and distributing it, as well as specialized containers for water (bathtubs, sinks, and shower stalls) which make it fairly easy to use water for different purposes and to dispose of it afterward. Tap water may have been available to most people in the cities by the end of the nineteenth century, but the other parts of the water system were not widely diffused until the middle decades of the twentieth. Between 1900 and 1930, small electric and gasoline motors became available to run water pumps in rural homes; gas and electric companies began to promote the sale and to lower the price of self-sufficient hot-water heaters (they were self-sufficient because, unlike the earlier heaters—called "waterbacks"—they had their own heat source and were not attached to the kitchen stove); new technologies were introduced in the manufacture of sanitary fixtures (ceramic finishes over metal bases) which both lowered the price and eased the maintenance of kitchen and bathroom appointments; new processes (particularly a technique for alloying zinc with steel) also lowered the price of plumbing fixtures; and monopolistic organization in the pipe industry meant that plumbing systems became standardized.

By the end of the 1920s, in urban areas hot and cold running water had become the norm for middle-class American housing, and the architectural form of the modern bathroom had solidified.[40] Most urban and small-town middle-class families had hot and cold water taps in their kitchens; and at least one separate room had become a bathroom, equipped with two sets of taps (for sink and tub), ceramic tiles (made by the manufacturers of sinks and tubs), and water closets; the water was likely to be available at any hour of the day or night at sufficient pressure to make all those fixtures function. For rural families and for the urban poor, the introduction of water systems was delayed, as a result partly of municipal building codes and of rural electrification, some such families achieved access to the full water system during the decade of the 1930s; the postwar construction boom brought these amenities to many other families after 1945.[41]

In terms of the processes of housework, the introduction of modern water systems had multiple effects, some of which have been ignored by the conventional model. People of all ages and sexes no longer had to carry water long distances (which was back-breaking work), and women no longer had to heat water on stoves and carry it to the place where their laundry was to be done. In this sense, obviously, burdensome tasks were eliminated for all members of the household, and grateful they must have been for the change. In addition, the installation of indoor plumbing made it possible to improve personal cleanliness, family health, and, ultimately, public health as well—improvements that all of us who now take them for granted would be wise not to ignore.[42]

Women shared in the general lightening of labor that occurred when taps replaced pumps and hot water heaters replaced kettles, but the advent of indoor plumbing created a new task, one that had never existed before; because of the way households were organized at that time, that task naturally fell to women. By the 1920s and 1930s, most men were employed (when employment was available) outside their homes, and most children spent most of their youth in school. Adult women remained at home, and thus it was to them that the burden of cleaning the bathroom fell: in any event, women had traditionally been responsible for household cleaning, whether they were employed outside their homes or not. Cleaning a bathroom was not light work; and, given the frequency with which the room was used, and the seriousness of the diseases that might result from unsanitary conditions, it was not casual work either. The bathroom was not then just one more room to be cleaned, but a room that had to be thoroughly and frequently cleaned if the health of the family was to maintained.

Thus, if it makes sense to say that, in the absence of modern water-supply systems, women (and other members of the family) had to "produce" water for cooking and hot water for bathing and laundering, then it also makes sense to say that, *with* such systems, women have to "produce" clean toilets, bathtubs, and sinks. The item produced has changed, but the fact of production has not. Indeed, as we all know, standards of personal and household cleanliness have increased markedly during the twentieth century (sheets, underclothes, table linens are changed more frequently; floors, carpets, fixtures are kept freer of dust and grime); or—to put it somewhat more accurately—more people are becoming accustomed to living at standards of cleanliness that were once possible only for the very rich. "Increased standards of cleanliness," when translated into the language of production and consumption, essentially means "increased productivity." Women have always been responsible for keeping their families and their homes clean; with modern water (and other utility) systems, they became responsible for keeping them even cleaner. Given the stereotypical sex-role division of labor in the early twentieth century, it was inevitable that this work would fall to women. Hot and cold running water in the kitchen and the bath eliminated some of the hard labor that women had done, but it also eliminated some of the work that men and children had once done (and thus left them increasingly free to labor in other places) and created new chores and new standards (which women would have to undertake and to meet). The conventional model accounts for the first of these changes, but not for the second and the third.

The Household Utility Systems: Gas, Electricity, and Oil

Considered together, the other household utility systems had a similar impact on the work processes of housework, in part because they reached a stage of fairly complete development—at least in the United States—at about the same time as the water-supply system. The first American company to manufacture inflammable gas (by controlled combustion of coal—hence "coal gas") was formed in Baltimore in 1816, and similar organizations appeared in other cities within a decade after that.[43] Coal gas was meant to be used for lighting, replacing candles and oil lamps on streets, in workplaces, and in homes. By the outbreak of the Civil War, the manufacturing and distribution of gas was a major industrial enterprise in most American cities; new techniques for creating gases that would burn more efficiently were constantly appearing, and competition between local companies was keen.

After the Civil War that competition became even keener as the result of new developments external to the gas industry itself: petroleum (which, after refinement, yielded a fine illuminating fluid, kerosene) was discovered in Pennsylvania in 1859; and the electric light bulb (which, when connected to a system of electric generation and transmission, was an even better illuminant) was invented in 1879. The gas companies struggled along for decades, jumping on one bandwagon or another to solve their competitive problems: sometimes by merger; sometimes by trying newer, more efficient gases; sometimes by altering the gas fixtures themselves (the Welsbach mantle, which created light by the incandescence of a fabric rather than by direct combustion of a gas, was introduced in the 1880s and led to a brief resurgence of gaslighting which has come to be called the "gaslight era"); and sometimes—and this is crucial—by developing new appliances for heating and cooking by gas. Late in the nineteenth century, gas stoves, ranges, water heaters, and furnaces began to appear on the market, frequently either sold through the gas companies themselves or manufactured by their subsidiaries.[44]

As the twentieth century began, the gas companies became aware that their lighting business was eroding ever more swiftly and was unlikely to return; consequently, they began an active campaign to promote gas for heating. Partly as a result of their efforts, the transition was achieved rather swiftly: in 1899 roughly 75 percent of the gas being produced nationwide was used for illumination (the largest part of the remainder was consumed in industrial processes); but twenty years later, in 1919, only 21 percent was still used for this purpose, while 54 percent was consumed as domestic fuel.[45] The trade association of gas companies (American Gas Association, or AGA) subsidized development work on the improvement of gas stoves, hot water heaters, and hot air furnaces—a tactic that proved effective. In 1915, for example, the American Stove Company brought out the first effective oven thermostat; and at about the same time, stove manufacturers began to shift from cast iron to enamelized surfaces.[46] The gas companies also began to offer reduced rates to domestic customers who purchased heating apparatus—a useful technique first pioneered, ironically, by the electric companies. Some companies also began to convert from manufactured to natural gas (a mixture of organic gases located in underground deposits, which is considerably more efficient and less toxic), thus further lowering the cost of gas heating and making it more attractive to homeowners. By 1930 gas cooking prevailed over all other forms in the United States: almost 14 million households cooked with gas; while only 7.7 million still used the older fuels (coal and wood), 6.4 million used oil, and .875 million used electricity.[47] By 1930 gas space and water heating, although not as prevalent as gas cooking, were also becoming commonplace.

Electricity and oil, quondam competitors with gas, were equally a part of that modernization process. The scientific principle that underlies the electrical system was discovered, during the 1830s, by Michael Faraday, an Englishman; but little was done to develop the capabilities of either electric generators or motors until an American, Thomas Edison, invented the incandescent light bulb in 1879.[48] Edison was a clever inventor and a brilliant businessman; he realized that the light bulb was useless without a source of electricity—and that the enterprise that could corner the market on supplying both of them would be an enterprise to reckon with. He consequently set himself and his laboratory assistants to the task of developing not just the light bulb but also the lamp sockets, the household wiring, the meters, the underground cables, and the electric generators that would be necessary. In 1882 he opened the first central electric station in the U. S. (on Pearl Street, in New York City); and two years later, five hundred New York homes (in addition to several thousand businesses) were using electric lamps. In 1882, Edison also began companies for manufacturing generators (for customers who did not want central electric service) and light bulbs; for several years he had a virtual monopoly on electric service and manufacturing. From these small beginnings (actually not so small, as Edison had powerful investors on his side), a major industry enterprise was born. By 1900, the companies that Edison had formed to manufacture electrical goods had merged with another company to become General Electric; his generating enterprises were on their way to becoming what is now one of the largest utility companies in the world, Consolidated Edison of New York; cities all across the nation were being wired for electricity; the enormous hydroelectric plant at Niagara Falls had opened; and another major company, originally formed for the manufacture of airbrakes for railroads (the Westinghouse Corporation), had entered the field.

Westinghouse was responsible for the introduction and development of the alternating-current (a.c.) motor, which now powers many household appliances. Edison had originally shown little interest in electric motors; development of efficient ones was a complex task, and his staff had enough to do without taking it on. George Westinghouse, on the other hand, knew the railroad business and realized that a healthy future could be envisioned for his company if he could manufacture effective electric motors for use in streetcars and railroads. Consequently, in 1888 and 1889 he bought out the patents on alternating-current motors that had been invented by two Europeans: an Italian scientist, Galileo Ferraris; and a Hungarian engineer, Nikola Tesla. Within a decade after starting development work, Westinghouse's engineers had perfected the alternating-current motor so that it was reasonably compact and reasonably reliable. By 1910 (and in part as a result of work done in companies other than GE and Westinghouse), the a.c. motor was available in a wide range of sizes, small enough to run a fan and large enough to pull a subway car loaded with passengers.

The a.c. motor would not have invaded the household, however, if its price (and the price of electricity) had not been low enough to be affordable by householders of moderate means. This lowered price was accomplished earlier in the United States than in other countries that had started on the road to electric development, because standardization occurred much earlier here, and standardization inevitably lowers the cost of production, which then lowers the retail cost of goods.[49] So few American companies held the crucial patents on the manufacture of electrical goods that it was a relatively simple matter for them to agree on standardization—and then to ensure standardization by cross-licensing their patents.* The electrical utility companies fairly early on formed themselves into a national association (the National Electric Light Association, or NELA), as did the electrical manufacturers (the National Electrical Manufacturers Association, or NEMA), and thus also helped to ensure the spread of standardization. The federal government did its part, too, not so much by direct action but by encouraging cross-licensing as a technique to avoid charges of monopolistic control. The end result was that by 1910 the entire country had been standardized on one form of electric current (alternating current, generated at 60 cycles, transmitted at high voltages but stepped down, by transformers, before entering households at 120 volts); and since electrical manufacturers could anticipate a nationwide market for products made to the same standard, mass-production techniques became a worthy investment for them. The end result, for Americans, was that the price of electric energy and electric appliances fell markedly between 1900 and 1930 and remained, during all that period and for many years thereafter, markedly lower than similar prices abroad.

Thus, not surprisingly, while only 8 percent of the nation's residences were wired for electricity in 1907, this percentage had doubled by 1912 and doubled again (to 34.7 percent) by 1920.[50] At first houses were wired just for lights, but by 1920 there was also a significant number of electric appliances on the market. Electric fans had been available since the 1880s; and although they probably deserve credit as being the first electric household appliances, they were not significant reorganizers of household work. By 1900 small a.c. motors were being sold with the intention that householders would connect them to the foot treadles of sewing machines or the hand cranks of washing machines. A decade later, appliances based upon the electric resistance coil (toasters, irons, hot water urns, and hair-curling devices) were becoming popular, since the substitution of nickel-chromium alloys for platinum in those coils had made them simultaneously

*Cross-licensing is the exchange of licenses on patents by two or more manufacturers.

more reliable (the platinum coils had burned out fairly easily) and less expensive. Between 1910 and 1920, all-of-a-piece electric sewing and washing machines came on the market, as did the early forms of the electric vacuum cleaner (essentially an electric fan hooked up to a carpet sweeper). Electric refrigerators and dishwashers were also available by the time the United States entered the First World War but were little more than toys for the very rich—as they tended to be either extremely expensive or extremely unreliable. During the 1920s the prices of washing machines, sewing machines, and vacuum cleaners fell (as mass-production techniques were introduced) and the reliability of the refrigerator increased (as new designs crowded each other on the market). Electric cake mixers (essentially old-fashioned egg beaters attached to electric motors) and food grinders also became popular during this period. By 1930 electric stoves were beginning to compete effectively with gas ranges, because electromechanical thermostats had been introduced during the 1920s; these thermostats also increased the popularity of electric toasters, irons, and hot water and space heaters. During the 1930s the price of electric refrigerators plunged—partly because of the introduction of mass production in this section of the industry, and also partly because of stiff competition for sales during the Depression. At the end of the 1930s, the automatic washing machine was introduced; the fact that this machine could spin-dry as well as agitate eliminated the time-consuming chore of running wet clothing through wringers between each part of the cycle. Although this washing machine (along with the electric dishwasher and the clothes dryer) did not become common until after the Second World War, electric service and electric appliances had become widespread among different classes of the population and, along with gas appliances, had begun to cooperate in the process of reorganizing the structure of household work by the outbreak of the war.[51] In 1941, according to the Bureau of Labor Statistics, 80 percent of all the residences in the United States were wired for electricity, 79 percent of the housekeeping families in the United States had electric irons, 52 percent had power washing machines, a similar percentage had refrigerators, and 47 percent had vacuum cleaners.[52]

Twentieth-Century Changes in Household Technology

Oil and its associated appliances were introduced into American homes somewhat later than gas but earlier than electricity.[53] Petroleum was first discovered in western Pennsylvania in 1859; the entrepreneurs who exploited these first American oil fields were principally interested in using liquid coal as a substitute for the various animal and plant oils that were then being used to provide light. In the decade following the Civil War, these entrepreneurs learned how to refine crude oil and to transport and market the resultant product, which was kerosene. Kerosene lamps had three advantages over gas lights: they were portable, they provided a pleasanter and steadier light, and they could be used in households that had no access to gas service—which, in the last quarter of the nineteenth century, still meant the majority of the nation's households. As the oil companies further developed their skill in bringing kerosene to market, they also managed to lower its price, so that kerosene lamps acquired a fourth advantage—economy. In the last quarter of the century, kerosene was stiff competition for gas. As ironic as it may be to think of it now, the fortunes of the major oil companies were initially created out of the sale of kerosene, not gasoline (a refinery product which was nearly useless until the internal combustion engine was developed late in the century).

By the turn of the century, however, the petroleum refiners had come to realize—as had the gas companies— that the handwriting was on (or, rather, in) the wall: electricity was going to erode the market for kerosene fairly quickly. The refiners, already having well-established distribution networks keyed to the residential customer, were reluctant to give these up and began to take defensive action. Kerosene and gasoline stoves had been on the market for several decades, but now the refineries began to give them away free or at much reduced prices, in order to stimulate demand for their fuel. They also began to encourage furnace manufacturers to develop designs that would enable home owners to convert from coal to oil for central heating. These "oil burners" first went on the market during the 1920s, but they did not begin to make serious inroads on the domestic heating market until after the Second World War, when the price of home heating oil fell in relation to the price of coal, and when a series of disastrous strikes in the coal fields made the ready availability of that product somewhat suspect.

Central heating, with all that it entails for both comfort and convenience, had, however, become possible even before oil became the principal fuel used for this purpose.[54] During the second half of the nineteenth century, large coal furnaces for household use had come on the market, complete with plumbing systems (if they were to be used to provide heat by piping hot water or steam through a house) and venting systems (if they were to be used to provide hot air). By the turn of the century, certain automatic features had been incorporated in these furnaces (so that, for example, they did not have to be continually resupplied with coal during the day), but complete thermostatic controls were not available until the 1920s. By that time gas furnaces with similar features were also available and competitively priced, and in some cities "central heating" was available as a municipal service; steam was generated in large central plants and piped, underground, to individual houses and apartment buildings for a monthly fee.

Installation of central heating was always an extremely expensive undertaking. The furnace itself was a major investment (during the last decades of the nineteenth century, for example, a furnace cost as much as a teacher's annual wage), as were the labor costs for installation of pipes, radiators, and vents. In addition, owners of older houses often had to pay to have a special basement room dug and cemented for the furnace, since walk-in basements had not been standard features of nineteenth-century residences. Consequently central heating remained a comfort enjoyed only by those who were fairly rich until after the First World War when it began, partly as a result of the boom in construction of new houses for the middle classes, to trickle farther down the economic scale. The trickling process was slow, however, since central heating remained the most expensive of all improvements that could be made to an older house (or apartment building), and since the poor lived then (as they do now) in the oldest housing. In their careful study of living conditions in Muncie, Indiana, in 1925, Helen and Robert Lynd remarked that about half the dwellings in the city had central heating, and that these belonged to the members of what they called the "business classes": "most of the working class still live in the "base-burner and unheated bedroom era."[55] Ten years later, when the Lynds returned to study Muncie again, not much had changed: 80 percent of the less expensive homes and 94 percent of the less expensive rental units in the city were still being heated by stoves in individual rooms.[56] In this regard Muncie seems to have been fairly representative of the country as a whole. Central heating was not available to poor people until the years after the Second World War.

Thus, with the exception of central heating and some advanced electrical appliances, many Americans made the transition to modern fuels in many aspects of their daily life before the outbreak of the Second World War. The symbolic nineteenth-century kitchen—dominated by the great coal- or wood-burning stove—was transformed into the symbolic twentieth-century kitchen—dominated by the gas, oil, or electric range. Hand tools were replaced by power tools; human energy, by chemical and mechanical energy. Scrubbing boards were discarded, and power washing machines took their place; carpet beaters and sweepers were thrown away, and vacuum cleaners acquired. Gas lights and kerosene lamps were wired and fitted with electric bulbs. Coal and wood no longer had to be hauled into the kitchen, and ashes no longer had to be hauled out of it. Cast-iron stoves no longer had to be rubbed with stoveblack; kitchens and parlors were no longer plagued by a constant residue of greasy ash. Light and heat could now be obtained, at almost any hour of the day or night, without much attention to the maintenance of the appliance or to the supply of fuel (aside from paying the bills). Some terribly burdensome chores were either eased or totally eliminated when the new kitchen came into being, which is no doubt why most people seem to have acquired conveniences and appliances as soon as they were in a position to pay for them and, given the prevalence of installment-credit plans after 1918, sometimes even sooner than that.

The multitudinous chores that constitute housework were totally reorganized by these technological changes; and yet—as with the impact of the water-supply system—the impact of these changes on the nature and the amount of work that housewives had to do was ambiguous. Consider for a moment the three parts of the work process of cooking which are directly connected to the appliance that we call a stove: fuel must be supplied, pots must be tended, and, subsequently, the appliance must be cleaned. Modernization of the fuel-supply systems for stoves eliminated only one of those steps, the first; and *that* was the step which, in the coal and wood economy, was most likely to be assigned to the men and boys in the family. Or, consider the process of doing laundry: washing sheets with an automatic washing machine is considerably easier than washing them with one that has a wringer, itself considerably easier than washing them with a scrubboard and tub. Yet the easiest solution of all (at least from the point of view of the housewife) is to have someone else do it altogether—common practice in many households in the nineteenth century and even in the first few decades of the twentieth. Laundresses were the most numerous of all specialized houseservants; many women who did their own cooking, sewing, and housecleaning would have a laundress "in" to do the wash or, failing that, would send some of it "out" to be done.[57] "Out" might have been the home of the laundress herself, or it might—especially in the early decades of the century —have been a commercial laundry, business establishments that were especially numerous in urban and suburban communities.[58] The advent of the electrically powered washing machines (as well as of synthetic washable fabrics) coincided with the advent of "do-it-yourself" laundry, so that the woman endowed with a Bendix would have found it *easier* to do her laundry but, simultaneously, would have done *more* laundry, and more of it herself, than either her mother or her grandmother had.[59]

I could multiply examples endlessly, but these two should suffice to reveal the reasons that modern fuel-supply systems did not necessarily lighten the work of individual housewives, although they certainly did reorganize it. Some of the work that was eliminated by modernization was work that men and children—not women—had previously done: carrying coal, carrying water, chopping wood, removing ashes, stoking furnaces, cleaning lamps, beating rugs. Some of the work was made easier, but its volume increased: sheets and underwear were changed more frequently, so there was more laundry to be done; diets became more varied, so cooking was more complex; houses grew larger, so there were more surfaces to be cleaned. Additionally, some of the work that, when done by hand had been done by servants, came to be done by the housewife herself when done by machine; indeed, many people purchased appliances precisely so that they could dispense with servants. It is not, consequently, accidental that the proportion of servants to households in the nation dropped (1 servant to every 15 households in 1900; 1 to 42 in 1950) just when washing machines, dishwashers, vacuum cleaners, and refrigerators were increasing just as markedly.[60] Finally, some of the work that had previously been allocated to commercial agencies actually returned to the domain of the housewife—laundry, rug cleaning, drapery cleaning, floor polishing—as new appliances were invented to make the work feasible for the average housewife, and the costs of labor (all labor, that is, except the labor of the housewife) continued to escalate in the postwar years.

Conclusion

Thus, the changes that occurred in household technology during the twentieth century had two principal effects. The first was to separate the work of men and children from the work of women, continuing a process that had begun in the previous century; and the second was markedly to increase the productivity of the average housewife. This conclusion can be put more succinctly by saying that, in the second phase of industrialization, American households and American housewives shifted not from production to consumption but from the production of one type of commodity to the production of another in even greater quantities. Prior to industrialization (which means, in the United States, prior to 1860), American households (and the adult women who lived in them) produced goods intended for sale in the market place, but they also produced goods and services that were intended for use at home: foodstuffs, clothing, medicines, meals, laundry, health care—and much more. During the first phase of industrialization (say, between 1860 and 1910), households stopped producing goods for sale. They did not, however (and this is the crucial point), cease to be productive locales: they continued to produce goods and services intended for use at home or, as the Marxists would say, for the production and the reproduction of labor power. During the second phase of industrialization (after 1910), those latter productive functions did not leave the home. The industrialization of the household did not entail, as that of the market had, the centralization of all productive processes; the household continued to be the locale in which meals, clean laundry, healthy children, and well-fed adults were "produced"—and housewives continued to be the workers who were principally responsible. What changed most markedly was the productivity of these workers: modern technology enabled the American housewife of 1950 to produce singlehandedly what her counterpart of 1850 needed a staff of three or four to produce: a middle-class standard of health and cleanliness for herself, her spouse, and her children.

Moreover, from the perspective of the household, the transportation system had developed in a direction that was precisely the opposite of the one taken by the food, the clothing, and the health systems. The shift from production to consumption of such goods as strawberry jam, petticoats, and medicine meant that less time needed to be spent in housework in order to provide the same standard of living; but the shift from the horse and buggy to the automobile canceled many of the potential benefits of this extra time.

Our commonly received notions about the impact of twentieth-century household technology have thus deceived us on two crucial grounds. They have led us to believe that households no longer produce anything particularly important, and that, consequently, housewives no longer have anything particularly time consuming to do. Both notions are false, deriving from an incomplete understanding of the nature of these particular technological changes. Modern labor-saving devices eliminated drudgery, not labor. Households are the locales in which our society produces healthy people, and housewives are the workers who are responsible for almost all of the stages in that production process. Before industrialization, women fed, clothed, and nursed their families by preparing (with the help of their husbands and children) food, clothing, and medication. In the post-industrial age, women feed, clothe, and nurse their families (without much direct assistance from anyone else) by cooking, cleaning, driving, shopping, and waiting. The nature of the work has changed, but the goal is still there and so is the necessity for time-consuming labor. Technological systems that might have truly eliminated the labor of housewives could have been built (as we shall see); but such systems would have eliminated the home as well—a result that (as we shall also see) most Americans were consistently and insistently unwilling to accept.

Chapter 5

The Roads Not Taken: Alternative Social and Technical Approaches to Housework

W E all tend to believe that the social arrangements with which we are familiar are the social arrangements with which everyone else is familiar; and if they appear to have been stable for long periods of time, we feel that there is good reason to believe that in some—almost biological—way these arrangements must be "best," either because they are most effective or most desirable, or even because they are prescribed by fate and are thus unalterable. The single-family residence, private ownership of household tools, and the allocation of housework principally to women have been normal arrangements in this country for more than a century, and most of us assume that they surely must be "best" for people in all walks of American life. We tend to make similar assumptions about pieces of machinery: if there is only one basic kind of refrigerator, or automobile, or television set, then that kind must be "best"; and if other kinds did not survive the competitive struggle of the marketplace, then they were not equipped to fulfill our needs.

Yet, over the years, many alternative social arrangements for housework have been proposed; and, at one time or another, the single-family residence, private ownership of tools, and the allocation of housework to women have all been challenged. These alternatives have had passionate defenders, and some have even been popular for short periods, but all have eventually failed. The same is true for alternative technical arrangements. Difficult as it may be to believe, there were many different kinds of household appliances on the market at one time, not just the restricted variety we now find (I am speaking here of *types,* not brand names); and these machines have also had their passionate defenders—a passion sustained, as the social arrangements were not always, by the desire for economic profit. In the end, however, these machines have also failed to win, as today's advertisers would say, "market acceptance." To understand why our households are organized as they are today, it is enlightening to explore the history of some of the possible alternatives that people, for good or ill, chose not to adopt—the roads, as a poet said, that were not taken.

Commercial Enterprises

The quintessentially American solution to the problem of housework is commercialization. At one time or another, entrepreneurs have attempted to pursue almost every aspect of women's work—from the care of infants to the care of the dead —as a business. Colonial cities—such as Boston, New York, Philadelphia, and Charleston—abounded with brewers, bakers, spinners, tailors, soapmakers, candlemakers, and dyers (most of them male) who undertook (for a price) to reproduce in their own places of business precisely the same work that many women of the time were doing at home for the benefit of their families.[1] During the early years of industrialization, some of those crafts became obsolete (candles, for example, were replaced by oil and gas lamps); but others—such as spinning, weaving, tailoring, soapmaking, and brewing—successfully weathered the conversion to large-scale, factory-based businesses. As industrialization proceeded, entrepreneurs began to experiment with commercial substitutes for other female skills; some of these experiments survived and flourished well into our own day, while others failed. The ones that succeeded, especially those concerned with the preservation of perishable foodstuffs and the preparation of foods for the table and of medicine for the sickroom, have been described in an earlier chapter; some of those that failed will concern us here.

Among the short-lived experiments were cooked-food delivery services, which were—unlike the modern enterprises that deliver pizza, wonton soup, or expensive exotic delicacies—intended to provide a family, on a contractual basis, with the basic meals that it needed seven days of the week. A scholar recently attempting an exhaustive treatment of the subject, has succeeded in locating records of nine such commercial establishments.[2] The earliest was founded in New York City in 1884; the latest in Flushing (in the borough of Queens, in New York City) in 1927; others were located in Pittsburgh, Pennsylvania, in Boston and Brookline, Massachusetts, in Mansfield, Ohio, and in New Haven, Connecticut. These establishments prepared meals in central kitchens and then delivered them to individual households at the time required; the householder had only to place the order, set the table, and (of course) pay the bill:

> Now let the cook lady strike; who cares? All I have to do is to step to the telephone or drop a post card and order dinner, have it served hot at the door, well cooked and of excellent variety, for less money

than you could do it yourself, to say nothing about wear and tear of nerves. It is emancipation, I say. . . . Be thankful there are those to blaze a trail out of the wilderness and lead the people into the promised land of delightful housekeeping. [An unattributed testimonial for the 20th Century Food Company, New Haven, 1901][3]

In the early days, delivery was accomplished in horse-drawn vans; in later years, in trucks. Some of these businesses experimented with new and different containers to keep the food hot for long periods; and one entrepreneur, who had formerly been an editor of *Good Housekeeping,* went into the business of manufacturing the containers on which he had acquired a patent, in the firm belief that cooked-food delivery services were the wave of the future.[4] He was, unfortunately, wrong. Although the records are by no means complete, none of the cooked-food delivery services appears to have been in business for much more than a decade, and most folded well before that. For whatever combination of reasons (and I shall return to this question later), cooked-food delivery services never became popular (the largest never serviced more than one hundred families), and none seems to have survived the difficult years of the Depression. Frozen T.V. dinners are our current, but not comparable, substitute.

THE COMMERCIAL LAUNDRY

Commercial laundries were longer-lived than cooked-food delivery services and, in their day, were considerably more popular, but they were eventually displaced as well. The origins of the industry are unclear. Some authorities say that the first commercial laundries appeared in the environs of San Francisco, California, in the late 1840s, to attend to the needs of the gold miners in the mountains; others, that such laundries were set up a decade or two earlier, in upstate New York, as an adjunct to the businesses that were then manufacturing detachable collars and cuffs for men's shirts; others, that they sprang up in many metropolitan areas to care for the linens used in hotels and boarding houses.[5]

Whatever the origins of the industry may have been, it is

clear that, in the years between 1860 and 1900, existing laundries expanded their services (especially to provide additional services to households), increasing numbers of entrepreneurs went into the business, and the businesses themselves increasingly depended on mechanized equipment. This equipment cleverly made use of the steam that was generated by the power source (a steam engine) to clean and rinse the laundry itself— hence, the terms *steam* and *power* laundry.[6] By 1900 there were commercial laundries in all major cities and in many rural and suburban districts as well. They offered diverse services, from "wet wash" (which meant that the drying and finishing were done at home) to fully finished (usually by hand) laundry. Some of these laundries were located in poor neighborhoods and were patronized by people who had no facilities for doing laundry in their own residences. The heyday of the laundry business seems to have been the decade of the 1920s. Between 1919 and 1929, gross receipts for power laundries virtually doubled; they declined somewhat during the Depression and war years, increased again immediately after the war, and then went into a long period of decline, from which they show no signs of recovering.[7] During the most prosperous years for the laundries, surveys undertaken by home economists demonstrated that, although few households (and only those with the highest income) "sent out" all their laundry work, very few families (and this was true even of poor ones) made no use at all of the commercial services. The items most commonly sent to commercial laundries were men's shirts and collars and "flatwork"—handkerchiefs, sheets, tablecloths, and napkins.[8]

In their day, the commercial laundries had both advocates and detractors. Those who argued in their defense believed, as Catherine Beecher and Harriet Beecher Stowe had, that laundry work was the most arduous, uncreative, and yet necessary part of women's work, and that, hence, "it would simplify the burdens of the American housekeeper to have washing and ironing day expunged from her calendar [and that] . . . whoever sets neighborhood laundries on foot will do much to solve the American housekeeper's hardest problem."[9] Detractors, such as Christine

Frederick, a household efficiency expert, argued that commercial laundries were expensive, that the rough handling frequently resulted in damaged or lost clothing (which only added to the expense), and that they might also be unsanitary, because either of disease-contaminated clothing or of disease-contaminated workers.[10]

Had all things been equal, it seems likely that the advocates would have eventually won out against the detractors (since few housewives implicitly regard their own time and energy as valueless, as Frederick did, and since lost socks and buttons notwithstanding, the commercial laundries continued to flourish); but things were not equal. Although no one seems able to be precise about how the industry was born, all commentators agree on what killed it: the electric washing machine. Wherever and whenever electric washing machine sales went up, commercial laundry receipts went down.[11] The decline of the commercial laundry is, in fact, one of the few instances we have of a household function appearing to be well on its way to departing from the home—only to return. Helen and Robert Lynd noticed this in Middletown in the mid-1920s. After noting that "the advent of individually owned electric washing machines and electric irons has . . . slowed up the trend of laundry work . . . out of the home to large-scale commercial agencies," they remarked in a footnote:

> This is an example of the way in which a useful new invention vigorously pushed on the market by effective advertising may serve to slow up a secular trend. The heavy investment by the individual family in an electric washing machine . . . tends to perpetuate a questionable institutional set-up—whereby many individual homes repeat common tasks day after day in isolated units—by forcing back into the individual home a process that was following belatedly the trend in industry toward centralized operation.[12]

Questionable or not, the practice of doing family laundry at home resurfaced with vigor; and today, commercial laundries are nothing but ghosts of their former selves, most of their trade being industrial rather than residential.

THE BOARDING HOUSE AND THE APARTMENT HOTEL

Two other commercial enterprises that some people thought "questionable," but that flourished for a time, were the boarding house and the apartment hotel.[13] Although we do not ordinarily think of these as businesses, that is what they were. The term *boarding house* here refers not so much to the common practice among poor immigrant families of "taking in boarders" (who were usually single and transient), but to the (to us) less familiar practice of converting what had once been a single-family home into a group residence with private bedrooms but "public" dining halls and parlors, all suitable for the use of middle-class people. Apartment hotels were somewhat more elaborate, usually larger, and always more expensive versions of boarding houses and were built *de novo,* rather than converted. Tenants rented suites of rooms for their private use; and various housekeeping services (laundry work, general cleaning, preparation of meals, telephone answering, and so on) were provided, sometimes as part of the rent, sometimes for an additional fee. The boarding house and the apartment hotel were dual attempts to profit from the fact that, between roughly 1870 and 1920, growing numbers of middle- and upper-class families either did not wish, or simply could not afford, to undertake the expense of running an independent household. In the 1870s, expensive apartment hotels were built in cities such as New York, Boston, and Hartford: the one in Hartford provided a centralized kitchen, a dining room, a laundry, and a barber shop.[14] Between 1901 and 1903, plans for ninety such hotels were filed with city officials in New York, and the editors of *Architectural Record* proffered the observation that "thousands of steady New Yorkers have been moving into them—people who are neither business nor social Bohemians."[15] In 1919, the thirteen-story Manoir Frontenac apartment hotel opened in Kansas City; it featured 103 expensive apartments, each outfitted with an electric grill-kitchenette for cooking breakfast and an electric dumbwaiter to deliver the other two meals from one of the building's three restaurants.[16]

During those same years, from 1870 to 1920, thousands of steady folk of lesser means had also been moving into boarding houses. No reliable estimate exists for the number of families who chose this form of dwelling, but it was sufficiently high to have engendered an angry response from social critics who believed, along with the editors of *Architectural Record,* that these institutions represented

> the consummate flower of domestic irresponsibility . . . the most dangerous enemy American domesticity has yet to encounter. . . . A woman who lives in [a boarding house or an apartment hotel] has nothing to do. She cannot have food cooked as she likes; she has no control over her servants; she cannot train her children to live in her particular way; she cannot create that atmosphere of manners and things around her own personality, which is the chief source of her effectiveness and power. If she makes anything out of her life at all, she is obliged to do it through outside activities.[17]

This last sentence reflects, of course, the principal reason that some people, especially feminists such as Charlotte Perkins Gilman, liked these institutions:

> This is the true line of advance; making a legitimate human business of housework; having it done by experts instead of by amateurs; making it a particularly social industry instead of a general feminine function . . . is good business. It is one of the greatest business opportunities the world has ever known.[18]

As it turned out, Gilman was wrong: like the cooked-food delivery service and the commercial laundry, the apartment hotel and the middle-class boarding house were not the greatest businesses the world has ever known; while some had more good years than others did, most of them were either defunct or in decline by the end of the 1920s.

THE FAILURE OF COMMERCIAL ALTERNATIVES

There are other "failed" commercial services that I might discuss (commercial vacuum cleaning, for example), but the central reason for discussing them would not change.* On the whole,

*Commercial vacuum-cleaning services, which existed in the United States and some European countries prior to the First World War, consisted of large compressors which were taken from house to house by horse-drawn carts; flexible tubing was attached to the compressors and run through the front door of the house, and various nozzles with which to do the cleaning were attached to the end of this tubing.[19]

although Americans have not objected to commercialization, they have applauded the commercialization of some household functions while resisting that of others. Funeral "homes" had no difficulty (apparently) in supplanting housewives as preparers of the dead for burial, and nursing homes seem to be succeeding in supplanting private homes as residences for the elderly who are ill; but many of the commercial day-care centers that commenced with such fanfare little less than a decade ago have collapsed. Most of us send (or, rather, carry out) our dry cleaning, but not our laundry. We allow strangers into our homes to wash our rugs and our upholstered furniture, but we insist on vacuuming those objects ourselves. On the surface, our behavior appears quixotic and inconsistent; if there is an underlying pattern explaining our acceptance of commercialization in some forms and our resistance of it in others, the pattern is exceedingly difficult to discern. One is tempted to argue, with the economists, that the underlying factor must be price: some things are brought to market at a price we can afford, while other things are not; hence, we buy the former because we can and avoid the latter because we cannot. This explanation is, at best, only partially adequate. Nursing-home care is very expensive, yet nursing homes thrive; infant care centers are also very expensive, but they do not thrive. Commercial laundries are only apparently more expensive than doing laundry at home (once the machine has been paid for); if the housewife's time is accounted for at even the minimum hourly wage, commercial laundry fees are not exorbitant: a man's shirt or a woman's blouse, washed, dried, ironed, and folded, currently costs $1.00 to $1.30, which represents 20 minutes of a housewife's time, when estimated at the current minimum wage, and 15 minutes when estimated at the current standard wage for houseworkers ($5.00 per hour).[20] Ever more families are bringing in two incomes, and ever more women are learning that their time is both literally and figuratively worth even more than $5.00 per hour, yet few—if any—households are rushing to patronize the remaining commercial laundries. Price is undoubtedly important in determining the choices that people make between competing ways of doing housework; but it is only one among many factors, as we shall see when we look carefully at some other "failed" social arrangements.

Cooperative Enterprises

While commercialization may have been a quintessentially American solution to the problems of housework, it was not the only solution that Americans attempted. Whatever the national commitment to individualism has been over the years, there have always been a few brave souls who preferred cooperation of one sort or another; and long years before the well-publicized hippy communes of the 1960s, many of these brave souls had tried their hand at some form of communal housekeeping.

"Communal" or "cooperative" housekeeping here denotes any social arrangement in which either some (or all) of the work or some (or all) of the expense involved in running an individual household is shared by a group of people who are not relatives. The cooperative or communal strain in our national character has made itself manifest in a wide variety of social institutions over the years. On a scale measuring the personal commitment required, these institutions would range from utopian socialist communities of the nineteenth century (where the participants totally renounced their former lives and gave themselves over to the group life) to the consumer cooperatives of the twentieth (where the cooperator only commits capital—and usually not much capital at that). All of these cooperative enterprises affected some aspect of women's work—sometimes intentionally, other times only by accident. If the cooperative strain in our character had become dominant, the social and technical systems through which housework is now performed would have been shaped very differently.

In the earliest days of settlement, some of the American colonies were organized as communes. In Jamestown, Virginia, for example, all tools, foodstuffs, and arable land belonged to the joint stock company that had financed the venture, and the settlers shared the work equally. Nonetheless, there was never much doubt that the principles of private property and individual ownership would dominate the economic life of the colonists. What cooperation there was in the colonial period took the form of neighborly sharing: a certain amount of the work was jointly performed by neighbors in barn raisings, in quilting, husking, and scutching (that is, preparing flax so it could be woven into linen) bees, and similar communal undertakings. Some tools were also shared: one housewife might lend her baking oven; one husbandman, his scythe; but the actual owner or the ultimate user of the barn, the quilt, the oven, or the scythe was never in doubt.

Late in the eighteenth century and then with increasing frequency in the first half of the nineteenth, certain religious groups began to advocate more radical forms of communal housekeeping. The Shakers (United Society of Believers) who settled in Mount Lebanon, New York, in 1787 may have been the first and the most famous of these groups, but they were not, by any means, alone. The Rappists were organized in Economy, Pennsylvania, in 1805; the Separatist Society of Zoar, in Ohio in 1817; the Society of True Inspiration (also called the Amana Colony), in Buffalo, New York, in 1843; the Perfectionists (later the Oneida Community), in Putney, Vermont, in 1848; the Jansonites, in Illinois in the same year; and later still, the Huterite Brethren, in South Dakota in the 1870s.[21] All these groups took their inspiration from the Sermon on the Mount and from the asceticism and communism preached by Jesus's earliest disciples. Each community practiced some form of shared work, shared property, and communal housekeeping. The Shakers slept in sexually segregated dormitories and worked at sexually segregated tasks; but all of what they defined as women's work (cooking, sewing, cleaning, laundering) was undertaken by groups of women working together, and assigned jobs were rotated periodically. In the Jansonite, Huterite, and Amana colonies, there were central dining rooms and nurseries, but each family occupied its own living quarters, although all the quarters were identical. The Perfectionists had what they called a "unitary household" but, unlike the Shakers, provided private sleeping quarters for couples, although they did not believe that the same individuals should be "coupled" to each other for long periods. Since the members of these communes were pooling their economic resources, they could afford to install the most modern housekeeping equipment. The writer Charles Nordhoff, who visited many of these communities in the 1870s, remarked that "a communist's life is full of devices for ease and comfort."[22] Frequently what the members of the community could not purchase they could devise, because the practice of rotating jobs among themselves meant that different skills were frequently being brought to bear on different jobs. The Shakers invented, among other things, improved washing machines, the clothespin, removable window sashes, a round oven for more uniform cooking, and an apple parer that quartered and cored the fruit. The Amana Colony produced cradles that could rock six or seven children at a time and furniture that was scaled down for children's needs. The Oneida Community patented a lazy Susan for a dining table and an institution-sized potato peeler, as well as improved mop wringers and washing machines. As they took their inspiration principally from religion and not from social theory, few of these communities explicitly intended to lighten or to alter women's labor (although the Perfectionists were an exception), but the net effect of their social practices was just that.

In other communities that were motivated by social theory rather than by theology, sexual politics were much at issue. The Owenite socialists, the anarchists, and the Fourierist socialists (also called "associationists") formed nearly one hundred communities during the nineteenth and early twentieth centuries, in places as diverse as Red Bank (New Jersey), New York City, San Antonio (Texas), Palo Alto (California), Cheltenham (Missouri), and Corning (Iowa). In each of these communities, communal housekeeping was adopted either to liberate women so that they could participate in industrial employment, or to liberate families so that they could enjoy the comforts that pooled resources might produce. Families remained intact in these communities but did not dwell in traditional homes. Each family had a private residence (in some communities, a cottage; in others, an apartment in a larger structure) but could take advantage of common facilities for dining and for child care. The work of providing meals, clothing, laundry, household maintenance, and child care was undertaken by community members specially employed for those purposes. These socialists and anarchists disliked the individual household as an institution but not the individual family:

> The isolated household is wasteful in economy, is untrue to the human heart and is not the design of God, and therefore it must disappear. . . . When we say the isolated household is a source of innumerable evils, which Association can alone remedy, the mind of the hearer sometimes rushes to the conclusion that we mean to destroy the home relations entirely. . . . the privacy of domestic life, Association aims to render more sacred, as well as to extend it to all men.[23]

If women were released from the drudgery of household labor, it was argued, and if women and men were free to pursue the work for which their talents best fitted them, then the exhaustion and frustration of daily life would disappear, and the relations between husbands and wives, parents and children, would be vastly improved. Similarly, if the returns from the work of the community were shared equally among all families, without some profiting handsomely from the labor of others, then there would be no difference between rich and poor, and all families would be able to enjoy the leisure and the comforts that industrialization had the potential to provide.

Whether religious or political, whether socialist or anarchist, there was some kind of cooperating community, practicing some form of communal housekeeping, in virtually every state of the Union during every decade from the early years of the nineteenth century until the end of the Depression. The founders and the members of these communities were highly motivated propagandists, since frequently the survival of their communities depended on their ability to make new converts. Some communities published newspapers and magazines; some members wrote books and articles; still others were missionaries and circuit lecturers. Although relatively few converts were made, the message of the "communists" was certainly heard throughout the land.

Not surprisingly, somewhat more modest experiments in cooperative housekeeping began to appear, spearheaded not by "wild-eyed" radicals but by fairly ordinary middle- (or upper-middle-) class people who could see some of the benefits that might accrue to cooperative housekeeping, but were not interested in giving their whole lives to it. In Cambridge, Massachusetts, in 1869, for example, Melusina Fay Pierce, then the wife of a Harvard professor, managed to persuade other respectable Cambridge families to invest in the Cambridge Cooperative Housekeeping Society. They rented a building not far from Harvard Square, installed equipment, and hired workers so as to function as a cooperative laundry and grocery store. The society collapsed after two years, without ever opening its planned cooperative kitchen.[24]

In the 1880s, community dining clubs (consumer cooperatives, where the work was done by employees), cooperative kitchens (producers' cooperatives, where the work was done on a rotating basis by the women whose families would eventually consume the meals), and cooperative cooked-food delivery services began to appear and continued to be established in one community or another until the mid 1920s; the longest lived of these survived for somewhat more than two decades; but, on the average, they lasted for only four to five years.[25] Early in the twentieth century, cooperative laundries became popular; these were simply commercial laundries operating under cooperative ownership. In Chatfield, Minnesota, for example, a cooperative laundry was established in association with a cooperative creamery; shares were sold at five dollars apiece; modern equipment (steam coils, centrifugal extractors, mangles, specialized ironers) was purchased, and a staff of nine persons employed. Farm families could (and did) send their wash to town with their cream; town families paid a surcharge of 10 percent for pickup and delivery. After six years of existence, 224 families had become patrons.[26] In New York City, a similar enterprise was set up by a social welfare agency to provide laundry services for poor families who were willing to pay a nominal membership fee.[27]

The most elaborate cooperative housekeeping venture of them all—and one whose failure suggests some of the reasons that others had difficulties—was the Evanston Cooperative

Housekeeping Association, founded in a wealthy suburb of Chicago by forty socially prominent families in 1890. This co-op owned its own building, which housed a commercial laundry and a cooked-food delivery service of "hotel standard." On its first day in business, the co-op delivered two hundred luncheons, but the experiment lasted a mere two months—killed, apparently, by an incompetent manager, a strike of servants (who believed, quite rightly, that some of them were going to be laid off), and the refusal of the wholesalers in Chicago, who feared a boycott by local merchants, to continue to supply raw materials.[28]

Like the Evanston Cooperative Housekeeping Society, most experiments in cooperative housekeeping were undertaken by people who were, if not wealthy, at least economically comfortable. There were, however, other kinds of cooperatives, like the New York City laundry mentioned earlier, that were set up by those who were middle class for the aid, the comfort, and the edification of those who were not. The principal intention behind these charitable cooperatives was to let them be controlled, eventually, by the cooperators themselves and, thus, to make the enterprise seem less demeaning as being less of a charity.[29] In Chicago, Jane Addams helped a group of single female factory workers establish a cooperative boarding arrangement for themselves, and various unions in New York City subsequently followed her example.[30] In Boston, Ellen Swallow Richards (one of the founders of the discipline of home economics) and several philanthropists established the New England Kitchen, a storefront community kitchen which prepared nutritious meals for immigrant families and trained immigrant housewives in American kitchen practices; the Kitchen failed to achieve its dream of becoming a cooperative because the immigrant families simply did not like the food the Yankee ladies were preparing.[31] In cities throughout the land, cooperative laundries and cooperative day nurseries were not uncommon in the years before the First World War. During the war, some of these expanded; and in certain locales, soup kitchens were added. One editorial writer in the *Ladies' Home Journal* expressed the hope that, after the war, all these cooperatives might be put on a self-supporting basis for use by the whole community:

[They] gave a new suggestion of the possibility of the eventual emancipation of women from the duplication in every household of equipment and labor for tasks that can be done cooperatively, thereby freeing the homemaker for the things that have to do with the higher life of the family.[32]

The heyday of the cooperative communities was in the years just before and after the Civil War; the heyday of communal housekeeping in one or another of its more modest forms, in the years of Progressivism, roughly between 1890 and 1930. Few of these alternative social arrangements lasted for long; few fulfilled the high hopes of their founders, and few survived the decade of prosperity and the Red Scare, the 1920s. We see the remnants of these arrangements today in a few communes scattered in rural districts, in a few cooperative nursery schools in cities and suburbs, in scattered cooperative supermarkets and credit unions, and in an occasional neighborhood food-buying cooperative that has managed to survive the entry into the job market of most of its female cooperators. A working mother of today, hard pressed to manage cooking, laundry, and child care, may close her eyes and dream about how much easier her life would be if there were a municipal laundry (with pickup and delivery) in town, a cooperative dining club up the block, and a cooperative day-care center around the corner; but recent history gives her few grounds for being sanguine. In the context of American culture, cooperative enterprises—however sensible on paper—have turned out to be difficult to sustain; and few of their members seem to have kept up the fight for long.

Part of the problem, no doubt, was economic: cooperators frequently could not raise the capital that they needed to get started; and some experiments in cooperation were ended when the cost of labor or the cost of raw materials turned out to be higher than everyone had anticipated, or when hard times made it difficult for the cooperators to continue paying their share or patronizing the service. But economics was only part, and perhaps a rather small part, of the problem. More at the hub of the matter were difficulties with the human material. Cooperation is not easy, as is well known by anyone who has survived five or more years of a marriage or tried to encourage cooperation in a group of recalcitrant nine-year-olds. It is hard enough when the task at hand is to win a baseball game or plan an advertising campaign or team-teach a course or build a new house. It is harder still when the task at hand strikes close to the individual human psyche, when the question is not how to build a house for someone else but how to build it for yourself; not how to serve a meal to strangers but how to serve it to your family; not how to train other people's children but how to train your own; when, in short, the task is not work but *house*work. Time and again cooperative communities died because internal arguments resulted in the departure of some of the cooperators or because members of the younger generation were not interested in following the cooperative paths of their parents. Limited cooperative ventures probably failed because their members found that they simply could not cooperate; one woman's husband did not like her to serve meals to another woman's husband, or one cook was preparing food in a fashion that the other cooks could not tolerate, or someone's notion of correct childrearing was widely at variance with someone else's, or the foods that were thought nutritious by one were considered barbaric by another.

Even under the best of circumstances, the survival of a cooperative venture is inherently—almost logically—problematic. When two ventures compete with each other (say, two companies that are both producing refrigerators, or two restaurants that are both serving fast food) and one fails (for whatever reason), there is still a reasonably good chance that the other will survive. Unfortunately, when two individuals (or two organizations) agree to cooperate with one another, and one partner subsequently reneges on the agreement, the whole enterprise collapses; one party can sustain a cooperative arrangement about as easily as one hand can clap. Thus, the chances of success for cooperative communities or even for cooperative kitchens were not high to start with, and social conditions in the United States during the period when cooperation was popular were not propitious. People in the mainstream of American society were almost always suspicious of "cooperators"; in the early nineteenth-century, cooperators were regarded as "godless heathens," and as such they were occasionally subjected to physical abuse. Later in the century, they were regarded as "free-lovers" and were driven out of town; in the twentieth century, especially in the 1920s, they were accused of being "reds," which meant the possible loss of their jobs and the certain loss of their social standing. Yet, even in the absence of overt hostility, the existence of the mainstream encouraged the failure of cooperative ventures, for whenever cooperation became too difficult or too frustrating, an erstwhile cooperator could always retreat to join the majority; there was always some place else to go.

The Domestic Servant

If most Americans voted with their feet to reject the commercialization and the communalization of some aspects of housework, many of them considered infinitely more attractive another alternative social arrangement—the maid. Although hard data on the subject are difficult to find (for reasons that will soon become clear), at no time in our national history have even half of the households in the nation been able to have such help full-time; but many more households, ranging fairly far down the economic ladder, have employed domestic servants seasonally, occasionally on a part-time basis. Employment of a servant is the most conservative of all alternative social arrangements for doing housework, because it is the only one that retains the single-family residence as well as the functions that any given family regards as crucial to its collective existence. This very conservativism may help to explain why, despite the expense involved, employment of a servant has always seemed attractive. For over three hundred years, American housewives have been telling each other that they would willingly trade in every one of the advantages of living in North America if they could only find a good maid. These housewives may not have regarded themselves as perceptive social critics, but they were unwittingly making a valid historical connection, for the social conditions that have made North American culture unique, and uniquely advantageous, are precisely the ones that have made good maids hard to find.

Over the years, there have been many different forms of household service.[33] During the first century or so of our existence, a large proportion of young women immigrants were indentured servants, trading a set number of years of employment in domestic service for the money that they needed to obtain passage across the ocean. In the centuries before industrialization, public authorities regularly sent young orphan girls to domestic service in "foster" households; and other young girls whose families were intact but poor went into service in return for room, board, and clothing. During the nineteenth century, wage labor began to replace these more or less medieval forms of employment, except of course in the antebellum South, where vast numbers of enslaved blacks performed domestic service without any hope of release. Elsewhere in the United States, however, unmarried women, many of them recent immigrants who would otherwise have had no residence on these shores, were earning a living (such as it was) as servants who resided in the homes of their employers. In 1870—the first year in which the employment of women was carefully recorded by census takers—fully one half of all women who were employed for wages were employed as domestic servants—roughly one million women, or one twelfth of the total labor force.[34] In the early decades of the twentieth century, the nature of the domestic servant labor force itself began to change.[35] As a result partly of the cessation of immigration, and partly of the expansion in industrial employment, young white women began to reject domestic service in favor of other kinds of work. Once having been predominantly white and single, the servant labor force in the twentieth century became increasingly black and married. This demographic change was accompanied by a change in the conditions of the labor. Married women preferred day labor to live-in work; and as the wages of such laborers continued to rise (since the supply was shrinking in relation to the demand), employers increasingly found that day labor was all that they could afford. Subsequently, with the introduction of income taxes, Social Security deductions, and contributions to unemployment funds, domestic work has been gradually forced into the underground economy. For the last few decades, employers and employees alike have been unwilling or unable to pay these taxes, and a vast amount of paid domestic labor is unreported and hence unrecorded. One consequence of this situation is a lack of information; another consequence is a lack of benefits. Domestic service today carries with it neither the benefits that used to accrue from having a free roof over one's head nor the benefits (such as Social Security pensions) that are now considered an essential part of legitimate wage earning.

In the past, as in the present, there have been impermanent, transient, or part-time forms of domestic service: rural girls who hired themselves out to cook and clean for farm families during the busy weeks of harvest; college students who regularly baby-sat for professors' children or came in occasionally to serve at dinner parties; women who, when their husbands were unemployed or temporarily disabled, picked up other people's wash and did it in their own homes; housekeepers who took over the management of a widower's household until he could find another spouse; suburban housewives who earned extra money by cleaning other people's homes a few days a week. Such employment has been difficult for census takers to enumerate, either because it has been deliberately unreported, or because people have been embarrassed to admit to it, or because irregular employment simply has not been inquired about in the census interview.

The variant forms that domestic service has taken, and the inherent difficulties that exist in enumerating it, render all statistical data on this subject dubious, except insofar as they suggest general trends. Prior to industrialization, it seems likely that one third to one half of the nation's housholds included resident domestic servants, but we have no way knowing how many households employed nonresident or temporary assistants. During the nineteenth century, the relative number of housholds employing full-time servants probably fell, but the absolute number was still fairly high, by twentieth-century standards, as the existence of at least one full-time maid was the *sine qua non* of middle-class status for a houshold. During the twentieth century, the ratio of servants to households has been falling, and in some locales, at some periods of time, it fell precipitously: in New York City, for example, there were 188 servants for every 1,000 families in 1880, 141 in 1900, and 66 in 1920.[36] Although day labor has been the most common form of domestic service in the twentieth century, so much of it is unreported as to make generalization virtually impossible, except to say that there are far fewer live-in servants than there used to be, and such servants have long since ceased to be required in middle-class households.

In any event, servants have always been something of a mixed blessing, for, as long as there have been settled communities on these shores, there has been a "servant problem." A household that has come to depend upon the work of a servant can be thrown into complete turmoil if the servant quits—and servants were forever quitting. Indentured servants were forever running away or asking to be released from their indenture in order to marry promising young men. Farm girls were forever getting lonely for their families or were never able to understand the sophisticated ways of the cities. Immigrant girls were, from the point of view of their employers, "forever dirty," "unreliable," "insubordinate"—and unable to understand instructions given to them in English. Black women were similarly, "forever drinking" or "coming late to work" or going off to "take care of a sick sister in North Carolina." Women who kept servants were forever worrying about the one who was just about to leave or the one who had just come to stay, and were forever giving each other advice about how to deal with the complex problem of finding and keeping competent helpers. Such women, from 1680 to 1980, counted themselves lucky if they "found someone good," and if "someone good" stayed on for more than six months. In the 1630s, Mary Winthrop Dudley of Boston complained in a letter to her mother about "what a great affliction I have me withal by my maide servant. . . . She hath got such a head and is growen soe insolent that her carriage . . . is insufferable."[37] Eighteenth-century newspapers carried advertisement after advertisement for recovery of "my servant who hath run away."[38] In 1832,

Frances Trollope, the English novelist's mother, complained that she could not engage a servant by the year in Cincinnati because, as one purportedly told her, "I hope I shall get a husband before many months . . . besides, mayhap I may want to go to school."[39] In the South at the turn of the century, housewives complained that they could not find competent help because "the agents from the North and West are offering high wages and taking away all the well-trained reliable colored people."[40] In Muncie, Indiana, in 1925, the refrain was somewhat different: "It is easy to get good girls by the hour but very difficult to get any one good to stay all the time . . . [and] the best type of girl, with whom I feel safe to leave the children, wants to eat with the family."[41] And, of course, some variant on each of these complaints—that servants are hard to find; that the ones that can be found are not reliable or competent; that, once hired, they become insolent; or that they will not work to the conditions that employers set—can still be heard today.

Employers seem always to have been perplexed about why they could neither find nor keep acceptable servants; they frequently protested either that "domestic service is good for a girl's health and for her moral character," or that "it prepares a girl for her ultimate career in the home," or that it "provides a haven for the homeless girl in this hazardous and heartless world."[42] Yet the employers' quandry seems to have been a grand case of self-deception, since the causes of the "servant problem" were, in every age, fairly easy to perceive. The work itself was sheer drudgery, since the whole point of employing a servant was to have someone do the work the housewife herself did not wish to do. The conditions under which the work was done were abysmal when gauged by whatever standards were thought to be appropriate in any given time; whether they were working or resting, servants were expected to occupy the parts of the house into which the family itself would not deign to set foot. Live-in servants were expected to be at work or on call before the family arose from bed and after it went to sleep. They were allowed little time off; the standard, until recently, was one evening a week and one day every two weeks. And ultimately, if the system of domestic service had worked in the way in which employers wanted it to work, the employment of domestic servants would have denied to those servants precisely that social arrangement that the employers themselves were trying to preserve—that is, private family life. Employers restricted the social lives of their servants, not just because they wanted to preserve their own homes from unwanted intruders, or because they wanted to keep their servants at work as much as possible, but also because they dearly wished that their unmarried servants would remain unmarried.[43]

Yet, even if the conditions of domestic service had been vastly improved, a servant class was not likely to have developed in this country. Domestic servants took the phrase "land of opportunity" literally to mean "the opportunity to cease being a domestic servant" or, if that was not possible, "the opportunity to see to it that my children do not become domestic servants." In the years before industrialization, the opportunity to escape domestic service existed because land was cheap and the ratio of women to men was low; a female indentured servant stood a reasonably good chance of being proposed to by a formerly indentured servant who now had enough money to buy a piece of land or to buy out the indenture of his intended wife. In the years during and after industrialization, the opportunity existed because the same unskilled and cheap female labor that some people wanted in their homes, other people wanted in their factories. The dark satanic mills did not look nearly so dark or nearly so satanic to young women who knew what it was like to work in some of America's dark satanic kitchens. In the factories, the work day may have been long, but it was not nearly as long as the work day in service; and when the work was done, it was at least done: a factory hand had her free time and her domicile to herself. Almost everyone who ever inquired into the matter discovered that unskilled women preferred factory work to household labor—a state of affairs that Frances Trollope remarked on as early as the 1830s.[44] In the 1890s, a sociologist asked a number of factory employees who had been in service why they preferred the factories when domestic service was more remunerative (because of free room and board). One former servant replied succinctly:

> In the first place, I don't like the idea of only one evening a week and every other Sunday. I like to feel that I have just so many hours work to do and do them, and come home and dress up and go out or sit down and sew if I feel like it, and when a girl is in service she has very little time for herself, she is a servant. In the second place a shop or factory girl knows just what she has to do and can go ahead and do it. . . . Of course I don't mean to say the domestics don't have a good time, they do; some of them have lovely places and lay up money, but after all, what is life if a body is always trying to see just how much money he or she can save?[45]

Domestic work was regarded, as it still is, as demeaning work for an American. Servant girls complained that young men almost automatically treated them as if they were wanton women, that working girls in other occupations were reluctant to socialize with them, and that their families were frequently reluctant to admit to the nature of their daughters' employment.[46] A Maine housewife, who was interviewed in a study of domestic employment, illustrated the problem better than a hundred sociologists could have done when she remarked:

> My husband has a servant who acts as his stenographer. She is welcome anywhere in society. I have a servant who does my work and although she is a graduate from Robinson's seminary in Exeter, she cannot even look inside anybody's house.[47]

Servants illustrated it themselves, even more graphically, in their strident objections to the most obvious symbols of subordination: American servants resolutely refused to wear livery and resented being called by their first names:

> Of course when I am with a mistress and she knows me, I am glad to be called Mary, but why should every mistress do it before she even engages us, and why should it be done in such a way that the iceman and grocer's boy and every Tom, Dick, and Harry always call us that? I am Mary to every guest in the house and every stranger

who appears at the kitchen door; in fact, how can I respect myself when no one else shows me any![48]

The great promise of American political life, the promise that all people would be treated equally, was taken by servants to mean that employers simply could not be permitted to control, as they wished they could, every facet of a servant's life. "Vhat *fur* you call she mistress," a German cook protested when an American-born parlormaid attempted to improve her diction:

She iss no great lady over me to say to *was* I do. I my own mistress. I do so I vant . . . I only work *hier fur* money. I cook *fur* my business, *und* I take orders *fur* my business like girl in store. *Dies iss* Amerika. Cook *so gut wie* anybody who works for a living *hier [sic]*. [49*]

Small wonder that so many immigrants left domestic service as soon as they reasonably could, and small wonder that they tried (with considerable success) to see to it that, no matter how poor they were, their children never entered it. In 1900, 60.5 percent of Irish-born wage-earning women in the United States were servants, but only 18.9 percent of the children of Irish-born parents were.[50] "We came to this country to better ourselves," said the daughter of an Irish cook in Philadelphia in 1905, "and it's not bettering to have anyone order you around."[51]

Thus, one of the social conditions that enabled industrialization to proceed quickly in this country—namely, the existence of a relatively tractable unskilled work force—was the condition that made it difficult for middle-class Americans to find servants. The poor and the recently immigrated provided the labor on which our industrial base was built, and they provided that labor in part because working in a factory—whatever its hardships may have been—was better than living and working in someone else's house. Twentieth-century housewives may have wished to trade in their vacuum cleaners for a "good old-fashioned maid," but could not do it because the good old-fashioned maids preferred positions on the assembly lines to positions in the parlor. And what was true in the past continues to be true in the present; like their potential employers, the only home potential servants wish

*The transliterations and the emphases are the author's, who was the parlormaid.

to work in full-time is the home they call their own. We can have vacuum cleaners or live-in maids, but not both.

Failed Machines

If the landscape of American social history is cluttered with the remains of failed communes and cooperatives, the landscape of American technical history is littered with the remains of abandoned machines. These are not the junked cars and used refrigerators that people leave along roadsides and in garbage dumps, but the rusting hulks of aborted ideas: patents that were never exploited (the patent record contains literally millions of them); test models that could not be manufactured at affordable prices; machines that had considerable potential but that were, for one reason or another, actively suppressed by the companies that had the license to manufacture them; devices that were put on the market but that never sold well and were soon abandoned. The publications of the Patent Office and the "new patents" columns in technical magazines reveal that the ratio of "failed" machines to successful ones is high, although no scholar has yet devised a formula by which it can actually be determined. Some nostalgia buffs have even become collectors of these "rusting hulks," filling scrapbooks with advertisements for bizarre devices and selling extant versions of them to one another at flea markets and antique shows.

The women's magazines of the nineteenth and twentieth centuries are filled with such aborted ideas: an ice-making machine driven by a small water wheel; a rocking chair that simultaneously propels a butter churn and a cradle; individual household incinerators; central vacuum-cleaning systems; sanitary toilets that do not use water; fireless cookers. There was a vast array of devices, some ludicrous but many, at least on the surface, very sensible. What resident of a drought-prone area today would not be grateful for a toilet that does not use water? How many energy-conscious housewives would be unwilling to try out a fireless cooker? In what city and town, plagued by erratic and expensive garbage pickup, would a householder not be pleased to be the first on the block to own a household incinerator? Why are these items either no longer on the market or not there at prices that most households can afford? Why do we have popcorn makers and electric can openers but not gas refrigerators or inexpensive central vacuum cleaners? If we can put a man on the moon, why have we been unable to pipe our garbage disposals into our compost heaps?

The answers to these questions are not simple: they involve economic decisions made by complex social institutions operating over long periods. In order to find out why a particular patent was not exploited, one must discover something about the Patent Office, something about the inventor, and something about potential consumers; in order to find out why a particular test model was never manufactured, one must learn about the technical problems involved, the decision-making procedures within the company that developed the test model, the state of the general economy, the availability of resources, and so forth. Yet if one wants to learn why our houses and our kitchens are constructed in certain ways but not in others—that is, why household work is shaped by certain constraints and not by others—then an exploration of the forces that cause some machines to "fail" and others to "succeed" may well be in order. One such case, which I shall here consider as an example of all the others, was the rivalry between the gas refrigerator (the machine that failed) and the electric refrigerator (the one that succeeded).

THE REFRIGERATOR: GAS VERSUS ELECTRIC

All mechanical refrigerators create low temperatures by controlling the vaporization and the condensation of a liquid, called a "refrigerant"; when liquids vaporize they absorb heat and when they condense they release it, so that a liquid can remove heat from one place (the "box" in a refrigerator) and transport it to another (in this instance, your kitchen). Virtually every refrigerator on the market in the United States today controls the condensation and the vaporization of its refrigerant by a special electric pump known as a "compressor." Compression is not, however, the only technique by which these two processes can be controlled. The simplest of the other techniques is "absorption." The gas refrigerator is an absorption refrigerator. Inside its walls, a refrigerant (ammonia, usually) is heated by a gas flame so as to vaporize; the ammonia gas then dissolves (or is absorbed into) a liquid (water, usually), and as it dissolves it simultaneously cools and condenses. The absorption of ammonia in water automatically alters the pressure in the closed system and thus keeps the refrigerant flowing, hence making it possible for heat to be absorbed in one place and released in another, just as it would be if the flow of the refrigerant were regulated by a compressor. The absorption refrigerator, consequently, does not require a motor— the crucial difference between the gas refrigerator and its electric cousin. Indeed, with the exception of either a timing device or a thermal switch (which turns the gas flame on and off so as to regulate the cycles of refrigeration), the gas refrigerator need have no moving parts at all, hence no parts that are likely to break or to make noise.

The basic designs for both compression and absorption machinery were perfected during the nineteenth century.[52] The phenomenon of latent heat (the heat absorbed when a liquid changes to a gas and released when the process is reversed) was discovered late in the eighteenth century and explored in great detail in the nineteenth because of its importance both in the new science of thermodynamics and in the new technologies of the steam engine. In those same decades, the need for mechanical refrigeration was growing as cities began to expand, both in Europe and in the United States, and ever larger quantities of food had to be preserved for longer periods of time as people continued to move farther from the places where it was grown. Between 1830 and 1880, dozens upon dozens of mechanical refrigerating machines were patented—machines that would make ice as well as machines that would cool large compartments without making ice. By the end of that period, the fundamental designs for large-scale compression and absorption installations had been perfected, largely through inventive and commercial trial and error. As a result of all this activity, manufactured ice became available throughout the southeastern United States by 1890 and throughout the northeast (where natural ice was more readily available through much of the year) by 1910. By 1890, nearly every brewery in the United States had purchased a refrigerating machine to remove the heat generated during the fermentation of beer and to cool the finished product while it aged and awaited transportation. Before the nineteenth century had turned into the twentieth, meat packers were using mechanical refrigeration in the handling and processing of meat, cold-storage warehouses had begun to appear in cities, icemen were carrying manufactured ice through the streets, and refrigerated transport (which utilized manufactured ice in railroad cars and refrigerating machines on ocean-going vessels) was becoming increasingly common and less expensive.

Operating a commercial refrigerator was an ambitious undertaking. Few machines weighed less than five tons, and a substantial number of them weighed from one hundred to two hundred tons. All the compression, and some of the absorption, machines required a source of mechanical power; and, as the electric motor was not yet perfected, this source was most commonly a steam engine (although hot-air engines and water turbines were occasionally used), which itself might weigh several dozen tons. As automatic controls were primitive, the machine was tended night and day by skilled operators, and each machine required a staff of even more skilled people to perform normal maintenance activities. Designing these machines was no simple task, since each one was built to unique specifications. By the turn of the century, a new profession had emerged: the refrigeration engineer—a person who could design and maintain refrigeration equipment. The American Society of Refrigerating Engineers was formed in 1904; and the Refrigerating Machinery Association, which represented the interests of manufacturers, one year earlier, in 1903.

None of this activity affected American households directly, even as late as 1920. Indirectly, many Americans benefited from lower prices for ice and greater availability of fresh meat, poultry, dairy products, and eggs during the first two decades of the century, but mechanical refrigeration was not yet possible in the household itself. The technical obstacles to developing a domestic mechanical refrigerator were substantial: such a refrigerator would have to be small and light enough to fit somewhere in a household, automatic enough not to require constant supervision, reliable enough not to require constant servicing; and it would have to have a power source that could be operated by a totally unskilled worker. Ultimately, it would also have to be designed so that it could be mass-produced, and it would have to be safe: many of the refrigerants then in common use were either toxic or flammable, and "ice-house" accidents were regularly highlighted in the newspapers. That a potential market existed was clear, for the use of ice and iceboxes in American households expanded drastically after 1880. In Philadelphia, Baltimore, and Chicago, over five times as much ice was consumed in 1914 as in 1880; and in New Orleans, the increase was thirteen-fold; the dollar value of iceboxes manufactured in the United States more than doubled between 1909 and 1919.[53] In the early years (1910–20), neophyte manufacturers of domestic refrigerators had no difficulty finding investors willing to lend them money and large corporations willing to buy them out. Just before and after the First World War, the problems involved in initiating domestic refrigeration were technical, not financial or social, and appear to have been about as great for the absorption machine as for the compression one. Indeed, since, until about 1925, gas service was more widespread than electric service, one might guess that the absorption machine would have had the competitive edge.

The Electric Compression Machine The first domestic refrigerator actually to go into large-scale production, however, was a compression machine. The honor of being first seems to belong to A. H. Goss, then an executive of the General Motors Company; to E. J. Copeland, a purchasing agent for General Motors; and to Nathaniel B. Wales, a Harvard graduate who was an independent inventor.[54]* On 14 September 1914, Goss and Copeland con-

*In matters technological, the question of who was "first" is difficult to resolve, initially because one must be careful to specify "first at doing *what,*" and then because available accounts, embedded as they are in the history of extremely private enterprises, are frequently vague, often in conflict, and most commonly nonexistent. Most authorities say that the Kelvinator was the first successful domestic refrigerator, but they may do so only because, at some point, the Kelvinator Corporation donated one of its "first" models to the Smithsonian. A reporter for *Air Conditioning and Refrigeration News* (then, *Air Conditioner,*

tracted with Wales to do the development work on a domestic refrigeration machine. After creating several test models, Wales settled on a compression machine using sulfur dioxide as a refrigerant; he had originally worked on an absorption machine, but—for reasons that are unclear—those plans were dropped. On 13 May 1916, this enterprise was incorporated as Goss & Copeland Electro–Automatic Refrigerator Company; but a few months later, the name was changed to "Kelvinator." At this juncture, Wales left the enterprise. In 1917, Copeland developed a satisfactory automatic control device and a solution to the problem of gas leakage (sulfur dioxide is toxic); and in February 1918, the first Kelvinator refrigerators were sold.

The path that Goss and Copeland pioneered quickly became a beaten track. By 1923, when the officers of the General Electric Company decided to do a thorough study of the domestic refrigeration business, the mechanical engineer to whom they entrusted the job, A. R. Stevenson, was able to identify fifty-six companies that were already involved in the business.[56] Some of these, such as Kelvinator and its rival, Frigidaire (which had been founded in 1916 and purchased by General Motors in 1919), were heavily capitalized and had already produced several thousand refrigerators. Other companies had just entered the field and had only test models and/or faltering finances. In those early years, compression refrigerators dominated the field; and out of the fifty-six companies, only eight were yet either well financed or well on their way to large-scale production.

Yet, in 1923, even the compression domestic machine was still in its developmental stage: the machines on the market did not inspire every middling householder to reach immediately for a checkbook. They were, to start with, expensive: the price had fallen from its original peak; but in 1923, the cheapest still ran to $450—not an inconsiderable sum at a time when most people earned less than $2,000 a year. Furthermore, refrigerators were difficult to run. Electric utilities estimated that, once every three

---

Heating and Refrigeration News) asserted that the Isko Company (which was started "by Fred Wolf with the backing of . . . Detroit capitalists") went into business in 1912, and that the Guardian Frigerator Company (which later became Frigidaire) was started in 1916, but provided no date for the commencement of manufacturing in either case.[55] Lacking more complete information, Kelvinator remains "first."

months, they serviced the machines that they had sold: the tubes leaked; the compressors malfunctioned; the thermostats broke; and so did the motors.[57] All these early machines were, in addition, "separated" machines—and water-cooled ones at that. The refrigerating machinery was sold separately from the refrigerating compartment, which might well have been simply the icebox that a family had previously used; the machinery could be set up in the basement, say, and the icebox put in the kitchen. The compressor had additional work to do, since the refrigerant had to be moved a considerable distance, but it must have been a relief to householders to have the noise, the oil, and the serviceman in some remote part of the house. Water cooling (the standard technique in large commercial installations) was not convenient in the home. The water pipes froze in some locales in the winter time (turning a refrigerator back into an icebox); or the water frequently leaked into parts of the machinery where excess humidity created excess problems. F. C. Pratt, a vice president of G.E. in 1923, forwarded Stevenson's report to Gerard Swope, president of the company, with the following warning:

> There reads through Mr. Stevenson's report the important fact that all existing practice carries a more than normal hazard of being revolutionized by inventions of a fundamental character. So many active minds throughout the country are being directed to the solution of these problems that it would be perhaps surprising if some such inventions did not materialize. The business is a rapidly evolving one, making real strides from the developmental to the commercial stage.[58]

Pratt was right, as it turned out. In the decade between 1923 and 1933, inventions that would profoundly alter the design of domestic refrigerators did, in fact, materialize; and, again as he predicted, they materialized in more than one quarter. In Sweden, for example, two young engineering students, Carl G. Munters and Baltzar von Platen, figured out how to design an absorption refrigerator that would run continuously and thus would not require expensive automatic controls; this machine (the Electrolux-Servel) went on the market in 1926. Engineers at Kelvinator and, later, at General Electric discovered techniques for dispensing with water as a cooling agent. In 1927, General Electric became the first manufacturer to make a hermetically sealed motor and to sell the box as an integral part of its refrigerating machinery. Within a year, other manufacturers followed suit and also began mass production of refrigerator boxes made from steel rather than from wood. In 1930, chemists at General Motors (which still owned Frigidaire) developed a series of artificial refrigerants (the Freons) that were neither toxic nor flammable; and in 1932, engineers at Servel designed an air-cooled absorption machine. By the middle years of the Depression, most of the fundamental innovations in domestic refrigeration design (with the exception of automatic defrosting, which came later) had been made.[59]

These innovations did not occur out of the blue. They were the end result of deliberate assignments given to a large number of highly trained (and highly paid) people, and of the equally deliberate expenditure of large sums of money not only to develop these ideas but to equip assembly lines that could realize them in production. The stakes were thought to be very high. The potential market for domestic refrigeration was enormous: by 1923, it was clear that every household in the United States was going to be equipped with either gas or electric service (and probably both in many places); and, thus, that if the price could be brought low enough, every household would become a potential customer for a refrigerator.[60] The potential revenues for the gas and electric utility companies would be even more enormous, since, unlike other household appliances, the refrigerator operates twenty-four hours a day. Thus, it is hardly surprising that the money and the time necessary to achieve these innovations was available—especially during the economically free-wheeling 1920s. Yet, to say that the stakes were high is also to say that the risks were great. Some manufacturers were going to succeed, and others were going to fail—and one of the failures would turn out to be the only manufacturer in a competitive position to keep the gas refrigerator on the market.

One of the manufacturers that succeeded, and whose success helped carry the compression refrigerator to dominance, was General Electric. By the 1920s, General Electric was an enormous corporation with vast resources and had its finger in almost every aspect of the electrical industry in the United States, from the design of large generating plants to the manufacture of light bulbs.[61] The refrigerator that General Electric introduced to the public in 1925 (called the "Monitor Top" because the working parts were located in a circular box that sat on top of the refrigerating cabinet itself) was the product of almost fifteen years of developmental work on the part of General Electric employees. In 1911, G.E. had agreed to manufacture a commercial refrigerator for the Audiffren Company, which held the American rights to a patent owned by a French monk, the Abbé Audiffren. Sometime during 1917, engineers at the Fort Wayne, Indiana, plant (where the Audiffren was manufactured) began to build test models of a modified Audiffren design, suitable for use in the household. Immediately after the First World War, G.E. found itself in poor financial condition; in 1922, the company was reorganized, and Gerard Swope was brought in as president. Swope believed that General Electric was going to have to enter the consumer electric market and, to this end, instructed A. R. Stevenson, who was then head of the engineering laboratories in the company's main headquarters in Schenectady, to review the current state of the refrigerator business.[62]

Stevenson's report, a model of engineering and econometric skill, provides glimpses of the factors that influenced decision makers at G.E. The report contained everything from engineering tests on competing machines to projections of the potential market for refrigerators sold at various prices. Stevenson had been asked to recommend a course of action to the managers of the company, and he did so without equivocating. Was it worth entering the domestic refrigeration business at all? Certainly Yes, concluded Stevenson. If it did, should G.E. purchase one of the many small companies already in the field (No) or make cross-licensing arrangements (our motors for your compressors) with one of the larger companies (No)? Should G.E. take advantage of the development work that had already been done at Fort Wayne and try to work with an Audiffren type of apparatus (Yes)? Was it worth spending the time and money that would be required to switch from water to air cooling? Absolutely, said Stevenson, not just because water cooling was a problem for home owners, but also because General Electric had to worry about the interests of its most important customers—not the home owners but the electric utility companies:

> the electric power bill of the air cooled machine would be about $1.30 more in six months than the water cooled machine. . . . Since the General Electric Company is entering this field for the benefit of the central station [the utility company that is generating electricity] it would seem wise to exploit a machine in which the total revenue would accrue to the central station rather than partly to the water works.[63]

Stevenson understood that General Electric would be assuming a considerable risk if it entered the refrigerator business; but he believed the risk to be worth taking for a number of reasons: he believed that there was a good chance that G.E. would be first, that the company had the resources to sustain the initial losses, that after this initial period the profits would be great, and finally that "widespread adoption [would] increase the revenue of the central stations, thus indirectly benefiting the General Electric Company."[64] G.E. stood to gain, both coming and going, from developing a successful refrigerator.

The managers of G.E. must have agreed with Stevenson. During 1924, a group of engineers worked on developing an air-cooled model of the original Fort Wayne design. In the fall of 1925, limited production began, and the "Monitor Top" was introduced to G.E.'s sales force and to the electric utility companies. During 1926, construction of an assembly line began (at a total cost of eighteen million dollars), and the design was modified again to allow for mass production. In 1927, a new department of the company was created to promote and market the machine; and within months of its establishment, the first mass-produced Monitor Tops had found their way into kitchens across the land. By 1929, fifty thousand Monitor Tops had been sold—a figure that may have been as surprising to the top management of General Electric (the company had anticipated sales of seven thousand to ten thousand per year) as it was to everyone else.[65]

Alternative Approaches to Housework

General Electric stimulated sales of its refrigerators by means of outlandish advertising and public relations techniques. Franchised distributors were appointed in the major cities across the country and given exclusive rights to sell and service their territories. Rex Cole, in New York, was famous for constructing a neon sign that could be read three miles away, and for staging promotional parades. Judson Burns of Philadelphia had his new store designed in the shape of a Monitor Top. When G.E. introduced its first all-steel cabinets in 1929, a novel "Pirate's Chest" sales campaign was broached:

> For some time previous to March 22 mysterious looking old iron-bound boxes closely resembling pirates' treasure chests had been on display in the windows of General Electric refrigerator dealers, with a sign saying that they would be opened on March 22. The night before, large door keys were hung on door knobs in the residential sections with an invitation to attend the opening the following morning.
>
> The event had been advertised in newspapers and through direct-by-mail literature. Many distributors and dealers arranged parties for the opening. A greater number provided radio programs. . . . In some cities the mayor was invited to open the box. In various stores, pirates swashbuckled inside and outside the sales rooms, and rode on floats with jazz bands.
>
> Promptly at 11 o'clock that morning, in the presence of crowds of onlookers, numbering from 200 to 800 each, the chests were unlocked and disclosed the new All-Steel G.E. Refrigerator.[66]

Special exhibition railroad cars toured the country, displaying refrigerators. Animated puppets danced in dealers' windows:

> The June ANIMATED Window Display dramatized the shortest "short story" ever produced . . . and the action takes place in a realistic stage setting in the interior of the G–E refrigerator.
>
> Prologue: A BRIDE IN JUNE. Stage set consists of an illuminated cathedral interior during a wedding ceremony.
>
> Act I: A SERVANT IN SEPTEMBER: A revolving stage discloses a second illuminated set consisting of a wearied housewife in an old-fashioned kitchen without electrical conveniences.

Act II: FREEDOM IN A G–E KITCHEN: The revolving stage shows a third set consisting of a glorified G–E Kitchen and the symbolical "Freedom" figure [a vaguely-Grecian female with arms extended in a gesture of leaping joyousness].[67]

The millionth Monitor Top was presented to Henry Ford in a special radio broadcast in 1931, and another one was sent on a submarine voyage to the North Pole with Robert Ripley (the originator of "Believe It or Not") in 1928. The most expensive media device of all was undertaken in 1935—a film that told "an interesting story in which comedy and romance are skillfully blended, all of which pivots on and revolves about the complete electric kitchen." An anonymous publicist waxed ecstatic:

It is of no avail to attempt to describe this picture, "Three Women." We can tell you that it is the most pretentious [sic], the most beautiful, the most effective commercial story ever told on the talking screen; that it is the first commercial Technicolor film ever made; that for gorgeous color and amazing realism it is on a par with outstanding examples of cinema artistry.[68]

The film ran for close to an hour and starred such Hollywood notables as Sheila Mannors and Hedda Hopper, Bert Roach and Johnny Mack Brown.

General Electric was not alone, either in these outlandish promotional schemes or in its effort to develop a successful compression refrigerator; the other major refrigerator manufacturers, just as anxious to attract consumer attention (especially during the straitened Depression years), were just as willing to spend money on advertising and promotion. The electric utility companies, which were then in a most expansive and profitable phase of their history, cooperated in selling both refrigerators and the idea of mechanical refrigeration to their customers. By 1940 the market for household refrigerators was dominated by the four manufacturers of compression machines which had at their disposal the financial resources of enormous corporations: General Electric; Westinghouse, which began to manufacture refrigerators in 1930; Kelvinator, which was then owned by American Motors; and

Frigidaire, which still belonged to General Motors.[69] Cross-licensing and mass-production techniques had made it possible for the manufacturers to lower their prices; installment plans and occasional price wars had made it possible for ever larger numbers of people to purchase refrigerators. Despite the Depression, and despite the still relatively high cost of refrigerators (when compared with other household appliances), roughly 45 percent of American homes were taking advantage of mechanical refrigeration by the time we entered the Second World War.[70]

The Gas Absorption Machine The manufacturers of gas absorption refrigerators were not idle during these years, but they lacked the large sums of money, the armies of skilled personnel, the competitive pressure, and the aggressive assistance of utility companies that the compression manufacturers had been able to command. When Stevenson surveyed the refrigeration business in 1923, he located eight prospective manufacturers of absorption refrigerators.[71] In the next several years, several of these went out of business—hardly surprising, since they had had little or no paid-in capital with which to work; the Common Sense Company, for example, was working with thirty thousand dollars in the same year in which Kelvinator had one million dollars.[72]

There seems to have been little question among knowledgeable people that the absorption refrigerator had the potential to be a superb machine for household use; and adjectives such as "ingenious" and "clever" were frequently appended to descriptions of gas refrigerators in the technical literature. "Thousands of people have examined this machine, among them a large number of engineers; in fact, generally speaking, the more technical a person is, the greater is the appeal made by the machine," wrote one commentator.[73] From the consumer's point of view, these refrigerators' chief advantages were that they were virtually silent (refrigerators with compressors once made a lot more noise than they do now—and they still hum noticeably); that, having few moving parts, they were potentially easy to maintain; and that operating costs could be kept fairly low, especially in locales where gas was cheaper than electricity. Stevenson's report on the Common Sense machine noted, for example:

The salesman at the People's Gas Company in Chicago claims that they have sold about fifty of these machines. Some of them have been in service for two years, and he claims that they have no trouble or service calls. . . . Mr. Robertson of . . . [G.E.'s] Chicago office, says that this ice machine is different from any other that he has seen, in that it has no rotating parts, and the machine appears to be very simple to maintain.[74]

Yet the absorption machine, like the compression machine, was going to require expensive development and promotion before it could be made commercially successful; all the absorption machines that Stevenson located were water-cooled, and there was a public prejudice against the use of ammonia as a refrigerant. It remained to be seen whether anyone was going to undertake the developmental work, which would be both time consuming and expensive.

By 1926, when the American Gas Association met in Atlantic City for its annual convention, only three manufacturers of gas refrigerators remained in the field; and of these three, only one —Servel—would succeed in reaching the stage of mass production.[75] In the early 1920s, Servel (whose name stood for "servant electricity") had been funded by a group of electric utility holding companies to manufacture and market compression refrigerators. But in 1925, it had purchased the American rights to the Swedish patents on the continuous absorption refrigerator, and had reorganized (with the injection of five million dollars from the financial interests that controlled the Consolidated Gas Company of New York) to devote itself principally to gas refrigeration.[76] Since it had a manufacturing plant already in existence when it purchased these new patents, it was able to commence production quickly; the Servel gas refrigerator went on the market in 1926 to the accompaniment of a good deal of publicity.

The other two manufacturers failed within a few years: they could neither compete with Servel nor sell the machines on which they held patents to any of the large corporations that might have had the resources to compete. The trials and tribulations of these small businesses are exemplified in the story of the SORCO refrigerator, which was one of the other two on display in Atlantic City in 1926.[77] SORCO was the creation of Stuart Otto, an engineer who had patented an absorption refrigerator in 1923. He owned a factory in Scranton, Pennsylvania, that produced dress forms for seamstresses, and persuaded twenty of the leading businessmen of Scranton to put up five thousand dollars apiece so that he could develop his machine and modify his factory to produce it. These early SORCO refrigerators were advertised in gas-industry periodicals ("Build Up Your Summer Load—and fill your daily valleys: Gas controlled entirely by time-switch to be set by your service man") and were sold to gas utility companies.[78] The results of the tests being more or less positive, Otto decided in the fall of 1926 that the time had come to attempt large-scale production:

> I was not able to raise the money from my stockholders when I informed them that $1,000,000 or more would be required. My only alternative was to buy out my stockholders. So I made an option agreement with them to pay them for their stock within a year. I then went about the country offering manufacturing companies non-exclusive licenses for the manufacture of my machines under our patents, of which some fifteen existed.
>
> I licensed Pathe Radio & Phonograph Co., Brooklyn, N.Y., Crocker Chair Company, Sheboygan, Wisconsin, Plymouth Radio & Phonograph Co., Plymouth, Wisconsin.
>
> Each of these companies paid me a cash down payment on signing of $25,000 and agreed to a guaranteed minimum of $35,000 per year royalty on a 5% of net sales, for 17 years.[79]

Otto had tried to interest General Electric and General Motors in his refrigerator. General Electric was, however, just about to bring out its own refrigerator; and General Motors had just purchased the patent rights on an English machine that utilized a solid rather than a liquid solvent.* Otto was trying to enter the national market with ludicrously small sums of money; the days in which David had any reasonable chance of succeeding against Goliath had long since passed. Within a few years, Otto was forced to acknowledge failure: "Unfortunately . . . we were not

---

*This refrigerator, the Faraday, was marketed, on a limited basis, by G.M. in the mid-1930s; but, as it was water-cooled and very expensive, G.M. soon dropped it.

financially able to carry the loads. After two years I managed to collect only a small portion of the accrued royalties."[80]

Thus, Servel was essentially alone: from 1927 until 1956, (when it ceased production of refrigerators), it was the only major manufacturer of gas-absorption refrigerators in the United States. Never as highly capitalized as its competitors in the field of compression machinery (G.E., after all, had invested eighteen million dollars just in its production facilities in 1927, when Servel's entire assets amounted to no more than twelve million dollars), Servel had entered the market somewhat later than the other manufacturers and was never able to compete effectively. The gas utilities, notoriously conservative companies, were defending themselves against the encroachments of electricity and were not helpful; they complained that Servel was badly managed, that its refrigerators were more expensive than comparable electric machines, and that the lack of another manufacturer meant a lack of models with which to interest prospective customers.[81] Servel did not succeed in bringing out an air-cooled refrigerator until 1933, six or seven years after the electrics had done so; and by then the race was virtually lost. For all its virtues as a machine, the Servel, even in its peak years, never commanded more than 8 percent to 10 percent of the total market for mechanical refrigerators.[82]

The demise of the gas refrigerator was not the result of inherent deficiencies in the machine itself. The machine was not perfect when it was first brought on the market, but it was no less perfect than the compression machine, its rival. The latter succeeded for reasons that were as much social and economic as technical; its development was encouraged by a few companies that could draw upon vast technical and financial resources. With the exception of Servel, none of the absorption manufacturers was ever able to finance the same level of development or promotion; and Servel never approached the capabilities of General Motors, General Electric, or Westinghouse. The compression refrigerator manufacturers came on the market earlier and innovated earlier, making it doubly difficult for competing devices to succeed. The fact that the electric utilities were in a period of growth and great profitability between 1920 and 1950, while the gas manufacturers and utility companies were defensive, conservative, and financially weak, cannot have helped matters either. If Stuart Otto had been able to obtain either capital or encouragement from the gas utilities, if Servel had been managed well enough to have innovated earlier, if either one of them had been able to command a chemical laboratory capable of discovering a new refrigerant, if there had been a sufficient number of gas-refrigerator manufacturers to have staged price wars, or license innovations to each other, or develop cooperative promotional schemes along with the gas-utility companies—well then, the vast majority of Americans might have absolutely silent and virtually indefatigable refrigerators in their kitchens. The machine that was "best" from the point of view of the producer was not necessarily "best" from the point of view of the consumer.

THE PROFIT MOTIVE AND THE ALTERNATIVE MACHINE

The case of the gas refrigerator appears, in many particulars, to be structurally similar to the cases of many other aborted or abandoned devices intended for the household. There were, at one time, dozens of different kinds of washing machine: contraptions that simulated the action of a washboard; tubs with sieves that rotated inside fixed tubs filled with soapy water; tubs that rocked back and forth on a horizontal axis; motor-driven plungers that pounded the clothing inside a tub. All these washing machines yielded, during the 1920s and 1930s, to the agitator within the vertically rotated drum, because of the aggressive business practices of the Maytag Company which owned the rights to that design. [83] The central vacuum cleaner, which technical experts preferred, quickly lost ground to its noisier and more cumbersome portable competitor, in part because of the marketing techniques pioneered by door-to-door and store-demonstration salesmen employed by such firms as Hoover and Apex.[84]

Furthermore, many of the companies that pioneered successful household appliances had already developed a sound financial base manufacturing something else. Fedders, for example, made radiators for cars and airplanes before it made air conditioners; Regina made music boxes before it made vacuum cleaners; Maytag made farm implements; Sunbeam made scissors and clippers for shearing sheep; Hoover made leather goods.[85] Alternatively, small companies with innovative ideas rarely succeeded unless they were purchased by, or made cooperative agreements with, much larger companies that had greater financial flexibility and the resources necessary to broach the national consumer market. Hotpoint belonged to General Electric, as did Edison Electric. Birdseye became part of General Foods; Norge, of Borg-Warner; Kelvinator, of American Motors. Bendix Home Appliances was a subsidiary of the Bendix Corporation, manufacturers of airplane parts. A larger corporation frequently purchased smaller ones or introduced new products when one (or several) of their old lines were failing. William C. Durant, of General Motors, for example, purchased Frigidaire because he wanted his salesmen to have something to sell when automobiles went off the consumer market during the First World War. Landers, Frary & Clark began to sell small appliances (under the name "Universal") when their cutlery trade fell off. Westinghouse went into refrigerators as a cushion against the Depression. Maytag started making washing machines because of seasonal slacks in sales of farm machinery.[86]

By itself, the gas refrigerator would not have profoundly altered the dominant patterns of household work in the United States; but a reliable refrigerator, combined with a central vacuum-cleaning system, a household incinerator, a fireless cooker, a waterless toilet (otherwise known as an "earth closet"), and individually owned fertilizer-manufacturing plants (otherwise known as "garbage disposals that make compost") would certainly have gone a long way to altering patterns of household expenditure and of municipal services. We have compression, rather than absorption, refrigerators in the United States today not because one was technically better than the other, and not even because consumers preferred one machine (in the abstract) over the other, but because General Electric, General Motors, Kelvinator, and Westinghouse were very large, very powerful, very aggressive, and very resourceful companies, while Servel and SORCO were not. Consumer "preference" can only be expressed for whatever is, in fact, available for purchase, and is always tempered by the price and the convenience of the goods that are so available. At no time, in these terms, were refrigerators that ran on gas really competitive with those that ran on electric current.

In an economy such as ours in the United States, the first question that gets asked about a new device is not, Will it be good for the household—or even, Will householders buy it? but, rather, Can we manufacture it and sell it at a profit? Consumers do not get to choose among everything that they might like to have, but only among those things that manufacturers and financiers believe can be sold at a good profit. Profits are always the bottom line, and profits are partly compounded out of sales—but only partly. Profits are also compounded out of how much staff time has to be spent, whether a marketing arrangement is already in place, how easily manufacturing facilities can be converted, how reliably an item can be mass-produced—and similar considerations. General Electric became interested in refrigerators because it was experiencing financial difficulties after the First World War and needed to develop a new and different line of goods. G.E. decided to manufacture compression, rather than absorption, refrigerators because it stood to make more profits from exploiting its own designs and its own expertise than someone else's. Once having gone into the market for compression refrigerators, G.E. helped to improve that market, not just by its promotional efforts on its own behalf, but by the innovations that it could then sell to, or stimulate in, other manufacturers. And having done all that, G.E. helped to sound the death knell for the absorption machinery, since only a remarkable technical staff and a remarkable marketing staff, combined with an even more remarkable fluidity of capital, could have successfully competed with the likes of General Electric, Westinghouse, General Motors, and Kelvinator.

Conclusion

Is there any rhyme or reason to be discerned in this diverse pattern of failed alternatives? Some attempts to commercialize women's work succeeded, but other attempts clearly failed. Virtually every communal or cooperative housekeeping experiment has failed. The effort—and it was at one time strenuous—to develop a permanent class of servants in this country has also failed. Some modern appliances have become part of our daily environment; but others, which seemed equally promising at their inception (and which many of us might still find useful), have disappeared. Anthropologists are fond of saying that "one case may be an accident, two a coincidence, but if there are three or more something structural is at work."[87] Is there a set of structural conditions that might help us to make sense of these apparently unrelated outcomes?

Governmental repression or censorship are not here the answer, however much, in other countries, either or both may be. Ever since we have existed as a nation, some American somewhere has been experimenting with some radical rearrangement of household functions, from people who wanted to move spinning and weaving into factories (at the time, they were regarded as radical), to those who wanted to communalize child care on self-sufficient farms, to those who wanted to replace laundresses with Laundromats. All of these enterprises confronted political obstacles of one sort or another. The entrepreneurs of the 1820s were as much convinced that the government was against them as were the flower children of the 1960s; but whatever obstacles confronted both groups were as nothing compared with the full-scale repression that governments and churches are capable of imposing. The very fact that historians can find contemporaneous printed accounts of all these experiments is itself explicit testimony that most Americans could have learned of their existence, and that neither the government nor the churches were capable of (or even interested in) suppressing information about them.

The combined forces of capitalism and patriarchy are not the answer either—or, at least not in a conspiratorial sense. Many scholars have argued that these two large-scale, pervasive social institutions have worked together to create and then to buttress the single-family home, the private ownership of tools, and the allocation of housework to women.[88] According to this argument, capitalism requires some agency that will produce and then reproduce a stable and pliant workforce; capitalism prefers this agency to be numerous, small households, each possessing its own tools, in order that there may be the largest possible market for goods; and prefers that women should find their proper "place" in these households, so that, in the event of a social emergency, they can be called upon as a reserve, but temporary, labor force. Patriarchy, the argument goes, prefers this arrangement as well, because it keeps women subservient, thereby making men at once more powerful and more comfortable.

The history of these failed alternatives teaches that, although this Marxist feminist argument contains profound truths, it is not the whole story. Capitalism and patriarchy exist, but they are not the sole determinants of our behavior. It is true that all of the successful alternatives to traditional modes of doing housework have been stimulated by the profit motive, and also that much of what goes on in American households is indeed intended to serve the triple purposes of getting people out to work in the morning, of raising children who will, when their time comes, also be able to get out to work in the morning, and of making men comfortable. On the other hand, it is also true that some profit-making enterprises did not make profits. Why should the powers-that-be have preferred one form of profitable enterprise to another? Why should cooked-food delivery services, commercial laundries, gas refrigerators, and apartment hotels have failed, while fast-food chains, washing-machine manufacturers, compression refrigerators, and ordinary apartment houses have succeeded? The commercial laundries tried every technique in the book to advance their sales, and so did the washing-machine manufacturers; but people across the land decided to patronize one rather than the other. At least between 1927 and 1956, gas refrigerators were easily available to anyone who wanted one, but most people apparently did not care to make the effort. Apartment hotels were as profitable (perhaps even more profitable) than apartment houses, but more people were willing to move into the latter than the former, even when rents in the latter were very, very high. The Marxist feminist argument seems adequate to explain why successful enterprises have come into existence, but not the fact of their success.

In addition, while the argument makes clear why men, children, and entrepreneurs should have an interest in maintaining the single-family home, it does not explain why, in each generation, millions of women have chosen to marry and to have children and to become at least part-time housewives and to cooperate in the purchase of a house and its attendant tools. If it is really true that capitalism and patriarchy have oppressed women by relegating them to "places" in the home, then it must also be true that, without the usual instruments of terror, capitalism and patriarchy have somehow induced millions upon millions of women, generation after generation, to cooperate in their own oppression. And if that is true, then women, as a class, must be either inordinately stupid or inordinately passive—a conclusion that is both historically unlikely and profoundly anti-feminist. Is it not odd that we have no records of either large-scale or frequent rebellions against such a presumably oppressive system? In point of fact, we do not even have records of more than an occasional sit-down strike. Even a goodly number of suffragettes who wore themselves out lecturing and parading—indeed, even those who went so far as to chain themselves to the gates of the White House and refused to eat in jail—eventually returned home to worry about what would be served for dinner the next night. Elizabeth Cady Stanton, for example, was one of the most radical feminists of her day; yet she remained firmly embedded in a middle-class family life, against which she only occasionally chafed.[89] A twentieth-century example of the same phenomenon was Anna Kelton Wiley, a suffragette who chained herself to the White House gates in 1919, but who, for almost ten years before and forty years after that outrageous act, devoted herself to maintaining not one, but two, residences for her family.[90] Were women such as Stanton and Wiley duped? Shall we believe that millions upon millions of women, for five or six generations, have passively accepted a social system that was totally out of their control and totally contrary to their interest? Surely there must have been at least one or two good reasons that all those women actively chose, when choices were available to them, to reside in single-family dwellings, own their own household tools, and do their own housework.

Alternative Approaches to Housework

The history of all these failed alternatives to housework suggests that when the choices were available (and capitalism, if nothing else, has surely tossed up choices), the majority of people —whether rich or poor, owners or workers, male or female— chose to preserve in both the realm of symbol and the realm of fact, those activities that they deemed crucial to the creation and the maintenance of family life. There are, of course, specific reasons why each of the proposed alternatives to housework failed. Commercial laundries failed because the automatic washing machine was invented. Cooked-food delivery services failed because the meals were too expensive for the budgets of most families. The Shakers failed, in the long run, because they did not allow their members to bear children and thus create a new generation of Shakers; and the Oneida Community eventually failed, in part, because of errors made by its charismatic leader. One cooperative kitchen may have closed because its members could not agree with each other, and another may have closed because the husbands of the cooperators were not enthusiastic about the arrangement. One household may have failed to retain its servants because it was particularly nasty to them; and another, because it could not afford to compete with the wealthier household up the road. The gas refrigerator may have failed to become popular because the Servel Corporation was underfinanced; and the central vacuum cleaner, because it was too expensive for the average home. Yet, in the end, all these alternatives to the single-family residence, the private ownership of tools, and the allocation of housework to women, failed. The common condition that underlies their failure is the fact that most people prefer to live in their own homes, with their own relatives, rearing their own children, regularly sitting down to meals together, decorating their quarters according to their own lights, dressing themselves according to their own tastes, and controlling the tools with which they have to do their work. When push comes to shove, most people will opt to increase the possibility of exercising their right to privacy and autonomy: so that they can sleep, eat, have sexual relations, discipline their children, clean their bodies and their clothes without interference; and so that they can construct long-term emotional relationships with people of their own choosing. And when further push comes to further shove, when decisions have to be made about spending limited funds, most people will still opt for privacy and autonomy over technical efficiency and community interest. Americans decided to buy electric refrigerators rather than gas refrigerators because the latter were more expensive, and the expense could not be justified in any terms that were meaningful to the life of the family. Americans have decided to live in apartment houses rather than apartment hotels because they believe that something critical to family life is lost when all meals are eaten in restaurants or all food is prepared by strangers; they have decided to buy washing machines rather than patronize commercial laundries because they prefer to wash their dirty linen at home; they have decided to live in single-family houses rather than in communes because they like the privacy; and they have decided that it is easier to argue with one or two people, all relatives, about what is to be served for dinner, than with fifty or sixty participants in a cooperative kitchen. When given choices, in short, most Americans act so as to preserve family life and family autonomy. The single-family home and the private ownership of tools are social institutions that act to preserve and to enhance the privacy and the autonomy of families. The allocation of housework to women is, as we have seen, a social convention which developed during the nineteenth century because of a specific set of material and cultural conditions. It is a convention so deeply embedded in our individual and collective consciousnesses that even the profound changes wrought by the twentieth century have not yet shaken it.

(1) Homestead, Pennsylvania, Lewis Hine, *c.* 1910.

Washday

In the old days, if you had neither running water nor any tools but a scrubbing board and tub, washing clothes was back-breaking work (1), so difficult that your children could do little but look on (2). During the nineteenth century, you could have purchased one of the many hand-cranked washing machines that were on the market (3)—but the simplest and easiest way to avoid the horror of washday was to hire a laundress (4) or to patronize a commercial service (5). Later, you might have been able to sit down while your internal combustion engine (6) or an electric motor (7) did the scrubbing for you—although you would probably still have had to empty and fill the tub by hand as well as wring and haul the wet wash. The automatic washing machine—"the successor to the washing machine," as its first manufacturer called it—did not come on the market until just before the Second World War (8). Although it (and its accompanying dryer) make washday less exhausting, today you are doing much more laundry than your grandmother did (9, 10), while alternatives to doing it yourself—commercial laundries, and laundresses—have disappeared, along with alternative machines, such as this combination washing machine and dishwasher (11).

(2) Lewis Jung, photographer,
no place indicated, c. 1930.

(3) Advertisement for a churn-ty[pe]
hand-operated washing machine, [...]
Courtesy of the New-York Historical Socie[ty]
New York City, Landauer Collecti[on]

(4) Advertisement for a washing machine,
showing two laundresses at work,
c. 1869. Library of Congress.

The Old City Laundry

No. 19 State Street.

BRIDGEPORT, CONN[.]

A few doors east of the Post Office.

Good as the best !
Cheap as the Cheapes[t]

All Work Warranted to give Satisfaction.

Work called for and delivered without extra char[ge]

PRICE LIST FOR 1878-9.

Shirts	10 cen[ts]
Collars and Cuffs, per dozen	25 ce[nts]
Undershirts and drawers	8 cen[ts]
Night Shirts	8 cen[ts]
Socks	4 ce[nts]
Handkerchiefs, per dozen	30 cen[ts]
Vests	20 cen[ts]
Pants, woolen	20 cen[ts]
Pants, linen	25 cen[ts]
Coats	from 15 to 25 cen[ts]
Ties	4 cen[ts]
Towels	3 cen[ts]
Towels, roller	6 cen[ts]
Napkins	2 cen[ts]
Table Covers	from 5 to 10 cen[ts]
Sheets	6 cen[ts]
Pillow Cases	3 cen[ts]

**All Shirt Bosoms, Collar[s]
and Cuffs Polished and mad[e]
to look as good as new.**

Ladies' Fancy Wear and Fam[-]
ily Clothes Laundered in
the Best Style at
very Low Rates.

Don't forget the place,

No. 19 State St.
WM. H. LORD.

Standard Print, Bridgeport, Conn.

(5) Price list for a commercial laundry, 1878–79.
Courtesy of the New-York
Historical Society, New York City,
Landauer Collection.

(6) J. C. Allen & Son, place and photographer unknown, *c.* 1910.

The

HAPPY DAY

ELECTRIC
Home Laundry Machine

MANUFACTURED BY

ATIONAL SEWING MACHINE COMPANY

BELVIDERE, ILLINOIS

(7) Advertisement for an early electric washing machine, *c.* 1910. Courtesy of the New-York Historical Society, New York City, Landauer Collection.

WHY RISK HIS HEALTH
with germ-laden clothing

when a BENDIX HOME LAUNDRY costs only $99.50*

Washes . . . Rinses . . . Damp-Dries

Diapers, petticoats, shirts and other underthings that touch baby's skin should be absolutely sanitary. Doctors recommend Bendix Home Laundry for sanitation because it removes more harmful germs than other home washing methods. YOU get rid of the unpleasant task of washing baby's soiled clothing by hand.

Hands Need Never Touch Water

Simply toss in the soiled clothes, take them out fresh, sweet and line-dry. No more slaving over an old-fashioned washer! And no more worry over tragic washday accidents. There are no exposed moving parts on Bendix to catch hair or hurt fingers. Start enjoying Bendix NOW . . . costs less than many ordinary washers. Ask your dealer for a Free Home Trial.

THE SUCCESSOR to the WASHING MACHINE

FREE BOOKLET

(8) Advertisement for the earliest model of the Bendix, as it appeared in *Parents Magazine*, July 1940.

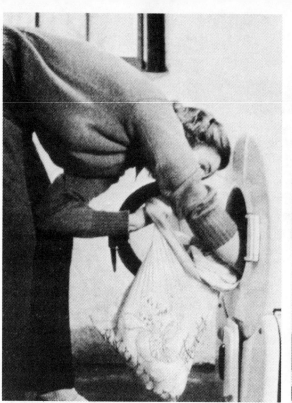

(9) Housewife washing diapers,
New York City, Suzanne Szasz, 1952.

(11) Advertising photograph for a converti
washing machine and dishwash
photographer and manufacturer unknown,
prepared by Earle Ludgin & Co., Chicago, 19

(10) Laundromat, photograph by Gus Pasquarella, for *Saturday Evening Post*, 4 May, 1946.

Chapter 6

Household Technology and Household Work between 1900 and 1940

I N the twentieth century, the proliferation of household technology has dramatically altered women's lives but has not in the least mitigated the assignment of housework to women. When the twentieth century opened, the vast majority of American women spent most of their waking hours feeding, clothing, cleaning, and sustaining themselves and their families; eighty years later, as the century is drawing to a close, the vast majority of American women are still spending many of their waking hours feeding, clothing, cleaning, and sustaining themselves and their families, albeit with markedly different tools.

Some of the reasons for this situation have already been discussed. The foundations for the technological systems that altered housework in the twentieth century were laid in the nineteenth and were built on the assumption that families would continue to live in single-family dwellings, and that adult women would remain at home to supervise, day and night, the activities pursued in those dwellings. The notion that women would do housework was almost literally cast in concrete—or, rather, in brass pipes and copper wires. Alternative technological and social systems which might have been built on different assumptions simply never became popular. In addition, each generation of twentieth-century families had, until recently, pressing reasons to believe that the assignment of women to work within the home was not only reasonable and wise but, in some cases, absolutely necessary.

Those latter reasons can best be understood by analyzing the history of twentieth-century household technologies comparatively, in terms of the different rates at which that technology diffused to the two great classes of the population and the different impact that technology had on the work processes in which housewives of the two great classes were engaged. This comparative analysis is especially meaningful when applied to the history of housework because people who do housework are constantly applying it to themselves: when women ask themselves whether they are successful as housewives, they frequently mean, "Am I successful when compared to someone else—to my mother, my grandmother, my neighbors, to women who are richer or poorer, smarter or dumber than I am." An understanding of the terms in which our twentieth-century mothers, grandmothers, and even great-grandmothers might have assessed their own housework, will provide some insight into why, despite all the technical and social changes that have occurred since 1900, we still label housework as "women's work" and still continue to accept the label.

To illustrate these terms, it will be necessary, much as it was in earlier chapters, to invent some hypothetical families. It will also be necessary to abjure the usual socioeconomic class terms for those families ("middle," "upper," "lower," "working") since those terms refer either to the work done, or to the income achieved, by the male head of a household. Language that suggests a standard of "living" rather than one of "working" might be more appropriate, because women's work is intimately bound up with categories that are usually associated with the former expression: diet, health, household equipment, amenities, education, and so forth. Following standard parlance, I might then distinguish the two great classes of the population as the "rich" and the "poor," always remembering, however, that here "rich" really refers to people who could, in any given time or place, afford to live decently or comfortably, rather than to those who were truly wealthy. Similarly, "poor" refers not only to those who are dependent, who must rely, at least sporadically, on public or private charity, but also to those whose household income derives from employment but is not large enough to achieve what is commonly regarded as the "decent" or the "comfortable" standard. Until recently there was a fairly simple way to distinguish intact rich families from intact poor ones: In households that were rich, wives and mothers did not have to undertake paid employment in order to maintain a decent standard of living; these were the households, to use common parlance again, that "had it made," and they frequently also, as we shall see, had a maid. In contrast, in households that were poor, adult women (and frequently children as well) either had to go out to work or to take piece work in; these were the households in which people constantly struggled to make ends meet.

While it is no doubt true that every family is unique, it is also true that, at any given time and place, families living within the range of a certain standard of living confront similar material conditions in their homes and similar public attitudes about what distinguishes a "good" or a "decent" home from one that is neither. Each of us may bring a unique combination of psychic and social factors to our work; but, in any given time or place, depending upon the class to which we belong, women tend to organize their kitchens in more or less the same way and to read the same magazines, newspapers, and books. If our work, at least part of the time, is housework, then no matter how different we may be from each other, our work processes will be fairly similar. Hence, although it is difficult for a historian to learn much about *what* individual women and men felt about the work that was (or was not) being done in their homes, it is somewhat easier to learn *how* that work was being done. Between 1900 and 1940, the differences in the work processes of housework between those who were rich and those who were poor, were striking—so striking, indeed, that they remained engraved, consciously and unconsciously, on the minds and in the behavior of later generations.

The "Golden Years" (1900–1920)

MATERIAL CONDITIONS FOR THOSE WHO LIVED COMFORTABLY

The matriarch in an average American family of the comfortable class would have been born sometime in the 1870s, would have borne her children around the turn of the century, and would have been managing her household in the "golden years" that ended as the First World War was drawing to a close. An insight into her domestic routine has been provided by the work of John B. Leeds and L. R. Dodge. Leeds was an economist who pioneered in what was, in his day, called "family budget studies": for his doctoral dissertation at Columbia University, he recorded, in minute detail, the living conditions of sixty intact families who were "earning enough for decency" between 1912 and 1914.[1] Dodge was a conductor on the New Haven and Hartford Railroad who kept a compulsively detailed record of every penny spent in his household from 1889 until 1945.[2] Dodge and his wife Maria were married in 1889, and the first of their three children was born in 1892. They purchased a home (in Milford, Massachusetts) in 1899, the same year their last child was born; thus their household was active between 1912 and 1914, the years in which Leeds was conducting his investigation of similar families. The picture that emerges from both Leeds's book and Dodge's accounts is consistent with the picture that emerges from pre-war women's magazines, from the *Journal of Home Economics* (which began publication in 1908), and from what one can still observe in extant homes of the period. Hence, the specific information in the work of Leeds and Dodge can be used to substantiate the history of this hypothetical family.

A "comfortable" housewife might have been described, in her day, as a "progressive sort of person." Like as not, she lived in a great city or its environs, or perhaps in a rural town with a college or a university nearby. Her home was a multistoried, rambling sort of house (stone, if in the city; wood, if anywhere else) with her husband, who might have been a professional man or a business executive, a high-level clerk or a skilled craftsman, and their three children (Leeds's 60 families had an average of 2¾ children each).[3] Her family's annual income ranged somewhere between $1,000 and $3,500. The Dodge family took in $1,202.77 in 1910, which is not far from the most frequent income among Leeds's families ($1,300); the lowest income that Leeds found was $700 for a farm family; the highest, $3,750 for the family of a professional man.[4] In these "comfortable" families, the housewife did not ordinarily work for wages; although if the household was particularly pressed, or she was particularly energetic, she might (as Mrs. Dodge did) keep hens, take in an occasional boarder, or give lessons in piano or French or fancy needlework (only four out of Leeds's sixty housewives had earned some money, and not very much at that, in the two years of his study).[5]

Early in her marriage, such a housewife probably cooked on a coal or a wood-burning stove and lighted her house with gas or kerosene lamps. If she lived in a city, she probably had running water in her house, but she may still have been heating it in a reservoir attached to her stove; if she lived in a town, she might still be pumping water from a well in her yard. Some time after the turn of the century, however, various improvements were made to her property which both increased its value and altered the pattern of her work. The Dodges installed a bathroom in their house in 1904—an amenity that was regarded as sufficiently normal by 1912 that Leeds did not even trouble to ask his sixty families whether they had one, even though he carefully inquired about everything else. The Dodges connected their house to the gas mains in Milford in 1913 and purchased a range for the kitchen at the same time; the charge for hooking up was $9.80 and for the range, $14.00.* Forty-two out of Leeds's sixty families had gas service (which was used primarily for ranges and hot-water boilers), and fifty-three had electric service. The Dodges were "wired" in 1914, at a cost of $15.50 for electric fixtures, $2.50 for a transformer, and $24.00 for a vacuum cleaner; no charge was recorded for installation of the service. Some form of central heating was not so likely: although fifty-one of Leeds's families had it, the Dodges did not; the only concession to modernization they were willing to make was to switch from a coal stove to an oil stove in their living room in 1934.† Irons, vacuum cleaners, and fans were fairly common appliances which comfortable people acquired soon after installing electricity for lighting; washing machines and refrigerators had not yet made their appearance. As Leeds put it, "In the washing of clothing the use of a wringer and washboard was assumed."[7]

With or without these conveniences and appliances, a comfortable housewife worked hard to provide the decent standard of living that she and her family expected; but she did not work alone, for she belonged, as Leeds expressed it, to the "one servant class."[8] Neither Leeds's respondents nor the Dodges were wealthy people, but they all employed domestic servants. At the upper end of the income scale, this servant might well have been a live-in maid; but at the nether reaches, she might have been a day worker who was paid to do the laundry or the heavy cleaning, or to help with seasonably heavy chores, such as spring cleaning. The Dodges, who were by no means extravagant, laid out between thirty and forty dollars a year to have their washing done—an expenditure that did not stop until 1934, when they finally bought a washing machine. Only one of Leeds's housewives reported doing all of her own wash, and none did all of her own heavy cleaning.[9]

The kind of working relationship that existed between such a comfortable housewife and her paid helpers (who were more than likely to be housewives in their own right, albeit in households of a much different sort) can be discerned in a mar-

*The price suggests that this was a device with burners but without an oven; if so, Mrs. Dodge continued to bake and roast in her stove, not an unusual practice at this time.

†On this occasion, Mr. Dodge, who rarely appended comments to his account, allowed himself the luxury of exclaiming, "Use no more coal!"[6]

velously detailed time sheet that was published in 1918 in the *Journal of Home Economics*. [10] Marion Woodbury, who carefully recorded her own daily routine, was the wife of a university professor and the mother, at the time of publication, of three small children, one still an infant. She described herself as a person who "did her own work"—a phrase that was, in those days, a euphemism for "not having a live in maid."* She did, indeed, do a lot of work (estimating ten-hour days, five days a week, and five-hour days on Wednesday and Sunday), but she did not do all the work that upkeep of her household required. On Mondays, she stripped all the beds, bathrooms, and tables in the house and put all the linens and the rest of the week's wash in to soak for the laundress who came on Tuesday (to wash and clean) and for half of Wednesday (to iron). Mrs. Woodbury herself then put the clean clothing and linens away on Thursday. In midmorning of most days, she spent an hour or so cooking, preparing lunch, and getting most things in order for dinner; but after those meals (which she ate with her children), a student came in to clear up the kitchen; this same student cared for the children when their mother was not at home (as she had social obligations connected to her husband's position at the university) and did most of the dusting and sweeping (although the housewife put the rooms in order before the student started) and the floor polishing; additional heavy cleaning (particularly of the bathrooms) was done by the laundress. Although Mrs. Woodbury purchased most of the clothing for her family, she still had a good deal of sewing, which occupied her in the evenings and on Tuesday afternoons, since garments frequently required alteration and repair. She also ordered many of her groceries over the telephone and went to market only once every two weeks, on Friday afternoons; thus, although their labor is not recorded on her schedule, her household took up a good part of the time of deliverymen as well.

The ubiquity of this kind of work process was amply testified to in other contemporary documents. Leeds described the laun-

---

*Actually the euphemism goes back a long way; it was frequently used in the middle decades of the nineteenth century, and one historian who has frequently encountered it explains it thus: "Doing her own work meant that a housewife supervised its completion, rather than doing it herself."[11]

dering practices of his sixty families as follows: "Five families send all clothing to a laundry to be washed, while nine send none. One-half of the families employ a laundress; sixteen families employ her for one day a week, eight for half a day, and several have clothing taken to the home of the laundress."[12] Christine Frederick, a housewife who used her own household experience as the basis for several popular books on housekeeping, concluded her report of how she organized some aspects of her work: "The washing and ironing are done by a woman who comes in on two consecutive mornings of the same week, as this plan allows for emergencies of rainy days, etc. and gives her time to clean my kitchen and bathroom—the heavy work."[13] Another author-housewife, Rebecca Gradwohl, described how she had managed her household (containing two school-aged children) without a maid: "The remainder of the housework was done by specialists. The washing was sent out to the laundry. Once a week a Japanese boy vacuumed and polished the floors, scrubbed the kitchen and thoroughly cleaned the bath."[14] Advertisers in women's magazines and the editors of those magazines knew precisely what their audience was like and how their homes were run. In the *Ladies' Home Journal* for 1 January 1918, "The Householders Dream of a Happy New Year" was a cartoon with the caption: "Mandy offers to stay for life and take less wages."[15] Throughout the monthly issues that year (and in all the preceding years since the *Journal*'s founding in 1883), domestic servants were repeatedly depicted: if you wanted to sell flannel baby clothes, you drew a baby held by a nursemaid; if you wanted to sell fabric, you drew a seamstress pinning up hems; shampoo, a maid washing her mistress' hair; talcum powder, "Nurse powders baby"; washing soap, a laundress hanging up clothes.

Yet even the presence of domestic servants did not make a comfortably situated housewife into a lady of leisure. At the technological level that most of these families had achieved, the upkeep of a decent home still required the labor of at least two adults, and the housewife herself was certainly one of them: "progressive" women were women who had "other interests" but still devoted most of their time and energy to the care of their homes and families. The housewives in Leeds's study spent an average of fifty-six hours per week doing housework; Marion Woodbury clocked herself at sixty hours.[16] Their work alternated between what we might call manual labor (cooking, baking, straightening rooms, sewing) and managerial labor (ordering foodstuffs, supervising household assistants, teaching children, doing the household accounts), and they did as little as they possibly could of the heavy labor that was considered demeaning for women of their station (scrubbing floors, hauling laundry, beating rugs, washing windows, ironing). Depending upon the ages of the children and the affluence of the household, a housewife of the comfortable classes was left at least some free time for other activities. She might serve on church committees, raise money for charitable endeavors, keep the accounts of her husband's business, do some of his clerical work, or entertain at luncheons and dinner parties.

Both her household work and her outside activities enabled her family to maintain its comfortable standard of living. Her home was capacious, orderly, and clean. All the members of the household wore clothing that fitted properly, and they changed it with some frequency. Meals were served at set times, on clean plates; and the diet was varied enough to keep everyone reasonably healthy. Children of this class had acquired the rudiments of education even before they entered school, and their progress in school was carefully monitored. Their mothers had other interests and enough time to indulge them (especially after the children had passed infancy); but these interests were of such a nature that when some member of the household was ill, the wife and mother could easily drop her other responsibilities to undertake the nursing that was required, and in those years it could well have been required for weeks on end. When funds were short, this comfortably situated housewife had various means to augment the family purse, but her activities did not threaten either the family's health or its level of comfort. She was, as she might have said at the time, not only "decent" but also the mainstay of "decency" in her community, even though she might have had difficulty in defining precisely what "decency" was.

MATERIAL CONDITIONS FOR THOSE WHO WERE STRUGGLING TO MAKE ENDS MEET

Yet such a comfortable housewife was by no means the average American housewife of her time. However modest her annual household income may have been, she still belonged to an élite; and nothing lay closer to the heart of her élite status than her ability to live comfortably. Historians and demographers have struggled mightily with the problem of assessing just which portion of the population could achieve this particular standard of living in the early decades of the century (when there was no income tax statement to give the government even a rough approximation of the distribution of incomes across the land), but even the most sanguine guesses do not approach 50 percent of the population.[17] In the golden years before the First World War (and, indeed, for many years thereafter), the "other half" was considerably more than half of the population. Social workers and sociologists of the day also struggled mightily to define what "minimum decency" meant as a standard of living and to coin a term that would adequately describe the portion of the population who were forced to live at or below that standard. Yet those who lived in poverty surely had no difficulty in knowing precisely what the living conditions were that separated them from the comfortable classes, and surely would have had little difficulty in explaining what it meant to be "uncomfortable," whether or not common usage would have applied that term to their situation.

The matriarch of a hypothetical hard-pressed family might have lived in a tenement in a large urban area, a dilapidated frame house in a small city, a row house in a company town, a collapsing farmhouse on a small plot of land, or even a log cabin in the woods. She shared this dwelling with her husband (if he had neither died nor deserted), a fairly large number of children, and probably several other people, some related to her, some not: perhaps an in-law, or a cousin who was lodging with her until finding a job and a spouse; or boarders whose rent helped to make ends meet; or an orphaned niece or nephew.[18] Her husband might have been a tenant farmer or a day laborer or an unskilled factory hand or even a skilled factory hand in many of the highly competitive industries of the day; but his income was not sufficient to provide his family consistently with even the bare necessities of life, as his land might be unfertile, or he might be subject to periodic unemployment or disablement or might simply have been woefully underpaid. Unlike her comfortable contemporaries, such a housewife regularly needed a supplemental source of income. Whether it was hard labor in the fields, piecework, laundry or boarders at home, domestic service or drudgery in the factories, the money that she was able to provide was frequently essential for the survival of the family.

A housewife who was struggling to make ends meet was not likely to be filling out questionnaires or keeping records of her daily schedule, and her life certainly was not depicted in the widely circulated magazines and newspapers of her day. Fortunately for the historian, during the early years of the twentieth century, several new professions developed whose practitioners (social workers, home economists, public health officers) have left extensive and sympathetic accounts of what life was like in the households of the poor, especially the urban poor. What the social workers discovered is in reasonably close accord with what those few residents who left memoirs (either in fiction or in nonfiction) have said, and with what contemporary photographs reveal. When the distorting lens of nostalgia is removed, the reality is not pleasant to contemplate.

The entire family, plus its lodgers and boarders, resided in one, perhaps two, or—in very fortunate circumstances—four rooms, each of which had to serve multiple functions: some people had to cook while others slept; some had to work while others played; some had to bathe while others ate—all within the same four walls. Densities as high as two or three people to a room were not infrequently recorded in such cities as New York, Chicago, and Pittsburgh, or among tenant farmers (black as well as white) in the South. "A home I know well is a fair sample," wrote one social worker about a particularly prosperous family (the father earned twelve dollars a week, two children worked regularly in factories, and the mother made artificial flowers at home), "a four room flat, rent nineteen dollars, nine in family, . . . plus a boarder to help pay the rent."[19] Under such circumstances, there was little privacy. Each child shared a bed with two or three siblings, adults slept in the same room with children, boarders in the same room as members of the family. Domestic quarrels and domestic celebrations frequently spilled over into the streets and pubs. Children who needed a quiet place to study, or young people who were courting, or adults who needed some place to organize their thoughts either did without or went somewhere else.

Storage facilities in such homes were at a minimum. Kitchen cabinets simply did not exist (they were only just beginning to appear in many prosperous homes), and neither did closets. What storage there was might have consisted of a few shelves, some pegs, a box under the bed, perhaps a chest of drawers, perhaps an old trunk. Lacking storage, everything that was needed for living and for working was out in the open nearly all the time: the pots and pans jostled with the sewing machine, the clothing jostled with the broom, the table was rarely cleared (where else would the utensils be put?), the toys (such as they were) mingled with the shoes (such as *they* were), and together they occupied what little floor space was left when the requisite furniture for such a family was crowded into the small rooms in which they lived. Beds became chairs, and sometimes doors became beds; one table might be used for preparing food, for eating it, for stitching garments, or gluing artificial flowers, or butchering a chicken. The towel with which people wiped their hands might wipe a baby's bottom or the floor or the table or the pots.

Under such circumstances, cleaning up was surely a herculean endeavor, and straightening up (which always preceded cleaning in a comfortable household) was virtually impossible. Running hot and cold water, toilets, bathtubs, and sinks were conveniences that had not yet diffused to shacks in the countryside or to fourth-floor walkups in the cities. Only fifteen out of the ninety families that Margaret Byington studied near Pittsburgh had indoor toilets, and only 20 percent of the four hundred families that Robert Coit Chapin studied in New York had bathrooms.[20] Poor people carried into their dwellings the water that they needed for cooking and cleaning, and they heated it by the potful on their stoves. Living as they did in the filthiest districts, and laboring as they did in the occupations most likely to produce dirt and grime, their homes, even under the best of circumstances, frequently required cleaning. Some women, determined to keep their homes as orderly and healthful as they could make them, exhausted themselves at the task; while large numbers of others—perhaps less optimistic perhaps less brave, perhaps more realistic—just gave up and rarely attempted it.

Under such circumstances, a housewife had to struggle not only against the horrendous condition of her housing but also against the exigencies of the weather. The comforts of central heating were comforts that she could not hope to enjoy; most women still heated the rooms where they lived with the stove on which they cooked, and most of those stoves (in rural areas there was still an occasional open hearth) required coal or wood for fuel. During warm weather, the cooking area was uncomfortably hot, since the fire had to be kept burning for much of the day to cook food and heat water; and in cold weather, some part of the dwelling (often a substantial part) was miserably cold. Summer might find this housewife faint from the heat on laundry day, and winter might find her with fingers that could barely move from the cold, trying to mend a tear in a child's glove. If she lived in a city or a town, she and her children also had to cope with the job of obtaining the fuel that the stove required, since coal and wood did not come delivered to the poor woman's door, and either ethnic tradition or the long hours of her husband's labor meant that he, unlike his more prosperous contemporaries, rarely supervised fuel-related chores himself:

> After a day's work in the factory or the home, you will find at dusk in the woods—two or three miles from where she lives—the dark-eyed foreigner, gathering huge fagots of firewood and, bent under their weight and bulk, trudging home by unfrequented paths . . . sometimes furtively helping nature a little with a small axe.[21]

Where wood was not available, women and children carried heavy buckets of coal from curbside vendors up long flights of stairs or spent long, cold hours searching for "black gold" that had spilled from railroad cars or overfilled delivery vans. Mothers who were extraordinarily well organized and extraordinarily well situated may have been able to manage their stoves and their fuel effectively, but everyone else suffered the burdensome extremes of too much heat in the summer and too little in the winter.

With the lack of time, energy, equipment, and cash, cooking could not have been a particularly elaborate undertaking in the households of the poor. Home economists did not think to trouble housewives of this group with time-study questionnaires; and, not surprisingly, we have no record of a hard-pressed housewife who recorded her daily activities quite as self-consciously as Marion Woodbury or Christine Frederick did. Hence, it is difficult to know with certainty how much time was allotted to food-related tasks in poor households. Yet we do have dietary information about what was served in certain weeks in such households, budgetary information about what was purchased, anecdotal information about what was offered for sale, social workers' reports about the nutritional adequacy of what was eaten, and public health officers' concerns about the ways in which the food was prepared—all of which produce a picture different from the one conjured up by writers of television advertising copy for bread and bottled spaghetti sauce.

Their nostalgic re-creations of fragrant smells emanating from kitchens, of mothers who baked special breads and sugar-coated cookies, of large families gathered at large tables for many-course meals must surely stem from recollections of special occasions (such as Christmas or Sabbath), whose specialness was signaled by the devotion of so much labor to them. Under ordinary conditions, however, cooking seems not to have occupied enormous amounts of time, skill, or energy in the households of people who had to struggle just to make ends meet. The poorest of those knew frequent hunger; and even the more prosperous knew a markedly monotonous diet, much of it (at least in the cities) purchased ready-made. Bread came from the baker; sausages, salamis, salted fish, cheese, beer, and canned goods, from vendors; and macaroni from the family down the block. What cooking there was, on the farms as well as in the cities, was largely

—as it had been in the eighteenth century—one-pot cooking: either gruels, soups, or stews which could be boiled on top of the stove; or bacon, fish, or, occasionally, chops, which could be fried. "The principal articles of food in the account books," reported one social worker who had asked close to two hundred families living in New York City to keep track of their expenditures for a month:

> are meat, milk (fresh and condensed), baker's bread, butter, potatoes and tea. . . . potatoes are used freely, often a quart for a meal in large families. The vegetables are mostly canned corn or tomatoes, turnips, carrots and cabbage. Macaroni, beans, bread, vegetables and soup are the main food of the Italians. The poorer families live on bread, tea, soup or stew, and oatmeal.[22]

The poor in the countryside did not fare markedly better, despite their proximity to fresh fruits and vegetables. In the households of those who were comfortable, people had the time and the facilities to maintain a kitchen garden and an orchard and to put up their products. The poor, however, were likely to be hard at work on someone else's land during the times of year when these tasks had to be undertaken, and hence made do with cornmeal mush, bacon, and whatever game, fish, or wild fruits and vegetables they chanced upon.

In the neighborhoods in which such diets were commonplace, evidence of malnutrition was everywhere to be found, from children bent with rickets to adults lacking teeth. For babies, the diet of the poor was particularly threatening, since anything that they imbibed (other than mother's milk) was likely to be either contaminated or difficult to digest, and since a mother who was herself exhausted and malnourished was unlikely to have milk sufficient to feed a child, even if she were physically present to nurse one, as many mothers could not be. For this reason (as well as others), infant mortality was horrifying high among the poor; scarcely a child grew to adulthood without witnessing the death of a little brother or sister.

In such an environment, bathing and laundering must have been terrible trials. In warm weather the wash could be carried close to the water tap or the well, and if a portable stove were available (or an open fire could be made), the washing could be done without much hauling of heavy buckets, but the weather was not always warm, and the facilities were not always available. For most women, for most of the year, the labor of doing laundry meant carrying heavy buckets of water from tap to stove and from stove to tub, repeatedly overturning the tubs and refilling them, as well as carrying, scrubbing, wringing, and hanging the heavy fabrics that were the only ones cheap enough for poor people to buy. The labor of getting the family bathed was similar, lacking only the carrying, scrubbing, wringing, and hanging of the wash. A housewife who had to struggle to make ends meet usually could afford neither to send her washing out (assuming that there was a commercial laundry close enough to patronize) nor to hire a laundress (although when times were good, this might have been one of the first luxuries she allowed herself, as Margaret Byington discovered in certain households in Pittsburgh).[23] Even if a dwelling contained a sink, it was usually not deep enough for doing laundry and may not have had a drain. Public laundries were few and far between; and so, for that matter, were public bath houses, although in some cities special efforts were made by city governments and charitable organizations to provide them. The most fortunate families might have had a hand-cranked washing machine with a wringer, which had the advantage of being portable and labor saving; but as these cost fifteen dollars apiece, one was beyond the means of most families. The net result of the profound difficulty that washing and bathing presented was that precious little of it got done; underclothing might be changed only once a week, or even once a season; sheets likewise (if they were used at all, since featherbeds did not require them); outerclothes might do with just a brushing; shirts or shirtwaists might go for weeks without benefit of soap; faces and hands might get splashed with water once a day; full body bathing might occur only on Saturday nights (and then with a sponge and a wooden tub and water that was used and reused) or only when underwear was changed—or never at all. "Some women have a feeling that cleanliness is a condition only for the rich," one home economist remarked of the immigrant women with whom she worked:

> and if one is poor it follows as a matter of course that one is dirty. . . . Because the immigrant standard in this matter is so low, personal cleanliness is harder to teach than anything else. In order not to cause offense, the Educator has to impress upon the women the fact that the American climate demands more attention to details of toilet than in the old country.[24]

Whether in urban tenement or rural shack, the net result of the inability (surely not unwillingness, as this home economist implied) to launder and bathe frequently must have been unpleasant smells and unpleasant itches. The smells may not have bothered those who were accustomed to them (although it is difficult to imagine that the itches were not felt), but they certainly bothered those who were not, as John Leeds himself remarked:

> Many people do not sufficiently realize the extent to which the increase in cleanliness of home and person contributes toward the growth of democracy. So long as the upper classes felt the necessity of using smelling salts whenever approached by one of the common people, just so long would they despise the vile-smelling yokels. Cleanliness is not only next to Godliness, but it is essential to the establishment of the Brotherhood of Man.[25]

Leaving the brotherhood of man aside, cleanliness was essential to getting a good job, since the members of the comfortable classes, to whom Leeds referred, frequently encountered the members of the poorer classes only when they were seeking employees—whether as domestic servants, clerks, typists, shop-girls, or waitresses. Manuals for domestic servants and instruction booklets for shopgirls in department stores, magazines for boys and pamphlets distributed to immigrants at Ellis Island, all contained admonitions about the necessity of "keeping clean." For those who were poor, getting on in this world meant, many times, learning to control the smells and the itches, and it also meant that countless housewives were struggling to do laundry and to provide facilities for bathing. In this context, the laundry that hung from many tenement windows was more than just laundry; it was a signal and a symbol that the housewife had found the time to do the laundry, and *that* fact might well have meant that the fortunes and the prospects of the family were improving.

Aside from cooking, cleaning, managing fuel, and laundering, a hard-pressed housewife also cared for her children; and although the available data are not altogether reliable (since, in those days, births frequently went unrecorded by the authorities), it seems clear that such a housewife was pregnant more often, bore more children, and was considerably more likely to watch some of them die or suffer permanent injury before reaching adulthood, than were her contemporaries who had greater economic resources at their command.

Hungry babies cry and do not sleep for long periods unless sedated, and are likely to exhaust and to frustrate their already overstrained mothers. Diapers that are changed infrequently chafe, and diaper rashes hurt. Toddlers who must be bundled up against the cold, and who have cramped quarters in which to play, tend to be cranky and bad-tempered. When clothing is made of rough materials and does not fit properly, children become irritable (for that matter, so do adults); and when children become adolescents, irritation is augmented by embarrassment and anger at those who have failed to provide. The children who had to be put to tedious labor often had to be brutally reminded of their duties. For older children, the streets and the woods, however full of bustle and adventure, were also full of hazards —and in environments such as these, skinned knees, cut fingers, and bruised toes were likely to stay infected and sore for a long time. In the years before widespread vaccinations and the availability of antibiotics, children were frequently sick and required care for long periods, sometimes all through the night; for children who lived in unsanitary conditions and who had to manage without the care of physicians and without medication, even the mildest illness could become life threatening. Many American mothers watched their children go hungry, watched them die, watched them suffer the pains of illness, scorn, and overwork, watched some of them drift into lives of petty crime and prostitution—sorrowful cares, bearing down upon and darkening the minds of women who were already overburdened.

And the housewife of the poorer classes was truly overburdened. In addition to her household chores, she often bore the extra yoke of paid employment—and whether this was piecework at home, or labor in factories and fields, or the care of innumerable boarders, the additional work sapped her energy, wrecked her health, and made nearly impossible the performance of even the most trivial household chores. National statistics suggest that, in the years before the United States entered the European conflict, no more than 10 percent of all married women were employed in any given year, but in poverty-stricken communities, the percentages were much higher. In Fall River, Massachusetts, for example, one demographer has estimated that one third of all married women were employed in the mills between 1912 and 1914; while investigators in Passaic, New Jersey, found that one fourth of all the married women (the vast majority of whom were also mothers) worked in factories.[26] These figures probably underestimate the paid employment of married women in these communities, because they do not account either for women who took in laundry, did piece work at home, or kept boarders. In addition, women who were not employed during one week might very well be employed the next, since the sudden loss of a husband's wages (which could occur as the result of accident or illness or one of the many periodic downturns in a trade) could propel his wife into the labor market on short notice. Only one fourth of all married women might have been employed in any one year, but all women of the hard-pressed classes could anticipate being employed for long stretches of time during the years of marriage. And their employment did not mean that they would either be relieved of household cares or have sufficient cash to pay someone else to lighten the burden of those chores, as the investigators in Passaic noted:

Scarcely more than 1/5 of these breadwinning mothers had any help in the performance of household duties; the number having hired help even for washing and ironing regularly or irregularly was negligible. What help they did have came chiefly from older children or relatives or lodgers.[27]

Only 25 out of the 522 mothers who were studied in Passaic could afford to pay someone to care for their children; the remaining children were supervised by a neighbor or a relative, and fully one fifth of them (that is, the children of over 100 families) were either unsupervised or supervised by a child under the age of fourteen. Today, a married woman works to improve her family's standard of living. At that time, however, for poor families —for whom housing was substandard, and epidemic disease rampant, where laundering and bathing were laborious enterprises, and fuel gathering was the responsibility of women—the employment of a woman may have been necessary to put food on the table or pay the rent, but it was also a serious threat not just to the comfort but also to the health of her family. Indeed, it was a serious threat to her own health as well. In Fall River, Massachusetts, the mortality rate for married women millworkers was three times higher than for single women millworkers, and four times higher than for married women who did not work in the mills.[28] The common prejudice against married women's gainful employment (a prejudice still with us today) has its roots in the tragic conditions that underlay such statistics.

Thus, no matter how difficult it may have been for economists to quantify and for social workers to define the standard of living of ordinary Americans in the years before the First World War, to the people who lived through those years the difference between living "comfortably" and being "hard pressed," between "having it made" and "making ends meet," was distinct and intense, a matter of daily mundane experience, rather than a matter of complex computation or linguistic niceties. Here memoirist Elizabeth Stern recalls her reaction to a visit to the home of a school friend who lived in a better neighborhood:

> I could not believe that the woman who opened the door to my knock was my friend's mother. A woman in *white!* Why, mothers dressed in brown and black, I always knew. And this mother sang to us. She romped through the two step with us. . . . I had always thought that

mothers never "enjoyed," just worked. This strange mother opened a new window for me in the possibilities of women's lives.[29]

And novelist Thomas Bell, the child of immigrant Slovak parents, recalled his impression of "how the better half lived" through the mind of his fictional re-creation of his father, Mike Dobrejcak. Mike courted a young woman who worked as a nursemaid in the home of a local factory owner; the boy she cared for was seven or eight years old:

> a clean bright boy who asked Mike questions about the mill and liked to display the few Slovak phrases Mary had taught him. Mike was infinitely more impressed with the boy's good manners; he would have given a month of his life to be able to say "I beg your pardon" and "Excuse me" as naturally.

One day, when her employers were out for the day, Mary took Mike on a tour of the house:

> The Dexter's was the first private house Mike had ever set foot in which was wired for electricity. For that matter it was the first private house he'd ever been in that had a bathroom, a telephone, steam heat, and in the kitchen a magnificent icebox. . . .
>
> Mike's interest in houses, in house furnishings, was no greater than most young men's . . . but in the Dexter's dining room, in their parlor and bedrooms, he saw furniture, dishes and silverware which were desirable and beautiful in themselves and not merely as articles of use. For the first time he perceived how graceful the business of eating and sleeping and entertaining one's friends could be, and how one could be proud of one's possessions, the way one lived. . . .
>
> "Maybe it would have been better for me if I'd never seen it." . . . He sobered, "Ach! What would we want with such a fancy house! No one would come to see us; we'd lose all our friends."[30]

The symbols of decent living in the first two decades of this century were symbols that the labor of a housewife and her assistants could provide: white lawn dresses on women, white shirts on men, clean bathrooms and clean kitchens, families who ate in their dining rooms, children who went to school regularly, and mothers who could romp through the two-step. And these symbols, like all potent symbols, bespoke reality. Having a white lawn dress or a white shirt meant that the housewife was assisted by a laundress and that her children would know how to be clean enough to get a good job if they needed one. A clean bathroom and a clean kitchen usually meant that someone had been hired to clean; and it also meant that the comfortable family had some control over the diseases that could lurk in kitchens and bathrooms, and could thus suffer less illness, live longer, and have fewer children who died. Eating in the dining room meant that a housewife had help with the cooking and the serving; and it also meant ample diets, regular meals, and ritualized hospitality. Those who were forced by circumstances to eat in their kitchens were those who ate meagerly, took all their food from a common pot, rarely "set" the table, and had malnourished children. Parents who sent their children to school regularly did not depend upon their children's labor for income; such parents could try to help their children by teaching them at home, by supervising their schoolwork, by chaperoning them when necessary, and by socializing them into a world that stood ready to greet them. Parents who could not afford to live "decently" could not guarantee anything for their children, not even regular meals. A housewife who belonged to the more prosperous part of the population could see and touch and feel, both in symbol and in reality, the various comforts that she had achieved for herself and for every member of her family. The housewife who belonged to the poorer part, no matter how hard she might labor, was constantly undermined by forces over which she had no control.

Between the World Wars (1920–1940)

The second generation of twentieth-century women came to maturity during the First World War, bore their children during the Roaring Twenties, and struggled to keep their households functioning during the dreary years of the Depression. Enormous technological and social changes occurred between their mothers' time and their own; and these changes began —but only just began—to alter not only the work processes of housework but also the fundamental differences between women of the two great social classes.

MATERIAL CONDITIONS FOR THOSE WHO WERE STILL LIVING COMFORTABLY

During the 1920s and the 1930s, a housewife of the more prosperous classes did not regularly work for wages, despite the fact that she was better educated than her mother had been and more likely to have worked for a few years before marriage. Only one in forty of the "business class" housewives who were studied by Helen and Robert Lynd in Muncie, Indiana ("Middletown"), in 1925 had worked for wages in the previous five years.[31] The typical comfortable housewife of this generation lived in a house that was fairly similar to the one in which she had been raised (if she were lucky enough to have been the daughter of a prosperous father); it was spacious, perhaps a bit smaller than her parents' had been, lacking a spare bedroom or an old-fashioned parlor, but not much smaller; and it was equipped with many of the same modern conveniences (telephones, hot and cold running water, indoor plumbing, gas and electricity). By the end of the 1920s, the daughter was likely to have had one or two appliances that had not been available to her mother (perhaps an electric washing machine, or a refrigerator, or an automobile); but, even more significantly, she would have acquired the conveniences and the appliances earlier in her marriage, when her children were still young and the burden of her work was heaviest, and when her household routines (which are very resistant to change) were first established. In 1926, 80 percent of all the affluent households that were studied by market researchers in thirty-six American cities had vacuum cleaners and washing machines.[32] More than half of all the households in the United States had an automobile by 1930, and every single one of the business-class households of Muncie had one by 1925.[33] When the Lynds returned to study Muncie again in 1935, 40 percent of all the households whose assessed value was over two thousand dollars (a sum the Lynds regarded as the dividing line between adequate and inadequate housing) had a refrigerator.[34]

Taken together, the vacuum cleaner, the washing machine, the refrigerator, and the automobile had profound implications for the reorganization of work in the households of the prosperous. Possession of an electric washing machine meant that a "decent" housewife could do her wash at home and by herself without undue drudgery; these early washing machines did not go through their cycles automatically and did not spin the clothing semi-dry (they had electrically powered wringers), but they did eliminate a good deal of the hauling and the hand wringing that had once made laundry work inconceivable for a woman of "status." The vacuum cleaners of the day were heavy instruments; but since they could be wheeled, they eliminated not only the drudgery but also the stooping that had once been associated with heavy cleaning and thus eliminated the perceived necessity for a servant to undertake it. Vacuum cleaners also cleaned more thoroughly than brooms and thus made it possible for the young housewife to dispense not only with the horrors of spring cleaning but also with the women whom her mother had hired to help with it. The young housewife's refrigerator reinforced the tendency—which had actually commenced when either her basement or her mother's had been converted from a storage room to a furnace room—to purchase foodstuffs in small, rather than large, quantities and to dispense with delivery services provided by the retailer. The automobile served only to accelerate that trend as well as to create a host of other transportation services (such as taking children to parties and to doctors) that women of an earlier generation had not provided for their families. The average comfortable housewife of the generation before the First World War had done some of her housework herself and managed the labor of other people who did the rest of it; the average comfortable housewife of the generation that came to maturity after the war managed more appliances than people.

The availability of appliances and conveniences was one—but not the only one—of the factors that stimulated this reorganization. One study of the relationship between the acquisition of household appliances and the organization of household work in this period reported that, while most of the families of students at Mount Holyoke College had acquired four or five major appliances in the decade between 1919 and 1929, and 96 percent of the families had also decreased the amount of household help that they employed, only a small fraction of these attributed the decrease solely to the acquisition of the appliances.[35] The other families were probably responding to a new set of demographic factors (namely, a severe contraction in the available supply of servants) and to a new set of ideological factors (namely, new attitudes articulated in women's magazines and advice books during the 1920s). Subsequently economic factors also came into play (although they would not have been applicable to the Mount Holyoke families, who were interviewed in 1929), as the severe decline in income that many prosperous families experienced during the Depression led them to fire the servants that they had previously employed, and to decrease their patronage of commercial services that had previously performed domestic work.

The supply of servants was shrinking for many reasons. The European conflict and, after that, the immigration restrictions of the mid-1920s drastically reduced the influx of foreign-born young women, who had previously constituted the largest portion of the servant population. In addition, the expanding economy of the 1920s increased the opportunities in factories for women without skills. In Indiana, for example, the ratio of servants to households was 1 in 20 in 1920; and the business-class wives of Muncie reported that they employed approximately half as many servant-hours as their mothers had done, at roughly five times the wages (salaries for people in the middle-income ranges had roughly doubled in the same period).[36]*Only one quarter of the seven hundred urban households of college-educated women that were studied carefully by the United States Department of Agriculture in 1930 employed a domestic servant, as did only 17 percent of the three thousand middle-class families studied a year later by President Hoover's Conference on Home Building and Homeownership—percentages that would have been astounding twenty years earlier.[38]

*This estimate that salaries had doubled is derived from calculations made by the Lynds, who regarded it as a rough approximation.[37]

The Depression served to accentuate this pattern. Widespread unemployment meant that more women were available to perform domestic chores for pay, but the curtailment of incomes meant that fewer households were ready and able to pay for these women's services. The slight rise in the absolute number of servants recorded by the census during the 1930s (from 1,998,000 in 1930 to 2,412,000 in 1940) may reflect the fact that some small number of multi-servant (in other words, extremely wealthy) households were able to increase the number of servants that they employed during the Depression; many of these "new" servants may have been men who could no longer find employment in the factories and were hence willing to act as gardeners and chauffeurs.[39] In the pages of the public press during those years, the genteel housewife who had formerly kept servants, but was forced to let them go, became something of a social stereotype: "a college girl who in recent years has been obliged to live the anxious circumscribed life of the maid-of-all-work wife of a small-time lawyer with vanishing fees," as the journalist Anne O'Hare McCormick described a friend of hers in 1933.[40]* "Doing it yourself these days?" asked the makers of LaFrance bluing, over a picture of manicured hands immersed in a laundry tub; and apparently many people were.[42] The Secretary of the American Washing Machine Manufacturers Association reported in 1932 that, for the first time, washing machines were being sold on Fifth Avenue, and he remarked:

> Nothing could be more expressive of the changed social and buying conditions. An entirely new class, never before directly interested in the washing process or in the details of household economics has come into the buying market. . . . These housewives have the money to buy anything. . . . Now for the first time in their lives in many cases they are going to direct attention to every item of household expense.[43]

"Really doing it yourself" had once been considered demeaning, but attitudes were changing. In the early decades of the

*The constraints on housewives who previously employed servants were fictionalized in women's magazines as well: "But it would have been foolish to keep her [Dagmar, the maid]. As Lillian told Steve, plenty of other women were doing their own housework."[41]

century, women's magazines had repeatedly offered advice to housewives who were, for one unfortunate reason or another, coping with their homes singlehanded, but the emphasis in those articles had been on the word *unfortunate*. The housewife was told, for example, that if help was scarce, it was easiest to serve children the same food that adults were eating, although clearly it would be better for the former's digestion and your temperament if they ate with a nursemaid in the nursery; with luck, the servant shortage would soon pass.[44] "Decent" housewives were never depicted, in those years, as doing the heavy work of their households themselves; when instructions for proper laundry work or sanitary cleaning were proffered, a tell-tale "instruct your laundress" or "see that your maid" would always slip through. In the years after the First World War, as advertisements for refrigerators, washing machines, and vacuum cleaners replaced those for iceboxes, laundry tubs, and brooms, servants disappeared from the advertisements—to be replaced by housewives, neatly manicured and elegantly coiffured, but housewives nonetheless.[45] In those same years, the language used in the nonfiction material in women's magazines also underwent a subtle change, coming to imply that housework was to be thought of no longer as a chore but, rather, as an expression of the housewife's personality and her affection for her family. Laundering had once been just a task to be finished as quickly as possible; now it was an expression of love. The new bride could speak her affection by washing tattle-tale gray out of her husband's shirts. Feeding the family had once been just part of a day's work; now it was a way to communicate deep-seated emotions:

> When the careful housekeeper turns from the preparation of company dinner to the routine of family meals, she will know that prime rib roast, like peach ice cream, *is a wonderful stimulant to family loyalty*, but that it is not absolutely necessary for every day.[46] [Italics mine]

Diapering was now a time for building a baby's sense of security, and cleaning the bathroom sink became an exercise for the maternal instincts, protecting the family from disease.

Clearly, tasks of such emotional magnitude could not be relegated to servants. The servantless household may have been an economic necessity for some people in the 1920s and the 1930s; but, for the first time, that necessity was widely regarded, at least in the public press, as a potential virtue. And whether or not she regarded it as a virtue, the average comfortable housewife of this generation learned to organize the work in her household without the assistance of servants or with far fewer hours of assistance than her mother had had. Where a servant had been replaced by a vacuum cleaner, the comfortable housewife was spending more time than her mother had spent getting the floors and the rugs into shape; where a laundress had been replaced by a washing machine or a deliveryman by the household automobile, a housewife was spending time and energy on chores that, in her mother's day, had been performed by other people. No matter how a household chose to slice the cake of available resources in the interwar years, every decision to "do it myself" was a decision to increase the time that the housewife would spend at her work. In households that were prosperous, the labor saved by labor-saving devices was that not of the housewife but of her helpers. This is the most salient reason that every time-study of affluent housewives during these years (and many such studies were done, as these were the years in which home economists, like so many other Americans, were fascinated by "efficiency studies") revealed that no matter how many appliances they owned, or how many conveniences were at their command, they were still spending roughly the same number of hours per week at housework as their mothers had.[47] The most comprehensive of those studies, covering fifteen hundred urban and rural households, in the years 1924–25 and 1930–31, found a range of hours spent in housework from a high of sixty-one (for rural farm homemakers) to a low of forty-eight (for college-educated urban women living in large cities)—figures that were not markedly different from those reported by Leeds and Woodbury twenty years earlier.[48]

This second-generation prosperous housewife had also expanded certain aspects of her job description, which could not be mediated by technology at all—namely, those aspects having to do with the care of her children. Infant care was much more complex than it once had been, because in an effort to combat infant mortality (which had been scandalously high in the United States in the pre-war period)*—mothers were watching scrupulously over their children's diets, weighing them several times a day, and repeatedly carrying them to physicians' offices for checkups. Child care no longer consisted of teaching young children to read, write, and add and in seeing to it that children were adequately clothed and regularly fed; it now also involved attending child-study meetings, becoming involved in the local schools, reading books and magazines about children, supervising them in playgrounds, and transporting them to lessons and social events.

> I accommodate my entire life to my little girl. She takes three music lessons a week and I practice with her forty minutes a day. I help her with her school work and go to dancing school with her.

> My mother never stepped inside the school building as far as I can remember, but now there are never ten days that go by without my either visiting the children's school or getting in touch with their teacher. I have given up church work and club work since the children came. I always like to be here when they get home from school so that I can keep in touch with their games and their friends. Any extra time goes into reading books on nutrition and character building.

> I put on roller skates with the boys and pass a football with them. In the evenings we play cards and on Sundays we go to ball games. My mother back East thinks it's scandalous.[50]

Experts repeatedly suggested that a mother was the single most important person in a child's life, and that the child raised by nursemaids was a child to be pitied. The young boy raised by servants would never learn the upright, go-getting resourcefulness of the truly American child, would never become a useful member of the egalitarian republic, and would probably fail in the business world; his sister, deprived of the example of her mother, would not know how to manage the myriad appliances of the modern kitchen, would never learn how to decorate a

---

*The infant mortality rate was 100 per 1,000 live births in 1915 (one of the highest in the Western world), 71.7 in 1925, and 55.7 in 1935. By comparison, in 1978 it was 13.8.[49]

pineapple salad or wash silk underwear in an electric machine, and might thus never be able to capture a husband. Even more worrisome was the thought that children raised by nursemaids might never reach adulthood because they would be tended by persons who were unfamiliar with the latest medical and nutritional information. Mothers were being asked to take more of a hand in the rearing of their children, and many mothers were responding to the challenge.[51]

Thus, the comfortably situated housewife of the interwar years expended most of her time and energy, just as her mother had, in the interests of her family. Even during the worst years of the Depression, she continued to run her household "decently"; her husband was still employed, the family was not on relief; they still owned their own home, and they still kept it up; the interior was orderly, the meals arrived regularly, the children stayed in school, the family went to church, their health—whatever strain they were under—remained reasonably stable.[52]

But something subtle had changed. Emily Post summed it up better than anyone else when she added a new chapter to the fifth edition (1937) of the famous etiquette book that had first appeared in 1915. This chapter dealt with the problems faced by "Mrs. Three-in-One"—the woman who had to be guest, waitress, and cook at her own dinner parties.[53] Like her mother she understood the rituals of gracious entertaining, knew how to make guests comfortable in her home, knew precisely which foods should be served on which occasions, knew how to reflect the status of her household in her own behavior. But unlike her mother, either because of inclination or circumstance, she was also a manual laborer: she had to chop the onions, roll the pastries, manipulate the cooking times, arrange the platters, carry them to the table, carve the roast, remove the dirty plates, pour the coffee—all the while appearing as if she were not doing any of these tasks. As part of the process of reallocating the time she spent in household work, she had ceased managing the labor of others and had substituted her own. This transformation, which might properly be called the "proletarianization" of the work of economically comfortable housewives, did not occur overnight. Its fullest effects would not be felt until the next generation had reached maturity, but the handwriting was on the wall. In an effort to sustain the standard of living to which an earlier generation had been accustomed, the properous housewife of this generation started down the path of "doing it herself," the implications of which would not become entirely clear until her daughter had completed the journey.

MATERIAL CONDITIONS FOR THOSE WHO WERE STILL STRUGGLING TO
MAKE ENDS MEET

Meanwhile, during these decades, many Americans—in fact, still the majority of Americans—were struggling, as their parents had, to maintain their families at something over the level of mere subsistence. The fabled "prosperity" of the 1920s was more apparent than real, more intermittent than continuous, for the families of industrial workers, small farmers, day laborers, and skilled craftsmen. Industrial productivity—particularly of consumer goods—multiplied during the 1920s and then multiplied again. Automobiles were appearing in ever more front yards, radios proliferated, the number of pages devoted to advertisements in newspapers and magazines trebled and then quadrupled. In communities across the land, however, more than half of the households were still living below—and, in some cases, far below —what was then defined as the minimum standard of "health and decency." Helen and Robert Lynd calculated, for example, that in Muncie in 1924, $1,920.87 was required to achieve this standard for a family of five (the estimate included the cost of rent, food, fuel, clothing, insurance, union dues, and other such items as well, significantly enough, as one full day per week of paid household help), and that somewhere between 70 percent and 88 percent of all the households in town, in that year did not attain it.[54] Similarly, in 1926, in Zanesville, Ohio, 70 percent of all families had incomes below $2,000.[55] Wages for skilled and unskilled workers and prices for agricultural goods were indeed better in the 1920s than they had been in any previous decade; but the problem, for the families of men so employed, was that good wages and prices could not be depended upon to be continuous: factory workers were likely to be laid off at a day's notice when business was slow; farmers had good seasons but also bad ones; day laborers were paid only during certain seasons of the year; illness and accident could strike at any moment and, in the absence of guaranteed sick leaves and adequate workmen's compensation, could cripple a family for substantial periods. A nationwide study conducted by economists at the Brookings Institution in 1929—when the boom had presumably been booming for close to a decade—revealed that 59 percent of the nation's families appeared to be living below a minimally decent standard; needless to say, that figure went up, rather than down, during the next decade.[56]

There were, to put it simply, still more "uncomfortable" people than "comfortable" ones during the supposedly gay 1920s, and there were considerably more during the depressing 1930s. During the 1920s, sheer subsistence may not have been as much of a problem as it had been for an earlier generation; but families still found that, periodically, they needed two incomes in order to get by. Fifty-five out of 124 "working class" wives studied by the Lynds in Muncie had worked for wages between 1920 and 1924: "the mister was sick and I had to"; "it takes the work of two to keep a family nowadays"; "we are always needing extra money."[57]

Admittedly, some of that extra money was being spent on goods and services that would have been totally out of reach twenty years earlier. The hard-pressed housewife of the 1920s was not investing in luxuries (although some contemporary critics accused her of doing so); but when times were good, she and her husband were trying to create for themselves the standard of living to which more prosperous families had become accustomed before the First World War. With the help of building-and-loan associations, these families were buying their own houses; in Zanesville, for example, where 70 percent of the households earned less than two thousand dollars, 79.9 percent of them were owners rather than renters of their dwellings.[58] The houses in which the second generation of hard-pressed housewives lived were neither spacious nor elegant (a typical one would have been a four-room, one-story bungalow), but they were likely to be wired for electricity (73.7 percent of the houses in Zanesville), outfitted with running water (90 percent), perhaps a bathroom with indoor toilet and a tub (60 percent), piped gas (96 percent), a gas range (89.6 percent), and a telephone (69 percent); and if things had gone particularly well for the family, or if there was more than one continuous breadwinner, there might even be a car (48 percent of the families in Zanesville had one at a time when only 30 percent of the families were living above the poverty level).[59] Those social critics who disparaged these expenditures (because "money was being wasted on luxuries," or because "the pressure to conform and to consume is everywhere more intense," or because "people are today so willing to put themselves into debt to satisfy expanded wants") were uniformly members of the more comfortable classes. From the point of view of those who had known the discomforts of poverty in their youth, these amenities were not so much amenities as basic decencies too long withheld. To own one's own home meant to be out from under the thumb of a landlord who could evict a family at a moment's notice; to have electric lights meant an end to eyestrain, kerosene explosions, and the need to clean lamps; to have running water, an end to exhausting labor; to have a toilet, an end to the discomfort of a privy on a snowy night and to typhoid fever in the summer; to have a telephone, the possibility of easy communication with members of one's family; to have a gas range, the end to coal dust all over the kitchen; to have an automobile, the possibility of a Sunday in the country (is that luxury?) and also, of finding a job on the other side of town in case the plant close to home shut down (is *that* a luxury?).

In the period after the First World War, the diffusion of these amenities, combined with public health measures that were becoming more prevalent (purification and inspection of milk, water treatment plants, sewers for poor neighborhoods, diphtheria innoculations, regular refuse collection, fortification of certain foods with vitamins, certification of meat and poultry supplies) meant that the standard of living for this generation was considerably higher (or rather the standard of death and illness considerably lower) than it had been for their parents.[60] Nationwide, the infant mortality rate continued to fall—in part, at least, because milk and water ceased to be contaminated; and physicians learned how to control diarrhea, tuberculosis, congenital syphilis, and diphtheria (which had all been major killers of infants). Some of the dreadful epidemic diseases that had either killed or debilitated adults and older children in an earlier generation (cholera, typhoid fever, smallpox) were virtually eradicated by the 1920s; and other diseases (such as tuberculosis, rickets, syphilis, and dysentery) were vastly diminished in their destructive power: in Chicago the death rate from typhoid fever had gone as high as 174 per 100,000 population in the latter years of the nineteenth century, but was down to 2 per 100,000 in the 1920s; tuberculosis, which had been the second most prevalent cause of death in the United States in 1900, had declined to tenth by 1930, and the death rate from tuberculosis dropped by an incredible one third (from 150 to 98) just in the four years between 1918 and 1922; Salversan was being widely used to control syphilis, and cod liver oil (however awful it may have tasted) and fortified flour and margarine (whatever natural food buffs today may think of them) were just as widely used to control rickets. All of this, needless to say, went a long way toward easing a poor housewife's concern about the health of her family and toward relieving her, as her mother could not have been relieved, of the difficult work of caring for those who were ill.

The trouble was that neither the amenities nor the public health measures did much to lighten the burden of her other chores. While the hard-pressed housewife may have entered the twentieth century in terms of electricity, running water, and pasteurized milk, she had not entered it in terms of birth control. In 1924, for example, the Lynds found that in Muncie all of the business-class housewives approved of the use of contraceptives, but that only half of the working-class housewives did. Thus, not surprisingly, only one business-class home among those the Lynds studied had six or more children, but there were seven such working-class homes.[61] In the 1920s, although the birth rate was dropping nationwide, the poor continued to have markedly more children than the "comfortable". In the 1930s, although the birth rate in urban areas dropped off markedly for all classes of the population, that in rural areas—where many such housewives lived—was as high as it had ever been.[62] Nothing is, of course, better calculated to increase the burden of housework than the presence of children, especially small ones. When there are eight or nine mouths to feed (or even five or six), cooking is a difficult enterprise, even if it can be done at a gas range; and the drudgery of laundry (especially if there are diapers) is not greatly eased by having the hot water come out of a tap instead of a pot. The electric appliances that would have made some aspects of housework markedly easier simply remained too expensive for those who were still struggling to make ends meet. Even when electric service was available, an electric washing machine cost between sixty and two hundred dollars (a month's wage for a workingman), and only the more expensive models would have been truly labor saving, since the less expensive ones had small tubs, which had to be emptied and filled manually, and hand-cranked wringers. Small wonder, then, that in 1926 only 28 percent of the homes in Zanesville had electric washers, and that the vast majority of them were in affluent homes. What was true for the washer was true also for the vacuum cleaner (only 52.6 percent of homes, of whom slightly more than half were affluent homes) and mechanical refrigeration (.4 percent).[63]

In any event, in both the 1920s and the 1930s, a substantial number of poor housewives were either rural or black or both and thus lacked access to amenities, public health measures, and appliances. Among the tenant farmers that Martha Hagood studied in 1934 in Tennessee, only eight out of two hundred households could afford electric service (although the area in which they lived was considered progressive in rural electrification), and not a single one had running water—at a time when 83 percent of all urban and rural non-farm residences were electrified.[64] In "Plainville," a rural town studied by James West in 1940, only three homes had bathrooms, and they belonged, respectively, to the funeral director, the veterinarian, and the mayor.[65] The Farm Housing Survey, undertaken by the United States Department of Agriculture in 1934, revealed that, for example, only 20 percent of the farmhouses in Missouri had a kitchen sink with a drain, that only 7 percent of those in Kentucky had a bathroom, that only 25 percent of those in the state of Washington (which was considered a particularly prosperous agricultural state) had flush toilets, and that only 17 percent of those in Ohio (which was also fairly prosperous) had electricity.[66] On farms across the land, the birthrate was still high, the average length of life still low, the "old-fashioned" diseases still appallingly prevalent, and various discomforts, both of body and of mind, were part and parcel of daily experience.

Even the hard-pressed housewife who had access to amenities, and had invested in appliances, could not be certain that they would be there when most needed. The washing machine, the car, and the living-room furniture were all likely to have been bought on installment plans, the house carried a mortgage, and the utility companies presented their bills monthly. Thus, in bad times, when her husband was out of work or disabled, and she was forced into the labor market—precisely the time when she dearly needed her washing machine to do the laundry or her car to reduce her trips to market—the family was more than likely to have fallen behind in its payments; and, as a result, the electricity might be turned off or the car repossessed. The Lynds described the technological condition of working-class homes, under the best of conditions, as a "crazy quilt":

> A single home may be operated in the twentieth century when it comes to ownership of an automobile and vacuum cleaner, while its lack of a bathtub may throw it back into another era and its lack of sewer connection and custom of pumping drinking water from a well in the same backyard with the family "privy" put it on par with life in the Middle Ages.[67]

The quilt must have been even crazier when conditions were not the best. No small part of the horror of the Depression was the reality of eviction and repossession, when the amenities that working people had struggled hard to provide for their families were suddenly taken away from them, and when a housewife had to go back to coping with the same material conditions that had undermined her mother: hungry children, crowded rooms, unsanitary dwellings, excessive cold, and a despondent husband.[68]

To make matters even worse, the hard-pressed housewife of this generation had begun to read—as her mother probably had not—many of the magazines that were addressed to her more affluent contemporaries; and the daughters of both classes were taking the same home economics courses in school.*Through these various sources of information, such a housewife learned about ways to feed her family, furnish her home, do her laundry, and otherwise conduct her daily life—ways that were approved of by "experts," and that would have been totally foreign to her mother: nutritionally balanced meals, carefully structured family budgets, four-hour intervals between infant feedings, cabinets and extensive work surfaces in kitchens, completely tiled bathrooms, percale sheets, and many, many more. Unfortunately many of these products were very expensive; and if the price was not beyond the hard-pressed housewife's means at a particular moment, it may well have been beyond her ability to plan for. How do you make out a budget when you cannot predict what your income will be next month? How do you feed an infant on a four-hour schedule when you have a toddler who eats all the time, a husband who gets his breakfast at six in the morning and returns home hungry at seven at night, and a school child who eats at seven, at noon, and at five o'clock?

If inability to rearrange her life in the "recommended" fashion were not enough to make the struggling housewife feel inferior, the women's magazines were delivering yet another message deliberately calculated to make her feel even worse: to wit, that if her family were not socially accepted, if her children and her husband were not healthy, if her home were a breeding ground for germs, if she herself looked old and tired before her time, or if her babies failed to gain weight—or, worse yet, if they died— she was entirely to blame, since remedies for those conditions were easily at hand and easy to apply.† If such a notion had ever crossed her mother's mind, it was at least not confirmed, over and over again, on almost every printed page. In her mother's day, when copywriters composed advertisements for soap or sheets or sealing wax, they thought in terms of the ingredients in the

*Women's magazines (such as the *Ladies' Home Journal*) were more widely diffused in this period than they had ever been before; and general interest magazines (such as the *Saturday Evening Post* and the *Literary Digest*) ran much the same kinds of advertisements as the women's magazines, as did those women's magazines (such as *True Confessions* and *Red Book*) that were specifically intended for working-class readers.[69]

†A content analysis of the advertisements in the *Ladies' Home Journal* in the years between the wars reveals that "guilt" was among the top three appeals used; the other two were "celebrity" and "social status."[70]

product, or the cleanliness of the factory where it was made, or the various ways in which a clever housewife could use it. In the years between the wars, they thought about "guilt" and did so intentionally, because psychologists were telling them that "guilt," "embarrassment," and "insecurity" would sell goods faster than any other pitch.[71] Thus, the hard-pressed housewife was being told that if she failed to feed her babies special foods, to scrub behind the sink with special cleaners, to reduce the spread of infection by using paper tissues, to control mouth odor by urging everyone to gargle and body odor by urging everyone to bathe, to improve her children's schoolwork by sending them off with a good breakfast, or her daughter's "social rating" by sending her off to parties with polished white shoes—then any number of woeful events would ensue, and they would all be entirely her fault: not God's will, and certainly not a result of the greed of capitalists or the cupidity of public officials. This message was reiterated so frequently, and the visual material accompanying it was so blatant, that it could not have failed to make an impression on such a housewife and, at the very least, to undermine her self-confidence. Small wonder, then, that some of these housewives went out to work even when their husbands had steady jobs: with the additional cash, these wives could at least purchase the clothing, the cosmetics, the appliances, and the sundries that the magazines were suggesting would so markedly improve a family's way of life and a mother's own peace of mind.*"I began to work during the war," one housewife in Muncie reported,

> when everyone else did; we had to meet payments on our house and everything else was getting so high. The mister objected at first, but

*Whether women of the lower economic classes worked for "pin money" or out of real economic necessity is a question that has been endlessly debated, one commentator's pin money invariably turning out to be another commentator's "real necessity." The most recent analyses of working women in the interwar years are no exception: Winifred Wandersee sees married women's workforce participation as a result of the "pursuit of luxury"; while Alice Kessler-Harris sees it as an effort to maintain or to improve a family's standard of living.[72] Kessler-Harris seems to me to be right; the "rising expectations" of this period were the expectations of working-class people that they had a right to the same conveniences and amenities that had long been associated with the standards of the more comfortable classes. What Wandersee seems to regard as luxuries were washing machines, automobiles, additional changes of clothing, a four-room apartment, and a chance for children to stay in school longer than their parents had.

now he don't mind. I'd rather keep on working so my boys can play football and basketball and have spending money their father can't give them. I have felt better since I worked than ever before in my life . . . We have an electric washing machine, electric iron, and vacuum sweeper. I don't even have to ask my husband anymore because I buy these things with my own money.[73]

Older cultural values may have suggested that a working wife was a sign of economic distress and social disorganization in a family (which no doubt is why many "misters" didn't approve of their wives going out to work, and why many wives avoided such work), but newer cultural values suggested that it was the responsibility of both parents to improve the standard of living of their children; and some women no doubt concluded, as had the mother just quoted, that they could achieve this aim faster and more surely with cash in their pockets than with bread dough on their hands.

Thus, while the comfortably situated housewives of this generation were slowly marching down the road to proletarianization, their less comfortably situated contemporaries were heading toward greater productivity. Improvements in technological systems were having the same effect on the households of people with small incomes as they have in giant factories and offices: an increase in the goods or services that can be produced for the person-hours that are being expended. Low-income housewives worked very hard in the interwar years. None of the working-class wives of Muncie reported spending less than four hours a day on cooking, cleaning, and laundering (marketing and child care were not even inquired after), and most reported seven or more hours a day, seven days a week.[74] Yet for some of those housewives, some of that hard work was paying off, some of the time. If a hard-pressed mother of this generation had more cash than her mother had had, then her children ate better than she had as a child; since more fruits and vegetables were available, fresh and cheap, at more seasons of the year, their diet was more varied and more healthful. If she and her husband had managed to buy a house, then it was, like as not, more spacious than the one in which she had been raised, and it was better ventilated, warmer in the winter and cooler in the summer, and more likely to have running water and a toilet. With the running water and a hot-water heater and a sewing machine, she could keep her children cleaner, better dressed, more comfortable, and possibly even healthier than she had been as a child, without spending much more time than her mother had spent in the doing of it. She certainly could not afford to pay the wages of human servants; but when times were good, she was beginning to invest in electrical appliances and she knew that they, too, could increase her productivity: that a washing machine meant the ability to change the sheets every week or underwear every day, and a vacuum cleaner meant that dust could be kept from accumulating in the house.

Conclusion

In the years between the two world wars, there were still many differences between the two great segments of the population—not the least of which was that, for those who were poor, any gain in their standard of living in one year was likely to be lost in the next. In some communities, at some times, the gap between the standard of living of the two classes was as great as it had ever been: the poor still begot many children and took them out of school early, still lived with filth and ate in their kitchens, still suffered ill health, lost their teeth and smelled bad, still handed down their clothes and took their shoes from the ragpile. But in other communities, at other times, the ability to live at a minimum standard of health and decency was no longer the privilege only of those who were affluent. Public health was improving, housing conditions were better than they had been, various amenities and conveniences were becoming more widely diffused; and even those who were poor in relative terms could profit from some of these changes. All of them worked together to make hard-pressed housewives more productive and less uncomfortable than their mothers had been and to make their housework bear fruit in improving the health and the prospects of their families. The gap between those who could afford to live "decently" and those who could not may have been as wide as ever; but in the years between the wars, the average housewife of less than modest means was living, at least some of the time, at a higher standard than her mother had been able to attain. Looking back, we can readily understand why she, and her daughter in the next generation, believed that gas ranges, pasteurized milk, electricity, washing machines, fortified margarine, and vacuum cleaners had played a significant role in this accomplishment. We can also understand why these women continued to believe not just that their place was in their homes but that the work that they did there had enormous value. Small wonder then that these women, and their descendants, accepted the yoke of women's work in the home and viewed the modern tools with which they did it as liberating, rather than as oppressive, agents.

Chapter 7

The Postwar Years

THE social seeds planted during the 1920s and the 1930s came to fruition in the decades following the end of the Second World War, but with an ironic twist that no one had anticipated. The diffusion of affluence in the postwar years was accompanied by both the diffusion of appliances and the disappearance of servants. As a result, women who had been in comfortable circumstances before the war (and their children and grandchildren) were under increasing pressure (both economic and ideological) to shoulder the burden of housework alone; and women in families that were economically disadvantaged before the war (and *their* children and grandchildren) were ever more able to provide themselves and their families with basic amenities that their mothers could not have attained. The spread of affluence and the diffusion of amenities was accompanied not, as earlier commentators guessed, by an increase in leisure for housewives of both classes, but, rather, by increases in the amount of work that some housewives had to do, and in the level of productivity that others were able to achieve. In the first postwar generation, some women found that they were working harder inside their homes than their mothers had worked, because they employed fewer servant-hours than their mothers had employed; other women found that they were working just as hard as their mothers, but were achieving greater results. As time wore on, their daughters, members of the second postwar generation, discovered that they were working even longer hours than *their* mothers had worked, because of the double burden of housework and outside employment. Either way, the end result of the long historical process that began when the shooting stopped in 1945, has been more work for mother.

Today men, women, and children continue to demonstrate through their behavior that household work produces both economic and social value. At the end of a day of housework, weary women know that, whether what they have been doing all day is called "consumption" or "purchasing" or "maintaining our social status," it still takes time and energy. Infants still want to be fed when they are hungry, toddlers still want to be comforted in the middle of the night, and schoolchildren still want someone to be at home when the school day has ended. School nurses expect someone to be at home when a child becomes ill during the day, and plumbers expect someone to be there to open the door when a sewer has backed up or a radiator is leaking. Men still marry—and, if divorced, marry soon again—as if they knew (leaving aside considerations of companionship, sexuality, and affection, on the one hand, and of modern technologies, on the other) that the skills women possess are difficult to live without. The work processes of housework may have changed substantially since 1940, but the work itself has not gone away.

The Diffusion of Affluence: The Changing Face of Poverty

To say that the postwar decades have been decades of affluence is to say not that poverty has disappeared, but, rather, that its face has changed, as have the numbers of people afflicted by it. By

1960, the American who could afford to live at a "decent" and "healthful" level had become the average American; decency, cleanliness, rudimentary nutrition, and rudimentary healthfulness were no longer the privileges of an élite. The minimum subsistence budget that was used to determine welfare payments in New York City in 1960 specified a set of material conditions for family life that would have been regarded as fairly luxurious in 1910 and even, for that matter, in 1930.[1] A four-person family was permitted to rent a five-room flat, so that each member of the family who wanted to could be "alone in a room"—a luxury inconceivable to most poor families earlier in the century. The flat was to be outfitted with a complete bathroom (hot and cold running water, toilet, bath or shower, and a sink), a complete kitchen (sink with a drain, hot and cold water, refrigerator, and a gas or electric range), and central heat. Plain but adequate furnishings were allowed (each person was to have a bed and a complete set of eating utensils) as well as annual replacement clothing for the children (shoes that fit, dresses that were new and not made over from hand-me-downs). The diet for such a family was not to contain luxurious foods such as steak, but did allow meat, milk, fresh fruits, and vegetables to be served at least once a day. The family was also allowed an iron and a vacuum cleaner (although not a washing machine or a dryer) and linoleum (although not carpeting) to cover all the floors. That set of material conditions is doubly significant: first, because it was regarded as deprivation in terms of the general standard applying throughout the country in 1960: and, second, because it was luxurious in comparison to how people had lived in earlier decades.

As the standard of "minimum health and decency" has risen profoundly in the past forty years, so the portion of the population that has been unable to attain that standard has fallen. The horrors of poverty have not disappeared, but they are not nearly as horrible as they used to be, and not nearly as many people are beset by them. When computed in terms not of a specific rate of wages, but of standards of minimum decency and health established in each decade, the proportion of the population living at or below the poverty level has fallen from 33 percent (44 million

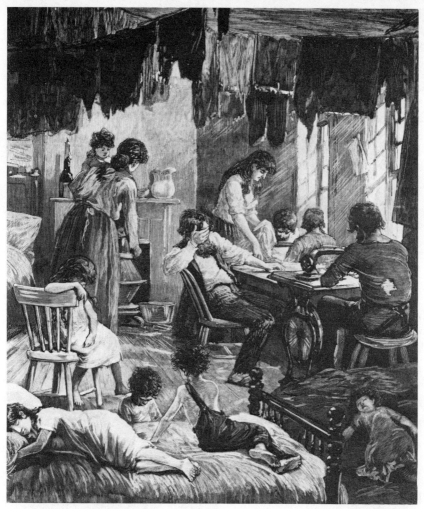

(1) "Homes of the Poor," by T. De Thulstrup, as it appeared in *Harper's Weekly*, 28 July 1883. Courtesy of the New-York Historical Society, New York City.

The Rich and the Poor

If you were a poor housewife before the Second World War, the tragedy of your poverty was apparent every hour of every day (1). You had to cook and launder and care for your children in the same room in which people slept and labored (note the bed beyond the curtains [2]), while your more comfortable contemporaries had separate rooms (3) for these activities. Your children slept when and where they could (4), while other people's children had rooms and possessions all to themselves (5). Mealtimes in the homes of the rich were filled with ritual and grace (6), while in your house people were grateful just to be fed (7). Because their bodies and their clothes could be kept clean, people, who were rich (8) looked different from you and your family (9), and were healthier as well. (Note that the photograph on the wall [9] is of two very well-kept youngsters.) Whatever other problems we may now have, one of the saving graces of the postwar world has been the elimination of these profound differences between the rich and the poor: we cannot really tell, from their clothing, their furnishings, or the nature of their activities, whether the people in these photographs (10, 11) are rich or poor, working-class or middle-class. Having forgotten the abject poverty of the "good old days," we try to re-create them in the open hearths and colonial décor of our electric and electronic kitchens (12).

(2) "Finishing Pants," New York City,
undated, Jacob A. Riis.
Jacob A. Riis Collection,
Museum of the City of New York.

(3) Kitchen of the Mrs. Burton Harrison Reside
New York City, photograph by Byron, 1
The Byron Collec
Museum of the City of New Y

(4) Tenement interior, Lower East Side,
New York City, photograph by Byron, 1896.
The Byron Collection,
Museum of the City of New York.

(5) A young girl's room, Edward Brandeis Reside
New York City, photograph by Byron, und
The Byron Collec
Museum of the City of New Y

Photograph by Ewing Galloway,
Parents Magazine, June 1933.

(7) Christmas dinner in a tenant farmer's house,
southeastern Iowa, Russell Lee, 1936.
Library of Congress.

(8) Syracuse, New York,
c. 1900, photographer unknown.
Courtesy of Phoebe Hoss.

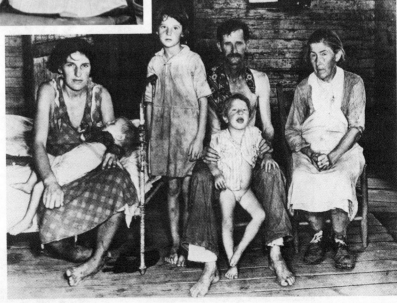

Sharecropper's family,
Hale County, Alabama,
Walker Evans, 1936.
Library of Congress.

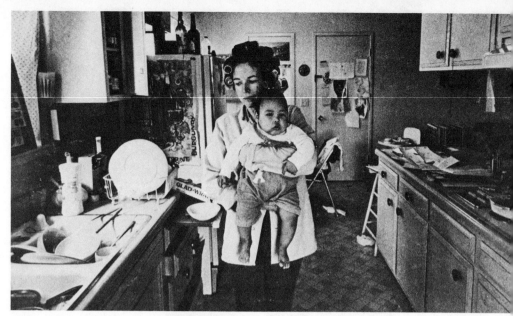

(10) Livermore Califor▪
photograph © 1972, by Bill Ow▪
from *Subu*▪

(11) Livermore, California,
photograph © 1972, by Bill Owens,
from *Suburbia*.

(12) Remodeled kitchen with open hea▪
Levittown, New Y▪
photographer unknown, *c.*1▪
Levittown Public Libr▪

people) in 1940 to 27 percent (41 million) in 1950, to 21 percent (39 million) in 1960, and to 11 percent (23 million) in 1970.[2] Although those who remain poor are justifiably angry that the so-called affluent society cannot provide more for them than it does, "those who remain poor" are a much smaller part of our population than ever before in history. Thus, when viewed in terms of the entire contemporary world and our own immediate past, the vast majority of Americans are staggeringly well-off. As we struggle to make ends meet from one paycheck to the next, we forget how really luxurious is the life to which we have become accustomed. Even if our minds forget, however, our behavior remembers, for the memory of poverty is enshrined in the habits of our housework.

The Diffusion of Amenities and Appliances

For many people the diffusion of affluence meant the diffusion of toilets, refrigerators, and washing machines, not Cadillacs, stereos, and vacation homes. In 1940, just as the Depression was drawing to a close and the economy was shifting to wartime production, one out of every three Americans was still carrying water in buckets, and two out of three Americans did not enjoy the comforts of central heating.[3] Forty years later, there were roughly eighty-seven million "year-round housing units" in the country: only one million of these did not have running water (1 out of 87). In 1940, only 53 percent of all households had any sort of built-in bathing equipment; thus forty years ago, taking a bath for just under half of all Americans involved a lot more work than just turning on a faucet. In 1980, only three million housing units did not have a complete bathroom. Similarly, in 1941—roughly thirty years after they had first come on the market, and twenty years after the prices had fallen to more or less reasonable levels as the result of mass production—only 52 percent of the families in the United States owned or had "interior access" to a washing machine.* Thus, just under half the families in the land were either still hand rubbing or hand cranking their laundry or using commercial services.[4] About the same percentage of families had mechanical refrigerators as had washing machines in 1941 (52 percent); but ten years later, this proportion had increased to 80 percent; and by 1980, access to mechanical refrigeration was virtually universal. Before the United States entered the Second World War, one third of the households in the country were still cooking with wood and coal, so that there was both back-breaking labor on someone's part to provide fuel and equally intense labor to provide cleanliness. By 1980, gas and electric cooking was common everywhere. Conversely, only one third of all the dwellings in the country had central heating in 1940. In 1980, however —even after the energy crises of the 1970s had sent millions of people out to buy coal stoves and kerosene heaters—only sixteen million of the eighty-seven million dwellings lacked central heating, and the vast majority of those were in parts of the country where such comforts were not necessary. In the forty years since the end of the Second World War, the amenities that were once reserved for just part of the population have become the basic standard for the lives of almost everyone.

Homogenizing Housework

Over, under, around, and through those statistics about the technological systems with which we live, lies a daily reality about the work processes of housework that we often forget. If the basic material conditions of life have become homogenized for all Americans (the fact that the less-than-basic material conditions have not is another matter, relevant to another book), so have the work processes of housework. In times past, housewives of the "uncomfortable" classes were manual laborers in their own homes, but housewives of the "comfortable" classes were both

*This last phrase refers to people living in apartment houses that had coin-operated machines in the basement.

managers and laborers. Nowadays, the general expansion of both the economy and the welfare system has led fewer people than ever before into the market for paid domestic labor;*and the diffusion of appliances into households, and of households into suburbs, has encouraged the disappearance of various commercial services. The end result is that housewives, even of the most comfortable classes (in our generally now comfortable population) are doing their housework themselves. Similarly, the extension of schooling for those who are young, the proliferation of school-related activities, and the availability of jobs for those who have finished their schooling has led to the disappearance of even those helpers upon whom the poverty-stricken housewife had once been able to depend. Hence, in almost all economic sectors of the population (except the very, very rich), housework has become manual labor: the wife of the lawyer is just as likely to be down on her hands and knees cleaning her kitchen floor as is the wife of the bricklayer or the garbageman. In 1914, the wife of a college professor had, as I described in chapter 6, two different kinds of household assistant (a laundress, who washed and did heavy cleaning; a student who cleared after meals, did light cleaning, and supervised the children when their mother was away) and did much of her marketing over the telephone. Forty years later, the wife of another college professor described her typical day this way:

I get up at 6 A.M. and put up coffee and cereal for breakfast and go down to the basement to put clothes into the washing machine. When I come up I dress Teddy (1–½) and put him in his chair. Then I dress Jim (3–½) and serve breakfast to him and to my husband and feed Teddy.

While my husband looks after the children I go down to get the clothes out of the machine and hang them on the line. Then I come up and have my own breakfast after my husband leaves. From then on the day is as follows: Breakfast dishes, clean up kitchen. Make beds, clean the apartment. Wipe up bathroom and kitchen floor. Get lunch vegetable ready and put potatoes on to bake for lunch. Dress

*Between 1940 and 1980, the number of households in the United States more than doubled, from roughly 35,000,000 to roughly 79,000,000 but the number of domestic servants fell from 2,400,000 to 1,200,000.

both children in outdoor clothes. Do my food shopping and stay out with children until 12. Return and undress children, wash them up for lunch, prepare lunch, feed Teddy and put him to nap. Make own lunch, wash dishes, straighten up kitchen. Put Jim to rest. Between 1 and 2:30, depending on the day of the week, ironing (I do my husband's shirts home and, of course, all the children's and my own clothes), thorough cleaning of one room, weekend cooking and baking, etc.; 3 P.M., give children juice or milk, put outdoor clothes on. Out to park; 4:30 back. Give children their baths. Prepare their supper. Husband usually home to play with them a little after supper and help put them to bed. Make dinner for husband and myself. After dinner, dishes and cleaning up.

After 8 P.M. often more ironing, especially on the days when I cleaned in the afternoon. There is mending to be done; 9 P.M., fall asleep in the living room over a newspaper or listening to the sound of the radio; 10 P.M., have a snack of something with my husband and go to bed.[5]

And just as striking were the comments of another housewife in the same decade—a twenty-four-year-old woman living in the then newly built Levittown, Pennsylvania; she was described by those who interviewed her as a member of the "working class." This housewife, whose grandmother might well have been grateful to have bread and soup on the table at night, described her day in terms virtually identical to those of the college professor's wife:

Well, naturally, I get up first, make breakfast for my husband and put a load of clothes in my washer while breakfast cooks. Then I wake him up, give him his breakfast and he's off to work. Then I make breakfast for the children. After the children eat I dress them and they go out to play. Then I hang the clothes up and clean lightly through the house. In between times I do the dishes—that's understood of course. Then I make lunch for the children and myself and I bring them in, clean them up, and they eat. I send them out to play when they're done and I do the dishes, bring the clothes in and iron them. When I'm done ironing it's usually time to make supper, or at least start preparing it. Sometimes I have time to watch a TV story for half an hour or so. Then my husband comes home and we have our meals. Then I do the dishes again. Then he goes out to work again —he has a part time job—at his uncle's beverage company. Well, he does that two or three nights a week. If he stays home he watches TV and in the meantime I get the kids ready for bed. He and I have a light snack, watch TV a while and then go to bed.[6]

In the 1950s (and the 1980s) the housewife of the "professional classes" and the housewife of the "working classes" were assisted only by machines. Few such women had paid household help, and fewer still had food or milk or clean laundry delivered to their doors. The differences between these women were no doubt profound—differences in levels of education, in families of origin, in annual household income; but those profound differences did not produce, as they would have done in the past, equally profound variations in the ways in which the women did their work.[7]

Apparently, also, there were no significant variations in the time that women spent at that work. One sophisticated statistical analysis of time-use data collected from a large national sample of households in 1965 found that the average American woman spent about four hours a day doing housework (or twenty-eight hours a week) and about three and one-half hours a day (or twenty-six and a half hours per week) caring for children (a fifty-four-hour week).[8] These figures were startling in two respects. First, they were not strikingly different from what Leeds had found for affluent housewives in 1912 or from what other researchers had reported for rural and urban housewives in 1935.[9] Second, these averages were not markedly affected either by the income level of the household or by the educational attainment of the housewife: women who managed on less than four thousand dollars a year in household income spent 245 minutes per day at housework and 207 at child care; while, at the other end of the income scale, housewives who could dispose of over fifteen thousand dollars put in 260 and 196 minutes at housework and child care, respectively. Housewives with college educations were logging in 474 minutes a day of housework and child care (a little under eight hours); and housewives who had not completed grade school put in almost equally tiring days of 453 minutes (or seven and one half hours).

Neither the working-class wife nor her middle-class contemporary could have expected her husband to help much with this work. For a while, in the 1950s, there was a hullabaloo in the popular press about "new husbands" in suburbia who were diapering babies and drying dishes and cooking barbecues and otherwise becoming "feminized." Again, in the late 1970s, a spate of books and national magazine articles appeared touting the virtues of "househusbandry," most of these articles written, it turned out, by free-lance writers and journalists who had decided to stay home for a while with their children when their wives went back to work. If the results of sociological studies are to be trusted, not much lay behind either one of those journalistic episodes. Men do very little housework; and the few "househusbands" there have ever been seem not to have stuck to it for long. Whether men are asked to estimate the time that they spend at housework, or wives are asked to estimate their husbands' time, or outside observers actually clock the amount of time that men spend at it, no one has ever estimated men's share of housework at anything higher than one and a half hours per day.[10] Housewives who are not employed in the labor market spend, roughly speaking, fifty hours a week doing housework; housewives who are employed outside their homes spend, again roughly speaking, thirty-five hours on their work in and for their homes. Men whose wives are employed spend about ten minutes more a day on housework than men whose wives "stay home", and men who have small children add yet another ten—a grand total, for these particularly helpful husbands, of just under eleven hours of housework a week.[11] Men who do housework tend not to do the same work that their wives are doing: they take out the garbage, they mow the lawns, they play with children, they occasionally go to the supermarket or shop for household durables, they paint the attic or fix the faucet; but by and large, they do not launder, clean, or cook, nor do they feed, clothe, bathe, or transport children.[12] These latter—the most time-consuming activities around the home—are exclusively the domain of women. In households that are particularly well equipped with appliances, men do even less housework, partly because they believe that the work simply cannot be onerous, but also because some of the "extra" appliances actually relieve them of sex-related, or sex-acceptable chores. In homes where there are garbage disposals, men give up removing the small quantities of garbage that still need to be carried to the curb; and in households where there are dishwashers, men cease providing whatever help with the dishes they had formerly profferred.[13]

Thus, there is more work for a mother to do in a modern home because there is no one left to help her with it. Almost all of the work that once stereotypically fell to men has been mechanized. Families tend to live a considerable distance from the place where the male head of the household is employed; hence, men leave home early in the morning and return, frequently exhausted, late at night. Children spend long hours in school and, when school is over, have "after-school activities," which someone must supervise and from which they must be transported. Older children move away from home as soon as they reasonably can, going off to college or to work. No one delivers anything (except bills and advertisements) to the door any longer, or at least not at prices that most people can afford; and domestic workers now earn salaries that have priced them out of the reach of all but the most affluent households. The advent of washing machines and dishwashers has eliminated the chores that men and children used to do as well as the accessory workers who once were willing and able to assist with the work. The end result is that, although the work is more productive (more services are performed, and more goods are produced, for every hour of work) and less laborious than it used to be, for most housewives it is just as time consuming and just as demanding.

The "Working" Mother

The modern technological systems on which our households and our standard of living depend were constructed on the assumption that women would remain at home, that they would continue to function as pre-industrial workers (without paychecks, time clocks, or supervisors), and that, as a corollary, they would not be tempted to enter the labor market except under unusual (and usually temporary) circumstances. Ironically, the last of these assumptions proved erroneous. In the postwar years, more and more married women, and more and more mothers, entered the labor force, the comforts of full-time wifehood and motherhood and the existence of washing machines and dish-washers notwithstanding.

In the decades after the Second World War, the national econ-omy shifted its focus from production to service, from manufac-turing to communication; and, in the process, jobs were opened up for which women were considered to be appropriate candi-dates: jobs as typists, clerks, and receptionists; as waitresses, store clerks, and stenographers; as teachers, social workers, nurses, administrative assistants; and, later, as computer programmers. To various women, at various times, those jobs and the salaries they provided, proved to be attractions too great to resist. In different households, the decision that wife and/or mother would "go back to work" or "continue working" was made at different times, determined either by what was going on in the world outside the family or by a particular family's development. Some women "continued to work" in the postwar years because they were reluctant to give up the life and the income to which they had become accustomed during the war; some women went home and had babies and did not re-enter the labor force until their children were grown and out of the house; other women never went back to work. As the years passed, some younger women decided not to interrupt their careers when their babies arrived, because the high level of education that they had attained, and the high salaries that they could consequently hope to command, seemed to compensate for the double burden of motherhood and career which they had to shoulder. Other women found that, whether or not they were graced with higher education and higher incomes, the growing pressure of inflation was so seriously eroding the purchasing power of their husbands' income that, small children or no, they had to go back to work. Furthermore, as a result of divorce, desertion, or the decision to remain single, other women, in increasing numbers, had no husband's income to fall back upon. The end result was that, by 1980, just over 40 percent of the total workforce was female (up from 25 percent in 1940), women with children at home constituted almost 20 percent of the labor force, and more than half of the nation's children under the age of six had mothers who were working full time.[14] Even though different women achieved the status of being "homemakers with jobs" at different times, very large numbers of them did achieve it; and if present trends continue unabated, even more of them will do so in the future.

WOMAN'S "PLACE"

It is hardly surprising that, in the immediate postwar years, many women struggled mightily with the decision to take a job, since cultural pressures of the most extraordinary kind were being brought to bear against the employment of wives and mothers. If many husbands and children opposed that decision even before they had had a chance to discover its consequences, they, too, can barely be blamed, since the public debates on the subject gave them not the slightest reason to believe that the venture would end successfully. In the 1950s and the 1960s, psychiatrists, psychologists, and popular writers inveighed against women who wished to pursue a career, and even against women who wished to have a job, and referred to such "unlovely women" as "lost," "suffering from penis envy," "ridden with guilt complexes," or just plain "man-hating."[15] Mass-circulation magazines almost never depicted a working wife, unless to paint her in derogatory terms: working mothers were blamed for the rise in juvenile delinquency in the 1950s, for the soaring divorce rate of the 1960s, and for the rise in male impotence in the 1970s. Women's magazine fiction of the day was populated by "glowing" pregnant women and "barren" working women, whose "hungers were not yet appeased, whose destinies were not yet fulfilled"; by children who felt abandoned when their mothers were not there to greet them on the day the teacher had finally given them an "A"; and by husbands who, while tempted by the career women in their offices, always returned to their less glamorous, but more feminine wives with a warm smile and a rose behind their backs. Betty Friedan, who worked for and wrote for some of those magazines in the postwar years, recalls:

> When you wrote about an actress for a woman's magazine you wrote about her as a housewife. You never showed her doing or enjoying her work as an actress, unless she eventually paid for it by losing her husband or her child, or otherwise admitting failure as a woman.[16]

Friedan might well have added that newspaper and magazine profits depended upon the sale of advertising space to manufacturers and retailers of consumer goods; and that in the postwar years, many advertising specialists and market researchers, who advised the manufacturers and the retailers, viewed the working woman as someone who was either too poor or too preoccupied to spend time and money in the stores.[17] Hence, profit-conscious editors, and the writers who desired their custom, were not inclined to enhance the image of the working wife, even if they happened to be one themselves.

Sociologists and other academic social scientists, rather than be left on the sidelines, joined in the debate about women's proper place by adopting what has come to be called the "functionalist" interpretation of the recent history of the family and then by broadcasting that interpretation in countless textbooks and lectures.[18] As I have explained in chapter 4, this argument suggested that since industrialization began, households have been deprived of their essential productive roles in the economy and, consequently, housewives have been deprived of their essential productive functions. Modern women are in trouble, the analysis continued, because modern technology has either eliminated or eased most of their earlier burdens, but modern ideologies have not kept pace with the change. One solution to the problem, the social scientists noted, would be for women to take their place in the market economy; but this solution, many of the experts argued, would be contrary to female instincts and biological needs and would interfere with the few remaining functions that housewives still perform at home—namely, socialization of young children and tension management. A better solution would be to create a new ideology, one that would rationalize the woman's situation and diminish the likelihood that she would suffer "role anxiety."

THE "BACKWARD SEARCH FOR FEMININITY"

Ironically, the ideology that became popular in the years when functionalism dominated sociology constituted a symbolic (but only a symbolic) reflection of the very set of conditions that had made it possible for many Americans to have the comfort both of indulging in ideological pursuits and of attending lectures in sociology. One perceptive observer referred to this ideology as the "backward search for femininity."[19] If women who lived before the Industrial Revolution had led happy, fruitful, and productive lives (as the sociologists were suggesting), then it seemed reasonable to assume that modern discontents could be wiped away if women would return at least to some of the conditions that had pertained in Martha Washington's day. In communities across the land (especially in those that were particularly affluent and, therefore, farthest removed from the horrors of pre-industrial conditions), people were acting out the sociologists' prescriptions by bearing numerous children (the baby boom appears to have been a result of a deliberate decision on the part of affluent couples to have more children than their parents had), by breastfeeding those numerous children, raising vegetables in their backyards, crocheting afghans, knitting argyle socks, entertaining at barbecues, hiding appliances behind artificial wood paneling, giving homemade breads for Christmas presents, and decorating their living rooms with spinning wheels. "I interviewed a woman," Betty Friedan reported,

in the huge kitchen of a house that she had helped build herself. She was busily kneading the dough for her famous homemade bread; a dress she was making for a daughter was half-finished on the sewing machine; a handloom stood in one corner. Children's art materials and toys were strewn all over the floor of the house, from front door to stove: in this expensive modern house, like many of the open plan houses in this era, there was no door at all between kitchen and living room. Nor did this mother have any dream or wish or thought or frustration of her own to separate her from her children. She was pregnant now with her seventh; her happiness was complete, she said, spending her days with her children.[20]

The wiles of the "backward search for femininity" apparently enticed men as well as women—as is nowhere more strikingly illustrated than in the writings of Kurt Vonnegut, whose novels ruthlessly dissect postwar mentality. In *Player Piano* (1952), Vonnegut created Paul Proteus, an archetypically unhappy "organization man" (an engineer working for a big electrical manufacturing company), who lives with his wife, Anita, in an archetypically "backward looking" home, replete with a huge fieldstone fireplace with candle molds over the mantel:

> Paul narrowed his eyes, excluding everything from his field of vision but the colonial tableau, and imagined that he and Anita had pushed this far into the upstate wilderness, with the nearest neighbor twenty-eight miles away. She was making soap, candles, and thick wool clothes for a hard winter ahead, and he, if they weren't to starve, had to mold bullets and go shoot a bear. Concentrating hard on the illusion, Paul was able to muster a feeling of positive gratitude for Anita's presence, to thank God for a woman at his side to help with the petrifying amount of work involved in merely surviving. As, in his imagination, he brought home a bear to Anita, and she cleaned it and salted it away, he felt a tremendous lift—the two of them winning by sinew and guts a mountain of strong, red meat from an inhospitable world. And he would mold more bullets, and she would make more candles and soap from the bear fat, until late at night, when Paul and Anita would tumble down together on a bundle of straw in the corner, dog-tired and sweaty, make love, and sleep hard until the brittle-cold dawn.[21]

Such erotic and historical fantasies were (and still are) potent cultural forces; they help us to understand not only why some people have difficulty coming to terms with the reality of their lives, but also why some people (most notably affluent housewives) are still spending so very much time at their work. People who believe that family solidarity can be bolstered by hand-dipped chocolates and hand-grown string beans are bound to spend a lot of time dipping chocolates and growing string beans.

In any event, even if these ideological props for full-time housewifery had not existed, historical experience itself would have militated against widespread enthusiasm for the entry of married women into the labor force. The adults who were worrying about these matters in 1950 (and even in 1960) had been children of the Depression; hence, they had good reason to remember that in their youth a "working mother" had been a person to be pitied, and her family had quite possibly been a family to be shunned. If "mother worked" during the 1920s and the 1930s, her family was more than likely to be poor, the father more than likely to be unemployed, the children more than likely to be dirty, the house more than likely to be in disrepair; when "mother worked," there were children who had no one to nurse them through illnesses, meals that were hastily thrown together from whatever could be found ready-made in the markets, poor teeth, clothing that did not fit, dirty floors, skin rashes, and bad breath. It hardly mattered that only a few of these symptoms of poverty were likely to have been directly attributable to the mother's employment, because the fact of her employment served as symbol for all of them. Similarly, at the other end of the economic scale, the presence of a full-time housewife served as symbol not just for the status of the family, but also for its degree of good health and for its decent living standards. Whether she actually did the work or whether she directed the work that was to be done, the presence of a full-time wife and mother meant careful supervision of the family's health, a well-appointed living room, white stockings, ironed hair ribbons, regular church attendance, Sunday dinner, birthday parties. All those small (and large) comforts both helped to demonstrate the family's status and to ensure that it did not fall. The postwar working-class husband who complained that he would be embarrassed in front of his friends if his wife went out to work, was as much a product of this historical experience as his middle-class contemporary who claimed that two well-organized dinner parties a month would do more for his family's annual income than the salary his wife would be able to earn at a job.[22]

THE ROLE OF THE MACHINE

In the end, whatever the complaints of husbands may have been (and there were many of them), and however ambivalent wives and mothers may have felt (as many of them did), by the time the children of the baby boom had come to maturity, the "working mother" had become the "normal American house-wife"; and many people believed that the widespread diffusion of modern technology was, in and of itself, responsible for this transformation. On common-sense grounds alone, a causal connection between the washing machine and the working wife seems justified: if it takes less time to do the wash with a Bendix than it did with a washtub, and to cook a meal since the advent of Birdseye, then housework must take less time (and certainly less energy) than it used to, and women must thus be tempted to fill their free time with paid employment.

The only trouble with this argument is that one empirical investigation after another has failed to find evidence for it; common sense, in this case as in many others, is not a reliable guide to the truth.[23] As we have seen, even with washing machines and frozen vegetables, housewives do not have much free time; 50 hours per week is ten hours more than what is now considered the standard industrial week. Housewives began to enter the labor market many years before modern household technologies were widely diffused; and the housewives then entering the workforce were precisely those who could not afford to take advantage of the amenities that then existed. Even in the postwar labor market the sociological variable that correlates most strongly with a married woman's participation in the labor force is her husband's income. And the correlation is strongly negative: the housewives who are most likely to enter the labor market are the ones who are least likely to have many labor-saving devices and household amenities. Indeed, in the early postwar years, some married women were entering the labor force precisely in order to acquire those attributes of affluence.[24]

Where the sociologists and economists have failed to find a causal connection, the historians may be able to suggest a substitute. The washing machine, the dishwasher, and the frozen meal have not been *causes* of married women's participation in the workforce, but they have been *catalysts* of this participation: they have acted, in the same way that chemical catalysts do, to break certain bonds that might otherwise have impeded the process. Most American housewives did not enter the job market because they had an enormous amount of free time on their hands (although this may have been true in a few cases). Rather, American housewives discovered that, for one reason or another, they needed full-time employment; and subsequently, they discovered that, with the help of a dishwasher, a washing machine, and an occasional frozen dinner, they could undertake that employment without endangering their family's living standards. The symbolic connection between "working wife" and "threatened family" was thus severed, not by ideologues but by housewives with machines. Working mothers discovered that, although they were weary when they left the office or factory, they could still manage to get a decent dinner on the table that night and clean clothes on everyone's back the next morning. Husbands discovered that they had been deprived of few, if any, of the comforts to which they had become accustomed, and that additional comforts (namely, ones connected with having more cash on hand) had appeared. Children discovered that they could, if need be, make their lunches and their breakfasts themselves.

Viewed from a national perspective, American housewives entered the labor market without destroying either the level of health or the level of comfort to which they and their parents had become accustomed. If the movement of married women into the labor force proceeded with what some social critics regarded as unseemly speed, it did so because many members of the generation that had been raised in the affluent society (those who were children of the baby boom, not of the Depression, and who came to maturity and began forming their households in the 1960s and the 1970s) saw little reason to worry about the various social ills that might result from cold cereal for breakfast, from an occasional meal in a restaurant, from slightly dirty bathroom sinks and unironed sheets. Modern household technology facilitated married women's workforce participation not by freeing women from household labor but by making it possible for women to maintain decent standards in their homes without assistants and without a full-time commitment to housework.

Conclusion

The work that women do when they are being paid to do it is easy to recognize, because there are so many standard indicators that allow us to account for it—personnel records, time clocks, pay sheets, and the like. On the other hand, the productive labor that is still being done in American homes is difficult to recognize, because the reigning theory of family history tells us that it should not be there, because the reigning methodology of the social sciences cannot be applied to it, because ordinary language has a penchant for masking it, and because advertisers have had a vested interest in convincing us that it has evaporated. Economists and sociologists do not consider housework to be "productive work," at least in part because they cannot measure it. They can easily quantify what people are consuming (how many cans of peas? how many dollars' worth of stockings?), but they cannot place a dollar value (to chose a particularly simple example) on a nutritious meal—and they cannot begin to estimate how many such meals are prepared in households throughout the year (in part, because the workers who prepare them are not paid nor are their hours timed). People who write advertising copy for microwave ovens, toilet bowl cleaners, and paper toweling seem to believe that they will lose their jobs if they confess that it still takes time to prepare food for the oven, scrub the brown stains out of the toilet, and wipe down counters after dinner has been consumed. Virtually every lecture on the history of the family, and every textbook on the sociology of the family, and every new inquiry into the state of the family begins with the sentiment that "households do not produce anything valuable any more." And, in our everyday conversations, we cannot even refer to housewives as "laboring" or as "working" or even as being "employed," without confusing our listeners, even though we all know that housework is work.

The technological systems that presently dominate our households were built on the assumption that a full-time housewife would be operating them, since very few people in the last one hundred years (when the foundations for these systems were being laid) wanted adult women to leave their homes in order to work in the labor market, or believed that adult women themselves would ever want to go out to work. In the earliest stages of industrialization, in the early decades of the nineteenth century, as some of men's work in the home was eliminated (fuel gathering, leather working, grain processing), some men were thereby freed to work (at least part of the year) in factories and offices. Some of women's housework was eliminated at that time also (principally spinning and weaving), but no one then expected or desired women to leave their homes to work for wages elsewhere (unless the women were single or exceedingly poor) because so much of what had always been considered women's work still remained to be done at home: cooking, sewing, laundering, cleaning, child care. In the next stages of industrialization, even more of men's household work was eliminated, as was much of children's work; but, again, no one expected or desired women to leave their homes in order to go out to work because, whether rich or poor, a family's sustenance and status still depended on the presence of a full-time homemaker. In this stage of industrialization (roughly from 1880 to 1920), the foundations for the modern household technologies were laid: municipalities began to supply households with clean water and ample sewers; gas and electric companies figured out how to bring in modern fuels; merchandisers and retailers developed new techniques for selling durable goods to households. Almost no one who participated in this process—whether rich or poor, whether female or male, whether producer or consumer—seems to have doubted that the individual household would be the ultimate consumption unit, and that most of the work of that household would be done by housewives who would continue to work, as they had in the past, without pay and without timeclocks. If the utility companies had had any reason to believe that households would stop functioning after five or six o'clock—as offices, stores, and many factories do—they would have had precious little motivation for trying to supply them with electricity, water, and gas. Similarly, if householders had believed that they would have to pay every adult woman for every hour that she labored in their homes, they would have had precious little economic incentive for preferring washing machines to commercial laundry services and automobiles to deliverymen. Whether for good or ill, women were the only workers whose "place" was still at home in the years when homes were becoming mechanized, and the vast majority of these women were housewives who were not paid hourly, weekly, or even annual wages. When, in the decades after the Second World War, our economy finally became capable of realizing the potential benefits of these technological systems, the individual household, the individual ownership of tools, and the allocation of housework to women had, almost literally, been cast in the stainless steel, the copper, and the aluminum out of which those systems were composed.

The implications of this arrangement and the ironies implicit in it became particularly clear to those millions upon millions of families who moved out of urban areas and into suburban ones in the postwar decades. The move to the suburbs carried with it the assumption that someone (surely mother) would be at home to do the requisite work that made it possible for someone else (surely father) to leave early in the morning and return late at night, without worrying either about the welfare of his family or the maintenance of his domicile. Having made the move and purchased the house and invested in the cars and the appliances without which the suburban way of life simply was not possible, people discovered that the technological systems in which they had invested (not only so much money, but also so much emotion) simply would not function unless someone stayed home to operate them.

When this "someone" had, however, decided that, for whatever reason, staying at home was no longer her cup of tea, neither the house nor the cars nor the appliances nor the way of life that they all implied could simply be thrown into the dustbin, nor did anyone wish to throw them there. All of these were long-term investments (consumer *durables*); and the technological systems of which they were a part (houses, roads, telephone lines, gas mains) were built to last for more than one lifetime. The transition to the two-income family (or to the female-headed household) did not occur without taking a toll—a toll measured in the hours that employed housewives had to work in order to perform adequately first as employees and then as housewives. A thirty-five-hour week (housework) added to a forty-hour week (paid employment) adds up to a working week that even sweatshops cannot match. With all her appliances and amenities, the status of being a "working mother" in the United States today is, as three eminent experts have suggested, virtually a guarantee of being overworked and perpetually exhausted. [25]

The technological and social systems for doing housework had been constructed with the expectation that the people engaged in them would be full-time housewives. When the full-time housewives began to disappear, those systems could not adjust quickly. Not even the most efficient working wife in the world can prepare, serve, and clean up from a meal in four minutes flat; and even the best organized working mother still cannot feed breakfast to a toddler in thirty seconds. Homes cannot automatically be moved close to a job or even close to public transportation, so someone still has to be available to drive the man of the family to the train or a child to the soccer field or to a party; and day-care centers cannot quickly be built where they have not existed before, so someone still has to leave a career behind for a while when babies are born—or find a helpful grandmother.

Indeed, given the sacred feelings that most Americans seem to attach to meals, infants, private homes, and clean laundry—and given the vast investment individuals, corporations, and municipalities have made in the technological systems that already exist—our household technologies may never evolve so as to make life easier for the working wife and mother. In the generations to come, housework is not likely to disappear. Barring a catastrophic economic or nuclear disaster, the vast majority of today's children will form families when they grow up, will buy houses, and will outfit those houses with tools for doing housework. Home computers may be added to the repertoire, but there will still be at least functional equivalents of cooking stoves and refrigerators, telephones and automobiles, washing machines and dishwashers. However much trouble these technologies may be, however much they may cost to obtain and then to maintain, and however much they may induce us to engage in amounts or forms of work that are often irritating and sometimes infuriating, the standard of living and the way of living that they make possible is one to which many Americans aspired in the past and that many are unlikely to forsake in the future. The washing machine may not save as much time as its advertisers might like us to believe, and electricity may not bring as many good things to living as the manufacturers of generating equipment would like us to think, but the daily lives that are shaped by washing machines and electricity are so much more comfortable and healthy than the ones that were shaped by washtubs and coal (or, before that, dirty clothes and open hearths) that we will probably not give them up.

Still, while enjoying the benefits that these technological systems provide, we need not succumb entirely to the work processes that they seem to have ordained for us. If we regard these processes as unsatisfactory, we can begin to extricate ourselves from them not by destroying the technological systems with which they are associated but by revising the unwritten rules that govern the systems. Some of these rules—to change our sheets once a week and keep our sinks spotless and greaseless, to wipe the table after every meal, to flush the toilet, brush our teeth, change our clothes and wash our hair, to give music lessons to our children and keep our dirty linen literally and figuratively to ourselves—generate more housework than may really be necessary. These rules were passed down to us by members of an earlier generation (our parents) and sprang from fear of the deprivations that poverty engenders and from a desire either to rise above those deprivations or to stave them off. Now that profound poverty has ceased to be an imminent threat for most of us, the time has surely come to re-evaluate the amount of time that we spend maintaining the symbols of our status.

Others of these rules—that, for example, men who dry dishes or change diapers are insufficiently masculine, that only women can properly nurture infants, that young girls should help their mothers in the kitchen and young boys assist their fathers in the garage, that husbands can undertake long commutes but wives cannot—ensure that the work processes of housework will be confined to members of only one sex, not only in this generation but in generations to come. These latter rules, connected as they are to aspects of our sexuality and our self-conception, are not easy to revise. Even those brave members of the postwar generations who learned to sever the bond between "working mother" and "social disaster" could not erase more than one social stereotype at a time; and when they chose spouses and formed households, they adopted virtually the same sexual division of household labor with washing machines and microwave ovens as had their ancestors with washtubs and open hearths: the men responsible for fuel and for lawns (those symbolic remnants of fields of waving grain) and the women responsible for cooking, cleaning, laundering, and child care. If centuries upon centuries of social conditioning have led us to prefer the private household and the individual ownership of tools, then centuries upon centuries of social conditioning also prepared these young women to be housewives and these young men to believe that the work of cooking, cleaning, and caring for infants would threaten their masculinity. Indeed, when the children of the baby boom were still children, when they were forming their sense of "what it means to be a woman" or "what it means to be a man," all the adults upon whom these adolescents might have been modeling themselves—their parents, the people down the block, celebrities, creators of plots for movies, authors of magazine articles and textbooks—were still engaged in the backward search for femininity and still suggesting (in the strongest affective terms) that dishwashers and diapers were objects to be manipulated by females, and that wrenches and lawnmowers were objects to be manipulated by males, and that the manipulation of inappropriate objects was, to put it anthropologically, sexually polluting.

The rules that stem from a fear of poverty, and the rules that stem from fear of sexual pollution, were the product of specific historical periods, with social and technological constraints of their own. The widespread diffusion of modern household technology and the widespread entrance of marrried women into the labor force have markedly loosened those constraints; and thus the time has come to begin changing the rules. We can best solve the problems that beset many working wives and their families not by returning to the way things used to be (since that is probably impossible and, in view of the ways things really used to be, hardly attractive), not by destroying the technological systems that have provided many benefits (and that much of the rest of the world is trying, for fairly good reasons, to emulate), and not by calling for the death of the family as a social institution (a call that the vast majority of people are unlikely to heed)—but by helping the next generation (and ourselves) to neutralize both the sexual connotation of washing machines and vacuum cleaners and the senseless tyranny of spotless shirts and immaculate floors.

Postscript:

Less Work for Mother

A S art mirrors life, so does scholarship; and a thoughtful scholar opens his or her life to the insights of scholarship. I am a scholar who has studied the history of housework, and also a working mother and housewife who lives in the suburbs and has three children. People frequently ask me—indeed, I frequently have asked myself—how my experiences as a housewife have shaped my research, and, conversely, how my research has shaped my behavior as a housewife. I think that these are important questions, deserving of an answer, because they are but special cases of the more general question, Can the study of history teach us how to live better? Unlike some other historians, I think that the answer to this question is Yes; and I can try to explain why I think so by telling a story, somewhat abbreviated but nonetheless true, about myself.

A few years after I had begun the research on which this book is based, I caught myself in the act of following one of the unwritten rules that I referred to at the end of the last chapter. One of my children dribbled egg yolk onto the front of her shirt; and, after putting her into her pajamas, I proceeded to throw her shirt into the laundry basket. "What are you doing that for?" I said to myself. "You know perfectly well that it's the soap manufacturers, and no one else, who foster such absurd notions of cleanliness, and that they do it so as to be able to sell more soap. You, of all people, should not be taken in by such foolishness. Take the shirt out of the laundry basket." "No, I don't think I will," my revery continued, "because whatever my feelings about soap manufacturers and advertising copywriters may be, I do not want my daughter to be laughed at in nursery school." The shirt got washed.

A year or two later, I caught myself, once again, doing the same thing, although perhaps this time the stain was chocolate rather than egg yolk. "Now wait a minute," quoth I to myself, "it's time for you to be a bit more honest about what you're doing. The other day your daughter dressed herself for school in a skirt that was absolutely filthy, and *you* were the one who made her take it off. She's very sensitive about what other children think of her, but she would have happily worn that skirt to school. You're the one who has the hangup about cleanliness. You're afraid that the parents of the other children and the teachers will think that you're not an adequate mother because you work." "That's true," my self-analysis continued, "but it's not a bad reason to wash that shirt. I've got a washing machine, I had to do a load of wash anyway, and I certainly don't want anyone to think less of me because I am a working mother or to pity my child for that reason." *That* shirt got washed, too.

Another two or three years passed (this research project went on for a *very* long time! Was I doing too much laundry?) and I was still putting into the wash shirts that had just been worn one day, and catching myself at it. "Now wait just one more minute," I finally instructed myself. "If it were truly the soap manufacturers or the other parents who were responsible for this silliness, I would have stopped it ages ago. The fact of the matter is that I cannot stand the sight of my children in dirty clothes. I associate dirt with poverty, with loss of control; and like a somnambulist,

I am walking through the rituals and responding to the symbols that really meant something seventy years ago. Isn't it time to lay that past to rest?" That shirt did not get washed—and neither did many subsequent ones.

Not long afterward, I was confined to bed with a serious illness for almost six months, and my husband was forced to assume some of the responsibilities of housework that had previously been mine. Since I could no longer trudge up and down the two flights of steps to our washing machine, he became the laundress in our family. No matter how many times or how patiently I explained the rules of laundry work to him, he persisted, during those months, in mixing the "dark" colors with the "light" ones and the "permanent press" with the "cotton." One day my nagging on this subject must have become even more than he could bear, and he pointed out to me rather sharply (to put it politely) that not a single piece of clothing had been ruined under his tenure, and that the rules for doing laundry were not unlike those that the Civil Rights statutes were intended to abolish: that is, rules propagated to create a spurious expertise, which allows one group of people to exclude another group from an enterprise that should be accessible to all. My husband was absolutely right; and since that time we have shared the laundry work between us, without abiding by all the rules and without causing any damage worse than one slightly pinkened undershirt. As near as I can tell, neither his masculinity nor my femininity (so far as these may be identifiable qualities) have been compromised in the process.

Many of the rules that tyrannize housewives are unconscious and therefore potent. However manufacturers and advertisers may exploit these unconscious rules, they did not create them. By exploring their history we can bring these rules into consciousness and thereby dilute their potency. We can then decide whether they are truly useful or merely the product of atavism or of an advertiser's "hard sell," whether they are agents of oppression or of liberation. If we can learn to select among the rules only those that make sense for us in the present, we can begin to control household technology instead of letting it control us. And only then is it likely that the true potential of that technology—less work for mother—will be fulfilled.

Bibliographic Essays

To the Reader

Each chapter of this book is based upon very different kinds of primary and secondary source materials. Rather than overburden the text with didactic notes, I have decided to provide, in the bibliographic essays that follow, some sense of the sources from which each chapter was drawn. Many of the works cited here are not specifically referred to in the text, but they were essential in my own research, and I hope that they will provide a useful guide for those who might like to explore further this fascinating subject.

Chapter 1. An Introduction: Housework and Its Tools

I was initially inspired to undertake the research on which this book is based, by an article that had first been published in 1965 but that I did not read until 1969: Alison Ravetz, "Modern Technology and an Ancient Occupation: Housework in Present Day Society," *Technology and Culture* 6 (1965): 256–60. With the possible exception of W. F. Ogburn and M. F. Nimkoff, *Technology and the Changing Family* (Cambridge, Mass., 1955), which is actually a textbook and not a report of scholarly research, Ravetz was, to my knowledge, the first person to raise serious scholarly questions about the historical relationship between household technology and household work. Since 1965, however, the subject has received a good deal of attention—partly because the women's movement has generated considerable research about many aspects of women's lives; partly because social scientists in general have recently become interested in many different forms of human labor; and partly because Marxist-feminist scholars have raised many questions about the ways in which traditional social analyses (including the analyses of traditional Marxists) have handled (or ignored) the work that slightly more than half the population engages in for a good part of every day. One of the most important of these Marxist-feminist scholars was Margaret Benston, whose article, "The Political

Economy of Women's Liberation," *Monthly Review* 21 (September 1969): 13–27, also served as an early stimulus to my research.

Among the many books that have appeared since 1969, and from which I have derived essential insights, are, in alphabetical order:* Sarah Fenstermaker Berk, ed., *Women and Household Labor* (Beverley Hills, 1980); Richard A. Berk and Sarah Fenstermaker Berk, *Labor and Leisure at Home: Content and Organization of the Household Day* (Beverley Hills, 1979); Barbara Ehrenreich and Deirdre English, *For Her Own Good: 150 Years of the Experts' Advice to Women* (New York, 1978); David Handlin, *The American Home: Architecture and Society, 1815–1915* (Boston, 1979); Dolores Hayden, *The Grand Domestic Revolution: A History of Feminist Designs for American Homes, Neighborhoods and Cities* (Cambridge, Mass., 1981); Helena Z. Lopata, *Occupation: Housewife* (London, 1971); Ann Oakley, *The Sociology of Housework* (New York, 1974); Ann Oakley, *Woman's Work: The Housewife Past and Present* (New York, 1974); Kathryn Kish Sklar, *Catherine Beecher: A Study in American Domesticity* (New Haven, 1973); Susan Strasser, *Never Done: A History of American Housework* (New York, 1982), which I read initially in its form as a dissertation, Susan May Strasser, "Never Done: The Ideology and Technology of Household Work, 1850–1930" (Ph.D. dissertation, State University of New York at Stony Brook, 1977); and, finally, Gwendolyn Wright, *Moralism and the Model Home: Domestic Architecture and Cultural Conflict in Chicago, 1873–1913* (Chicago, 1980).

During the 1970s, five other dissertations were completed that bore on topics related to the focus of this book. Although their authors have subsequently published several articles derived from the dissertations, the originals represent such an enormous body of research that they remain the best places to look for information and analysis: Sarah Fenstermaker Berk, "The Division of Household Labor: Patterns and Determinants" (Ph.D. dissertation, Northwestern University, 1976); Heidi Irmgard Hartmann, "Capitalism and Women's Work in the Home, 1900–1930," (Ph.D. dissertation, Yale University, 1974); Susan J. Kleinberg, "Technology's Stepdaughters: The Impact of Industrialization upon Working Class Women in Pittsburgh, 1870–1900" (Ph.D. dissertation, University of Pittsburgh, 1973); Charles Thrall, "Household Technology and the Division of Labor in Families" (Ph.D. dissertation, Harvard University, 1970); and Joann Vanek, "Keeping Busy: Time Spent in Housework, United States, 1920–1970" (Ph.D. dissertation, University of Michigan, 1973).

There are three essential sources of information about the history of household technology itself, none of which is completely accurate or inclusive, but each of which can at least provide the researcher with a place to start: Elizabeth Mickle Bacon, "The Growth of Household Conveniences in the United States from 1865 to 1900" (Ph.D. dissertation, Radcliffe College, 1942); Siegfried Giedion, *Mechanization Takes Command: A Contribution to Anonymous History* (New York, 1948); and Earl Lifshey, *The Housewares Story: A History of the American Housewares Industry* (Chicago, 1973). The bibliographic notes to Daniel Boorstin's three extraordinary volumes—*The Americans, The Colonial Experience* (New York, 1958), *The Americans, The National Experience* (New York, 1965), and *The Americans, The Democratic Experience* (New York, 1973)—abound in helpful references.

My understanding of the nature of technological systems has been drawn from my reading in general systems theory—in particular, Ludwig von Bertalanffy, *General System Theory* (New York, 1968), and Ervin Lazlo, *The Systems View of the World* (New York, 1972) —and from Jacques Ellul, *The Technological Society* (New York, 1964). The concept "work process" (or "labor process" as other authors would have it) is derived from Harry Braverman, *Labor and Monopoly Capital: The Degradation of Work in the Twentieth Century* (New York, 1974).

A recent history of household technology and household work in England appeared after this manuscript had been completed, but the interested reader will find that it is more useful than many other works on that subject because the author has made a concerted effort to locate primary sources that describe the lives of English women who were not members of the upper classes: Caroline Davidson, *A Woman's Work Is Never Done: A History of Housework in the British Isles* (London, 1982).

*Henceforth, unless otherwise indicated, all lists of secondary sources are in alphabetical order; those in chronological order are primary sources.

Bibliographic Essays

Chapter 2. Housewifery: Household Technology and Household Work Under Pre-Industrial Conditions in the Colonies and on the Frontier

This chapter discusses housework and household technologies under pre-industrial conditions, whether those conditions pertained in New England in the seventeenth century or in the Far West in the nineteenth; thus the primary and the secondary sources on which this chapter was based vary considerably. Among secondary sources that deal with women's lives and with family history during that nearly three-hundred-year span, I found the following most helpful: Daniel Boorstin, *The Americans, The Colonial Experience* (New York, 1958); Arthur W. Calhoun, *A Social History of the American Family* (New York, 1945); Lois Green Carr and Lorena Walsh, "The Planter's Wife: The Experience of White Women in Seventeenth Century Maryland," *William and Mary Quarterly*, 3rd series, 34 (1977): 542–71; John Demos, *A Little Commonwealth: Family Life in the Plymouth Colony* (London, 1971); Everett Dick, *The Sod-House Frontier* (New York, 1937); Alice Morse Earle, *Home Life in Colonial Days* (New York, 1898); Julie Roy Jeffrey, *Frontier Women: The Trans-Mississippi West, 1840–1880* (New York, 1979); Gloria Main, *Tobacco Colony: Life in Early Maryland, 1650–1720* (Princeton, 1982), which I was privileged to read in manuscript; Mary Beth Norton, *Liberty's Daughters: The Revolutionary Experience of American Women, 1750–1800* (Boston, 1980); Glenda Riley, *Frontierswoman: The Iowa Experience* (Ames, Iowa, 1981); Julia Cherry Spruill, *Women's Life and Work in the Southern Colonies* (Chapel Hill, N. C., 1938); and finally, Laurel Thatcher Ulrich, *Goodwives: Women's Lives in Northern New England, 1650–1800* (Boston, 1979).

Several secondary works based upon European sources have provided insights into pre-industrial conditions, and these were exceedingly helpful when I turned to the rich documentary material from the colonies and the frontier: Fernand Braudel, *Capitalism and Material Life, 1400–1800,* translated by Miriam Kochan (New York, 1973); J. Jean Hecht, *The Domestic Servant Class in Eighteenth Century England* (London, 1956); Olwin Hufton, *The Poor of 18th Century France, 1750–1789* (London, 1975); Olwin Hufton, "Woman and the Family Economy in 18th Century France," *French Historical Studies* 9 (1975): 1–22.

The preparation of food looms large in my discussion of pre-industrial households. What I learned on this subject from secondary sources has been derived from: Jane Carson, *Colonial Virginia Cookery*, Williamsburg Research Studies (Williamsburg, Va., 1968); Richard Osborn Cummings, *The American and His Food: A History of Food Habits in the United States* (Chicago, 1940); Elizabeth David, *English Bread and Yeast Cookery* (New York, 1980); J. C. Drummond and Anne Wilbraham, *The Englishman's Food,* revised by Dorothy Hollingsworth (London, 1957); Robert Forster and Orest Ranum, eds., *Food and Drink in History* (Baltimore, 1979); Marjorie Kriedberg, *Food on the Frontier: Minnesota Cooking from 1850 to 1900* (Minneapolis, 1975); Frances Phipps, *Colonial Kitchens, Their Furnishings and Their Gardens* (New York, 1972); and Reay Tannahill, *Food in History* (New York, 1973).

There is a special literature on the material culture of the colonial period and the frontier, some of it published by collectors of antiques and some by archeologists. For the historian's purposes, the best choices are the works of James Deetz, *In Small Things Forgotten: The Archaeology of Early North American Life* (Garden City, N. Y., 1977), and *An Invitation to Archaeology* (Garden City, N. Y., 1967); Mary Earle Gould, *Early American Wooden Ware* (Springfield, Mass., 1942), and *The Early American House: Household Life in America, 1620–1850* (Rutland, Vt., 1965)

The doctrine of separate spheres is actually a nineteenth-century phenomenon; but since I introduce it in this chapter, its bibliography belongs here: Nancy Cott, *Bonds of Womanhood: "Women's Sphere" in New England, 1780–1835* (New Haven, 1977): Ann Douglas, *The Feminization of American Culture* (New York, 1978); Kathryn Kish Sklar, *Catherine Beecher: A Study in American Domesticity* (New Haven, 1973); Susan Strasser, *Never Done: A History of American Housework* (New York, 1982); Barbara Welter, "The Cult of True Womanhood, 1820–1860," *American Quarterly* 18 (1966): 151–74; and Eli Zaretsky, *Capitalism, the Family and Personal Life* (New York, 1976).

Given the scope of this study, it proved impossible for me to investigate unpublished cookbooks, diaries, letters, and travelers' accounts for this entire period. Hence, what delving I did in the wealth of such sources was entirely in published form; and I present them here in approximate chronological order: Gervase Markham, *Country Contentments* [London, 1615] (New York, 1973); *The Diary of Joshua Hempstead, Covering a Period of Forty-Seven Years, from September 1711 to November 1758* (New London, Conn., 1901); Susannah Carter, *The Frugal Housewife or Complete Woman Cook* [c. 1750] (London and Boston, n.d.); Peter Kalm, *Travels in North America* [1753], edited by Adolph B. Benson [1937] (New York, 1964); Andrew Burnaby, *Travels through the Middle Settlements in North America in the Years 1759 and 1760*, 3rd ed. (London, 1798); Alice Morse Earle, ed., *Diary of Anna Greene Winslow, A Boston School Girl of 1771* (Boston, 1894); Albert C. Myers, ed., *Sally Wister's Journal* (Philadelphia, 1902); *Jemima Condict, Her Book, Being a Transcript of the Diary of an Essex County Maid during the Revolutionary War* (Newark, N.J., 1930); Karen Hess, *Martha Washington's Booke of Cookery* (New York, 1981); *Diary of Sarah Connell Ayer* [1800–1835] (Portland, Me. 1910); Fred Gustorf, ed. and trans., *The Uncorrupted Heart, Journal and Letters of Frederick Julius Gustorf, 1800–1845* (Columbia, Mo., 1969); Eliza Southgate Bowne, *A Girl's Life Eighty Years Ago*, edited by Clarence Cook (London, 1888); Fanny Kellogg, ed., *Tryphena Ely White's Journal, 1805* (New York, 1904); M. R. Lovell, ed., *Two Quaker Sisters: Lucy Buffum Chace and Margaret Buffum Lovell* (New York, 1937); Lora Case, *Hudson of Long Ago* [1811–97] (Hudson, O., 1963); "Letters of Mrs. Caroline Phelps of Lewiston, Illinois" [1816–73] *Illinois Historical Society Journal* 23 (1930–31): 55–98; Harriet Martineau, *Society in America* (London, 1837); Frances Trollope, *Domestic Manners of the Americans* [1832], edited by Donald Smalley (New York, 1949); Lydia Maria Child, *The American Frugal Housewife* (Boston, 1832); James Marryat, *Diary in America, With Remarks on Its Institutions* (Philadelphia, 1840); Elizabeth Farnham, *Life in Prairie Land* (New York, 1846); Harriet Bonebright-Closz, *Reminiscences of Newcastle, Iowa, 1848 as Narrated by Sarah Brewer-Bonebright* (Des Moines, Ia., 1921); Rebecca and Edward Burlend, *A True Picture of Emigration* [1848], edited by Milo Milton Quaife [1937] (New York, 1968); David T. Nelson, trans. and ed., *The Diary of Elizabeth Koren, 1853–1855* (Northfield, Minn., 1955); Charles Latrobe, *The Rambler in North America*, 2 vols. (New York, 1856); Pauline Farseth and Theodore Blegen, eds., *Frontier Mother: The Letters of Gro Svendsen* [1862–78] (Northfield, Minn., 1950); Lucy Leavenworth Wilder Morris, ed., *Old Rail Fence Corners: Authentic Incidents Gleaned from the Old Settlers* (Austin, Minn., 1914); and Phoebe Goodell Judson, *A Pioneer's Search for an Ideal Home: A Book of Personal Memoirs* [1925] (Tacoma, Wash., 1966).

Reading through all these primary sources would have been a superhuman effort for one person; I am delighted here to record my debt to Virginia Quiroga, who patiently sifted through bibliographies, filled out interlibrary loan requests, and read through many of these diaries and letters in order to locate material that I would find useful.

Chapter 3. The Invention of Housework: The Early Stages of Industrialization

This chapter places changes in the organization of household work into the context of changes in the general economy of the United States. My sources of information and analysis on the latter subject have been: James Leander Bishop, *A History of American Manufactures from 1608–1860*, 2 vols. (Philadelphia, 1864); Albert Bolles, *The Industrial History of the United States* (Norwich, Conn., 1879); Daniel Boorstin, *The Americans, The National Experience* (New York, 1965); Stuart Bruchey, *The Roots of American Economic Growth, 1607–1861* (New York, 1965); Alfred Chandler, *The Visible Hand: The Managerial Revolution in American Business* (Cambridge, Mass., 1977); Alfred Chandler, *Strategy and Structure: Chapters in the History of Industrial Enterprise* (Cambridge, Mass., 1962); Victor S. Clark, *History of Manufactures in the United States*, 3 vols. (New York, 1929); Chauncey Depew, ed., *One Hundred Years of American Commerce, 1795–1895*, 2 vols. (New York, 1895); Edgar W. Martin, *The Standard of*

Bibliographic Essays

Living in 1860 (Chicago, 1942); Albert W. Niemi, Jr., *U.S. Economic History*, 2nd ed. (Chicago, 1980); Nathan Rosenberg, *Technology and American Economic Growth* (New York, 1972); Nathan Rosenberg, *Perspectives on Technology* (New York, 1976); Geroge Rogers Taylor, *The Transportation Revolution* (New York, 1951); and Rolla Milton Tryon, *Household Manufactures in the U.S., 1640–1860* [1917] (New York, 1966).

For a topic of such apparent importance to the disciplines of women's history and American social history, surprisingly little has been written about the daily experiences of women in the nineteenth century. For my purposes the most useful texts on this subject were: Patricia Branca, *Silent Sisterhood: Middle Class Women in the Victorian Home* (Pittsburgh, 1975); Nancy Cott, *Bonds of Womanhood: "Women's Sphere" in New England 1780–1835* (New Haven, 1977); Carl Degler, *At Odds: Women and the Family in America from the Revolution to the Present* (New York, 1980); Peter Gabriel Filene, *Him, Her, Self: Sex Roles in Modern America* (New York, 1974); Anne Firor Scott, *The Southern Lady: From Pedestal to Politics, 1830–1930* (Chicago, 1970); and Kathryn Kish Sklar, *Catherine Beecher, A Study in American Domesticity* (New Haven, 1973).

For histories of household technology in the nineteenth century, the interested reader can consult the sources in chapter 1 as well as Walter Buehr, *Home Sweet Home in the 19th Century* (New York, 1965). For an idiosyncratic but nonetheless perceptive analysis of the impact of economic and social changes on American women in this century see, Charlotte Perkins Stetson Gilman, *Women and Economics* (Boston, 1898).

Women's magazines became fairly successful publishing ventures during the nineteenth century. For want of a lifetime to devote to reading them, I deliberately focused on those magazines that were addressed to an audience of urban, suburban, or rural middle- and upper-class women. Another whole book could (and should) be written from those numerous magazines and newspapers that were addressed (in whole or in part) to farm women. In any event, in the preparation of this chapter, I read random issues of the following publications, listed here with the dates on which they began and, in some cases, ended publication: *Godey's Lady's Book* (1828 to 1892); *Household Journal* (1860 to 1862); *Harper's Bazaar* (1867–1919); and *The Ladies' Home Journal* (1883–the present).

Cookbooks and household advice manuals are also invaluable sources of historical information, some of which has turned out, on more than one occasion, to retain its usefulness. Listed in chronological order, the nineteenth-century publications that served as essential background to this chapter were: Mary Randolph, *The Virginia Housewife* (Washington, D.C., 1824); *The Cook's Own Book: Being a Complete Culinary Encyclopedia . . .* (Boston, 1832); Lydia Maria Child, *The American Frugal Housewife* (Boston, 1832); Catherine E. Beecher, *A Treatise on Domestic Economy* (Boston, 1841); Sarah Josepha Hale, *The Good Housekeeper, or the Way to Live Well, and to Be Well While We Live*, 7th ed. (Boston, 1844); Mrs. E. A. Howland, *The New England Economical Housekeeper and Family Receipt Book* (Worcester, Mass., 1847); Catherine E. Beecher, *Miss Beecher's Domestic Receipt Book*, 3rd ed. (New York, 1848); Catherine E. Beecher and Harriet Beecher Stowe, *The American Woman's Home* (Boston, 1869); Mrs. E. F. Ellet, ed., *The New Cyclopedia of Domestic Economy and Practical Housekeeper* (Norwich, Conn., 1873); Juliet Corson, *Cooking School Textbook* (New York, 1879); Helen Campbell, *The Easiest Way in Housekeeping and Cooking* (New York, 1881); *Practical Housekeeping* (Minneapolis, 1883); Juliet Corson, *Family Living on $500 a Year* (New York, 1888); Mary Hinman Abel, *Practical, Sanitary and Economic Cooking Adapted to Persons of Moderate and Small Means* (New York, 1890); Fannie Merritt Farmer, *The Boston Cooking School Cookbook* (Boston, 1896); and Maria Parloa, *Home Economics* (New York, 1898). I found an invaluable guide to antiquated terminology in *The Grocer's Companion and Merchant's Handbook* (Boston, 1883).

The section on flour, milling, and baking bread and cake was derived in part from these cookbooks and in part from: Greville and Dorothy Bathe, *Oliver Evans: A Chronicle of Early American Engineering* [1936] (New York, 1972); Meryle Evans, "Whisking into Cake Heaven," *Food and Wine*, August 1979, pp. 45–48; Oliver Evans, *The Young Millwright and Miller's Guide* [1795] (New York, 1972); D. W. Garber, *Waterwheels and Millstones: A History of Ohio Gristmills* (Columbus, O., 1970); Siegfried Giedion, *Mechanization Takes Command: A Contribution to Anonymous History* (New York, 1948), pp. 169–209; Sylvester Graham, *Treatise on Bread and Breadmaking* (Boston, 1837); James Gray, *Business without Boundary: The Story of General Mills* (Minneapolis, 1954); Charles Byron Kuhlmann, *The Development of the Flour Milling Industry in the U.S.* (Boston, 1929); Hazel Kyrk and Joseph Stancliffe, *The American*

Baking Industry, 1849–1923 (Stanford, Calif., 1925); G. R. Stevens, *Ogilvie in Canada: Pioneer Millers, 1801–1951* (Toronto, 1957); John Storck and Walter Dorwin Teague, *Flour for Man's Bread: A History of Milling* (Minneapolis, 1952); Martha and Murry Zimiles, *Early American Mills* (New York, 1973).

The section on stoves, iron production, cooking, and heating was derived from: Eugene Ferguson, "An Historical Sketch of Central Heating" (unpublished, 1974); Eugene Ferguson, "Victorian Heating Systems and Equipment" (unpublished, 1974); Siegfried Giedion, *Mechanization Takes Command: A Contribution to Anonymous History* (New York, 1948), pp. 527–45; William John Keep, "History of Stoves" (unpublished, Baker Library, Harvard University); Josephine Pierce, *Fire on the Hearth: The Evolution and Romance of the Heating Stove* (Springfield, Mass., 1951); Alison Ravetz, "The Victorian Coal Kitchen and its Detractors," *Victorian Studies* 11 (June 1968): 428–45; Peter Temin, *Iron and Steel in Nineteenth Century America* (Cambridge, Mass., 1964); and Lawrence Wright, *Home Fires Burning, The History of Domestic Heating and Cooking* (London, 1964).

Almost all of the published diaries and letters that are listed in the bibliography for chapter 2, and that postdate 1800, provided material for this chapter as well; but additional such material was found, in rough chronological order, in: "The Original Diary of Mrs. Laura (Downs) Clark, of Wakeman, Ohio, from June 21 to October 26, 1818," *The Firelands Pioneer* (January 1920), pp. 2308–26; Lady Emmeline Stuart Wortley, *Travels in the United States, Etc., During 1849 and 1850* (New York, 1851); Donald Gordon, ed., *The Diary of Ellen Birdseye Wheaton* [1850–1858] (Boston, 1923); Oscar Osburn Winther and Rose Dodge Galey, "Mrs. Butler's 1853 Diary of Rogue River Valley," *Oregon Historical Quarterly* 41 (December 1940):335–66; Isabella Lucy Bird, *The Englishwoman in America* [1856] (Madison, Wis., 1966); Amelia M. Murray, *Letters from the United States, Cuba and Canada* (New York, 1856); Donald F. Danker, ed., *Mollie: The Journal of Mollie Dorsey Sanford in Nebraska and Colorado Territories, 1857–1866* (Lincoln, Neb., 1959); Robert C. Carriker and Eleanor R. Carriker, eds., *An Army Wife on the Frontier: The Memoirs of Alice Blackwood Baldwin, 1867–1877* (Salt Lake City, 1975); George L. Prentiss, ed., *The Life and Letters of Elizabeth Payson Prentiss* (New York, 1882); Edward Everett Hale, *A New England Boyhood* (Boston, 1900); *Told by Pioneers: Reminiscences of Pioneer Life in Washington*, 3 vols. (Olympia, Wash., 1936); and Berna Hunter Chrisman, *When You and I Were Young Nebraska* (Broken Bow, Neb., 1971).

Several manuscript collections of household accounts, diaries, and family letters were utilized in the preparation of this chapter; they are listed here, in chronological order, under the name of the archival depository in which they are located. At the New York Historical Society: *Diaries of Clara Burton Pardee* (1883–1938); *Diaries of Mrs. George Richards* (1883–1937). At the New York Public Library: *Diary and Account Book of Frederick E. Westbrooke* (1840–43); and *Diary of Caroline Dunstan* (1856–70); At the Queensborough Public Library, Long Island City Branch: *Hagner Family Papers and Account Books* (1790–1880); *Cook Family Papers* (1791–1934); *Rose Family Papers* (1825–1931); and *Correspondence of Anna Rose Cook* (1847–1920). At the Library of Congress: *Anna Kelton Wiley Papers* (1877–1964). At Cornell University, Regional History Archive: *Camp Family Papers* (1817–1953); *Mrs. Hayden's Diary* (1864); *Diary of Mary Bennet* (1866–74); and *Diary of John Berry* (1885–98). At the Schlesinger Library, Radcliffe College: *Hooker Family Letters* (1814–29); *Harriet Beecher Stowe Papers* (1863–1884); *Account Book of Chloe Sampson* (1819–64); and *Sally Joy White Papers* (1852–1909). In surveying these collections, I was fortunate to have the able assistance of David MacDonald, Valerie Park, and Virginia Quiroga.

Chapter 4. Twentieth-Century Changes in Household Technology

This chapter summarizes a body of research upon which I had once hoped to build an entire book. Unfortunately, when I began to study the history of individual appliances —such as the washing machine, the refrigerator, and the dryer—I had no idea that, in

Bibliographic Essays

order to paint a realistic picture of their development, I would also have to study the history of the companies that manufactured appliances, the history of utility delivery systems that provided fuel and water, and the history of price and income fluctuations for the entire twentieth century. The enterprise soon got out of hand. First, I thought I might solve the problem by limiting the number of appliances to be studied, but such limitation turned out to distort reality. Finally I decided that, in order to be able to say something cogent about each of the eight systems that, between them, define the material conditions under which household work is performed, I would have to summarize as best I could from the admittedly inadequate secondary sources that were available.

None of the secondary materials cited in the footnotes to this chapter is a definitive study of the history of even one of those eight technological systems. In order to create a history of the whole system in spite of the inadequacies in the secondary literature, I have combined, when they were available, individual company histories, with biographies of some significant innovators, with idiosyncratic accounts of the early development of some piece of equipment (idiosyncratic because they recount one individual's or one company's experience), with histories of one or another segment of an industry compiled to honor the anniversary of one trade association or another. Many of these sources lacked the usual scholarly apparatus of footnotes and page citations, and many of them were woefully uninformative (or even misinformative) about topics that lay outside (even just a little bit outside) the author's central focus. The reader who attempts a research project based upon any single one of those sources (or even a combination of them) is advised to tread warily.

My wariness has taken the form of not reporting anything in this chapter which I did not know to be true on the basis of the research that I had previously done in primary sources. That research effort began with an attempt to read one issue of *The Ladies' Home Journal* for every year from 1890 to 1970, focusing on the advertisements and the nonfictional material in order to get some idea of what was on the market at any given time and of what had then become "standard practice." Then I read selectively (the principle of selection frequently being the volumes that I could find bound or reproduced on microfilm in university libraries) in some of the trade journals that were or are prominent in this field, among them *Hardware Age* (1909–), *Electrical Merchandising Week* (1907–), *Merchant Plumber and Fitter* (1911–30), *Gas Age* (1883–), *American Gas Journal* (1859–), and *Air Conditioning, Heating and Refrigeration News* (1926–58). As some of these journals have changed names during their lives, I have given here the name under which the most complete entry can be found in the *Union List of Serials in Libraries of the United States and Canada*, 3rd ed. [New York, 1965]. Using its convenient annual index, I read selectively in *The Journal of Home Economics* (1909–) and also perused textbooks written by home economists who specialized in the sub-discipline of "household equipment"—most especially, Edith Allen, *Mechanical Devices in the Home* (Peoria, Ill., 1922), and the successive revised editions of Louise J. Peet and Lenore Sater Thye, *Household Equipment* (New York, 1934, 1940, 1949, and 1955). Since these sources gave me only a rudimentary idea of the extent to which either the pieces or the whole of a technological system had diffused to different segments of the population, I also frequently consulted the decennial editions of the *Census of Housing* (since 1940), *Historical Statistics of the United States, 1760 to 1960* (Washington, D.C., 1960), and many investigations of the standard of living of the poor, a partial list of which can be found in the bibliographic essays for chapters 6 and 7.

Several of the points made in this chapter which do not derive from secondary sources (for example, the point about the sexually stereotyped roles in transportation or about increased standards of cleanliness) are based upon my reading of diaries, letters, memoirs, and fiction; citations for these sources can be found in the bibliographic essays for chapters 2, 3, 6, and 7.

The notion that the history of the American family can be defined by the transition from "units of production" to "units of consumption" has had a long history, which, to my knowledge, no intellectual historian has yet tried to unravel. Early formulations of the idea can be found in the works of some of the founders of the discipline of economics in the United States—for example, Thorstein Veblen, *The Theory of the Leisure Class* (New York, 1899); and Simon Patten, *The Reconstruction of Economic Theory* (Philadelphia, 1912); as well as in the works of some of the founders of sociology—most particularly Helen Lynd and Robert Lynd, *Middletown: A Study in American Culture* (New York, 1929). Scholars who were creating a theoretical underpinning for home economics articulated the idea in the 1920s and 1930s—for example, Margaret Gilpin Reid, *Economics of Household Production* (New York, 1934), and Hazel Kyrk, *A Theory of Consumption* (Boston, 1923). By the 1950s, the transition from production to consumption had become the standard organizing idea for textbook treatments of the sociology of the family—for example, in Ernest W. Burgess and Harvey J. Locke, *The Family* (New York, 1950), in Paul B. Horton and Chester L. Hunt, *Sociology* (New York, 1964), and William Fielding Ogburn and Meyer Nimkoff, *Technology and the Changing Family* (Cambridge, Mass., 1955). By the 1970s, even Marxist historians had come to believe in this idea wholeheartedly—as in Eli Zaretsky, *Capitalism, The Family and Personal Life* (New York, 1977).

Within economics, the model was assailed fairly early in its history: see John B. Leeds, *The Household Budget: With a Special Inquiry into the Amount and Value of Household Work* (Ph.D. dissertation, Columbia University, privately printed, 1917). Within sociology, some of the most salient criticism occurs in William J. Goode, *After Divorce* (New York, 1956); Goode refers to the notion of the self-sufficient, productive, pre-industrial family as "the classic family of Western nostalgia" (p.3). Social historian Elizabeth Pleck criticizes the model in "Two Worlds in One: Work and Family," *Journal of Social History* 10 (1976):179–93; and I have criticized it, on grounds different from the ones presented in this chapter, in an earlier article, Ruth Schwartz Cowan, "The 'Industrial Revolution' in the Home: Household Technology and Social Change in the 20th Century," *Technology and Culture* 17 (January 1976):1–42.

My analysis in this chapter was influenced by Everett M. Rogers, *The Diffusion of Innovations* (New York, 1962). The only two articles that attempt, so far as I am aware, a similar "system-oriented" history of the diffusion of technology are: Mark H. Rose and John Clark, "Light, Heat, and Power: Energy Choices in Kansas City, Wichita, and Denver, 1900–1935," *Journal of Urban History* 5 (May 1979): 340–64; and Mark H. Rose, "Light and Heat in Denver and Kansas City: New Environments and the Social and Geographic Bases of Technological Innovation, 1900–1940 (unpublished). Unfortunately I did not see Thomas Parke Hughes, *Networks of Power: Electrification in Western Society, 1880–1930* (Baltimore, 1983) until my book was in press.

Chapter 5. The Roads Not Taken: Alternative Social and Technical Approaches to Housework

The first two sections of this chapter, on commercial substitutes for women's household labor and on experiments in cooperative and communal housekeeping were based almost entirely on secondary sources, many of which are cited in the footnotes to the chapter itself. These sections would have been much more difficult to write (indeed, might never have been written at all) had it not been possible for me to consult two very recent publications: Dolores Hayden, *The Grand Domestic Revolution: A History of Feminist Designs for American Homes, Neighborhoods and Cities* (Cambridge, Mass., 1981), and Susan Strasser, *Never Done: A History of American Housework* (New York, 1982). Although my theoretical perspective differs from the one adopted by these authors, I am indebted to Hayden for information about cooked-food delivery serves, cooperative and communal housekeeping experiments, and apartment hotels; and to Strasser for her invaluable chapter (chapter 8) on boarding houses. A reader with entrepreneurial inclinations might be fascinated to read a novel by one of America's leading feminist theorists, who imagined the possibilities for the complete commercialization of women's work: Charlotte Perkins Gilman, *What Diantha Did* (New York, 1910).

The history of domestic service in the United States is a vast, unresolved puzzle,

Bibliographic Essays

because the social role "servant" so frequently carries with it the unspoken adjective *invisible*. In diaries and letters, the "invisible" servant becomes visible only when she departs employment ("Mary left today"). In statistical series, she appears only when she is employed full-time, on a live-in basis; or when she is willing to confess the nature of her employment to a census taker, and (especially since the Second World War) there have frequently been good reasons for such confessions to go unmade. Several secondary sources can provide a good introduction to the history of domestic servants; but none, unfortunately, carries the story to the present day: Joseph A. Hill, *Women in Gainful Occupations, 1870–1920* (Washington, D.C., 1929); David Katzman, *Seven Days a Week: Women and Domestic Service in Industrializing America* (New York, 1978); Theresa McBride, *The Domestic Revolution: The Modernisation of Household Service in England and France, 1820–1920* (New York, 1976); Lucy Maynard Salmon, *Domestic Service* (New York, 1897); and George J. Stigler, *Domestic Servants in the United States, 1900 to 1940* (New York, 1946). None of these secondary sources substitutes for what can be learned from some of the essential primary sources, such as Helen Campbell, *Prisoners of Poverty: Women Wage Workers, Their Trades and Their Lives* (Boston, 1887); Lillian Pettengill, *Toilers of the Home, A Record of a College Woman's Experience as a Domestic Servant* (New York, 1903), and various letters from immigrant Polish servant girls to their parents in W.I. Thomas and Florian Znaniecki, *The Polish Peasant in Europe and America*, 5 vols. (Chicago, 1918–20). Many nineteenth-century travelers' accounts contain discussions of how different American servants were from their European counterparts; the most famous of these is Frances Trollope, *Domestic Manners of the Americans* [1832] (New York, 1949). In addition, virtually every issue of a woman's magazine from the mid-nineteenth century to the mid-twentieth contained an article about the "servant problem," or a series of advertisements illustrating the ways in which servants were idealized, or some fictional material suggesting the nature of the relationships between mistresses and maids. The nature of the "servant problem" can be discerned in Harriet Prescott Spofford, *The Servant Girl Question* (Boston, 1881); Gail Laughlin, "Domestic Service, A Report Prepared under the Direction of the Industrial Commission," *Report of the Industrial Commission on the Relations and Conditions of Capital and Labor Employed in Manufacture and General Business*, vol. 14 (Washington, D.C., 1901); or *First Report of the Commission on Household Employment of the YWCA* (Los Angeles, 1915).

My analysis of the competition between gas-absorption and electric-compression refrigerators was influenced by the work of several economists and economic historians; but it was stimulated by two rather iconoclastic articles—one by an intellectual historian and the other by a sociologist. The economists and economic historians are: Tom Burns and G. M. Stalker, *The Management of Innovation* (London, 1966); Alfred C. Chandler, *Giant Enterprise: Ford, General Motors and the Automobile Industry* (New York, 1964); Alfred C. Chandler, *Strategy and Structure, Chapters in the History of Industrial Enterprise* (Cambridge, Mass., 1962); Edwin Mansfield, *The Economics of Technological Change*; and Robert Sobel, *The Age of the Giant Corporation: A Microeconomic History of American Business, 1914–1970* (Westport, Conn., 1972). The intellectual historian was Daniel D. Luria, "Wealth Capital and Power: The Social Meaning of Home Ownership," *Journal of Intellectual History* 7 (1976): 261–82; and the sociologist was Bernhard J. Stern, "Restraints upon the Utilization of Inventions," in his book *Historical Sociology* (New York, 1959), pp. 75–101.

One of the reasons I chose to examine the history of refrigerating devices, rather than of laundering or cooking devices, was the existence of a superb secondary work on the subject: Oscar Edward Anderson, Jr., *Refrigeration in America: A History of a New Technology and Its Impact* (Princeton, 1953); and of the two collections of unpublished materials (on the General Electric and the SORCO refrigerators) that are described in detail in the relevant footnotes in chapter 5. Several other books provided either essential background or essential information for this section: Arthur Pound, *The Turning Wheel: The Story of General Motors 1908–1933* (Garden City, N.Y., 1934); *Report of the Federal Trade Commission on the House Furnishings Industries*, 3 vols. (Washington, D.C., 1923–25); and Bernard W. Weisberger, *The Dream Maker: William C. Durant* (Boston, 1979). Scattered articles about individual refrigerators and the refrigerator business in general were located in trade and business magazines through *The Applied Science and Technology Index* (called *The Industrial Arts Index* until 1958). The history of corporations involved in the manufacture of refrigerators was traced through *The New York Times* and through the annual editions of *Moody's Industrial Manual*. In-house publications of General Electric *(G.E. Monogram, On the Top)* and Westinghouse *(Westinghouse Electric News, The Westinghouse Magazine)* were also useful; I was fortunate to gain access to these through the collections of the Engineering Societies Library, New York City, and of the New York Public Library, and through the good offices of Dr. George Wise, of the General Electric Company, Schenectady, New York.

Readers who want to explore further the recent debate in Marxist circles about the relationship between capitalism, housework, and women can begin with Margaret Benston, "The Political Economy of Women's Liberation," *Monthly Review* 21 (September 1969):13–27; Renate Bridenthal, "The Dialectics of Production and Reproduction in History," *Radical America* 10 (1976): 3–11; Terry Fee, "Domestic Labor: An Analysis of Housework and Its Relation to the Production Process," *Review of Radical Political Economics* 8 (Spring 1976):1–8; Rayna Rapp, "Family and Class in Contemporary America: Notes toward an Understanding of Ideology," *Science and Society* 42 (Fall 1978):278–300; and Wally Seccombe, "Housework under Capitalism," *New Left Review* 83 (1973):3–24.

Chapter 6. Household Technology and Household Work between 1900 and 1940

The notion that an analysis by generations might be a reasonable way to analyze the changes in social and material conditions of housework first occurred to me after I had read Alan B. Spitzer, "The Historical Problem of Generations," *American Historical Review* 78 (1973): 1353–85.

My portrait of the standard of living of "comfortable" families in the first two decades of this century was drawn partly from the works of Leeds and Dodge (cited in the footnotes to the chapter) and partly from the nonfictional material in women's magazines expressly addressed to this audience—particularly *The Ladies' Home Journal* and *Woman's Home Companion.* The many "household reform" books written during these decades provide a rich source of details about work processes and attitudes, once one discounts the reformist material that they contain; Lydia Ray Balderston, *Housewifery* (Philadelphia, 1919); Martha B. Bruere, *Increasing Home Efficiency* (New York, 1913); Christine Frederick, *Household Engineering: Scientific Management in the Home* (Chicago, 1915); and Mary Pattison, *Principles of Domestic Engineering* (New York, 1915). I learned a good deal about comfortable living in small towns from Loren Reid, *Hurry Home Wednesday: Growing Up in a Small Missouri Town, 1905–1921* (Columbia, Mo., 1978); and about attitudes toward housing from Robert C. Twombley, "Saving the Family: Middle Class Attraction to Wright's Prairie House, 1901–1909," *American Quarterly* 27 (March 1975): 57–72.

Information about "poor" families during those decades came from very different kinds of source. I had at first hoped that some of the women's magazines that were addressed to this audience—*True Confessions,* for example, or *Redbook*—would be helpful; but the few issues from this period that I was able to find seemed to carry exactly the same advertising as the more expensive magazines, and the "true" stories were so outlandish (and so clearly written by free-lance authors) that I could not rely upon them as a mirror of reality. In the end, I was left with the writings of social workers and reformers who pioneered in the study of "social problems," and with fictional and nonfictional memoirs of persons who had lived in poverty in those years. Both kinds of account had to be read carefully—the former for ideological bias; the latter for the distortions of nostalgia. I have tried to correct for these difficulties by reporting only those points that sympathetic observers and participants seemed to agree on, and that are in rough accord with what contemporary photographs also recorded. Useful fictional accounts were: Thomas Bell, *Out of This Furnace* [1941] (Pittsburgh, 1976); Pietro DiDonato, *Christ in Concrete* (Indianapolis, 1939); Louis Forgione, *The River Between* (New York, 1928); Agnes Smedley, *Daughter of*

Bibliographic Essays

Earth [1928] (Old Westbury, N.Y., 1973); and Anzia Yezierska, *The Bread Givers* [1925] (New York, 1975). I found few memoirs that provided details about domestic concerns, but amongst those few were Elizabeth G. Stern, *My Mother and I* (New York, 1917); Rose Cohen, *Out of the Shadow* (New York, 1918); Harry Roskolenko, *The Time That Was Then: The Lower East Side, 1900–1914, An Intimate Chronicle* (New York, 1971); and Verna Mae Slone, *What My Heart Wants to Tell* (Washington, D.C., 1979). Social workers' reports are legion. On restricted topics, many articles can be found in such journals of the period as *The Survey, Charities,* the *Journal of Home Economics,* as well as in the publications of the Women's Bureau, U.S. Department of Labor. The broader studies that I found particularly helpful were Grace Abbott, *The Immigrant and the Community* (New York, 1917); Hugh T. Ashby, *Infant Mortality* (Cambridge, England, 1915); Wilbur O. Atwater and Charles Woods, *Dietary Studies in New York City in 1895 and 1896,* United States Department of Agriculture, Agricultural Extension Station Bulletin 46 (Washington, D.C., 1898); Josephine Baker, *Fighting for Life* (New York, 1939); Margaret Byington, *Homestead, The Households of a Mill Town* (New York, 1910); Robert Coit Chapin, *The Standard of Living among Workingmen's Families in New York* (New York, 1909); Michael Davis, *Immigrant Health and the Community* (New York, 1921); Edward T. Devine, *Misery and Its Causes* (New York, 1911); J. C. Kennedy, et al., *Wages and Budgets in the Chicago Stockyards District* (Chicago, 1914); C. F. Langworthy, *Food Customs and Diet in American Homes,* United States Department of Agriculture, Office of Experiment Stations, Circular 110 (Washington, D.C., 1911); Florence Nesbitt, *The Chicago Standard Budget for Dependent Families* (Chicago, 1919); Bertha Marie von der Nienburg, *The Woman Homemaker in the City: A Study of Statistics Relating to Married Women in the City of Rochester, New York at the Census of 1920* (Washington, D.C., 1923); *Tentative Quantity and Cost Budget Necessary to Maintain a Family of Five in Washington D.C., at a Level of Health and Decency,* United States Department of Labor, Bureau of Labor Statistics (Washington, D.C., 1919); and Robert M. Woodbury, *Infant Mortality and its Causes* (Baltimore, 1926).

On women and families during the interwar years, there is now a small, but helpful secondary literature—particularly William H. Chafe, *The American Woman: Her Changing Social, Economic and Political Roles, 1920–1970* (New York, 1972), and Winifred D. Wandersee, *Women's Work and Family Values, 1920–1940* (Cambridge, Mass., 1981). Women's magazines (especially *The Ladies' Home Journal, Woman's Home Companion,* and *American Home*) were once again important sources of information and insights, as was the *Journal of Home Economics. Parents Magazine,* which began publication in 1926, was both an indicator of, and a storehouse of information about, changing child-rearing practices in this period. Some works of fiction are also useful: Harriet Arnow, *The Dollmaker* (New York, 1954); Dorothy Canfield, *The Home Maker* (New York, 1924); John Dos Passos, *USA* (New York, 1937); Mary McCarthy, *The Company She Keeps* (New York, 1942); Mary McCarthy, *The Group* (New York, 1963); Sinclair Lewis, *Babbitt* (New York, 1928); Sinclair Lewis, *Main Street* (New York, 1932); and Tillie Olsen, *Yonnondio: From the Thirties* (New York, 1974).

Between 1920 and 1940, "community studies" became a popular form of sociological work, and many of these studies proved useful to me in writing this chapter: Margaret Jarman Hagood, *Mothers of the South: Portraiture of the White Tenant Farm Woman* (Chapel Hill, N.C., 1939); Robert S. Lynd and Helen M. Lynd, *Middletown: A Study in Modern American Culture* (New York, 1929); Robert S. Lynd and Helen M. Lynd, *Middletown in Transition: A Study in Cultural Conflicts* (New York, 1936); W. Lloyd Warner and Paul S. Lunt, *The Social Life of a Modern Community* (New Haven, 1941); W. Lloyd Warner and Paul S. Lunt, *The Status System of a Modern Community* (New Haven, 1942); W. Lloyd Warner and Leo Srole, *The Social Systems of American Ethnic Groups* (New Haven, 1945); and James West, *Plainville, U.S.A.* (New York, 1945).

Market research came into its own during these years as well; and although it is sometimes difficult to make judgments about the adequacy of the methods used by market researchers when they are assessing "attitudes" and "opinions," their work can provide useful information about material conditions and the variables that affect them. See, for example, *Woman's Home Companion, Women as Purchasers of Heating Equipment* (New York, 1924); Frederick E. Croxton, *A Study of Housewives Buying Habits in Columbus, Ohio, 1924,* Bureau of Business Research Monographs, no. 3, Ohio State University (Colombus, O., 1926); Mary E. Hoffman, *The Buying Habits of Small-Town Women* (Kansas City, Mo., 1926); R. O. Eastman, Inc., *Zanesville and Thirty-Six Other American Communities: A Study of Markets and the Telephone as a Market Index* (New York, 1927); MacFadden Publications, Inc., *86% of America: A Symposium on the Characteristics of The New American Prosperity as Related to the Wage Earning Masses* (New York, 1927); Time, Inc., *Markets by Incomes: A Study of the Relationship of Income to Retail Purchases in Appleton, Wisconsin* (New York, 1932); Cleveland Press, Inc., *Fourth Inventory of 5457 Cleveland Kitchens* (Cleveland, 1937); and Market Research Department of Fawcett Publications, *The Effect of Living Standards on the Consumption Trend of Grocery Store Products* (New York, 1939).

The literature of home economics expanded enormously between 1920 and 1940; and when one separates prescription from description, books written by home economists provide much useful information. Benjamin Andrews, *Economics of the Household* (New York, 1923; rev. ed., 1935); Lillian Gilbreth, *The Homemaker and Her Job* (New York, 1927); Hazel Kyrk, *Economic Problems of the Family* (New York, 1933); and Margaret Reid, *The Economics of Household Production* (Chicago, 1934) are among the most helpful of these books. Family budget studies were a popular form of investigation amongst economists and home economists during this period. Some of the most helpful are Leila Houghteling, *The Income and Standard of Living of Unskilled Laborers in Chicago* (Chicago, 1927); Jessica Peixotto, *Getting and Spending at the Professional Standard of Living* (New York 1927); University of California, Heller Commission, *Spending Ways of a Semi-Skilled Group, Cost of Living Studies IV,* University of California Publications in Economics (Berkeley, Calif., 1931); Faith M. Williams and Alice C. Hanson, *Money Disbursements of Wage Earners and Clerical Workers in Eight Cities in the East North-Central Region, 1934–1936,* United States Bureau of Labor Statistics, Bulletin 636 (Washington, D.C., 1940); Faith M. Williams and Carle C. Zimmerman, *Studies of Family Living in the United States and Other Countries,* United States Department of Agriculture, Miscellaneous Publication 223 (Washington, D.C., 1935); and Carle C. Zimmerman, *Consumption and Standards of Living* (Princeton, 1936).

Even before the Depression began, the federal government was starting to poke into everyday life, and some of the publications that resulted from this activity are invaluable sources of information. John M. Gries and James Ford, eds., *Reports of the President's [Hoover's] Conference on Home Building and Home Ownership,* 11 vols. (Washington, D.C., 1932); *Recent Social Trends,* President's Research Committee on Social Trends, 2 vols. (New York, 1933); *Farm Housing Survey,* USDA, Bureau of Home Economics (Washington, D.C., 1934); *The Young Child in the Home,* White House Conference on Child Health and Protection (New York, 1936); *Consumer Purchases Study,* USDA, Bureau of Human Nutrition and Home Economics (Washington, D.C., 1939–41).

Other works that were helpful but defy easy classification were Robert C. Angell, *The Family Encounters the Depression* (New York, 1936); Belle Boone Beard, *Electricity in the Home* (Bryn Mawr, 1927). Ruth S. Cavan and Katherine H. Ranck, *The Family and the Depression: A Study of One Hundred Chicago Families* (Chicago, 1938); Cecile Tipton LaFollette, *A Study of the Problems of 652 Gainfully Employed Married Women Homemakers* (New York, 1934); Ruth Lindquist, *The Family in the Present Social Order* (Chapel Hill, N.C., 1931); Winona Morgan, *The Family Meets the Depression* (Minneapolis, 1939); Abraham Myerson, *The Nervous Housewife* (Boston, 1926); Arthur Meier Schlesinger, *Learning How to Behave: A Historical Study of American Etiquette Books* (New York, 1946); Geoffrey Steer, "Freudianism and Child-Rearing in the Twenties," *American Quarterly* 20 (Winter 1968): 759–67; and Martha Wolfenstein, "Fun Morality: An Analysis of Recent American Childtraining Literature," in Margaret Mead and Martha Wolfenstein, eds., *Childhood in Contemporary Cultures* (Chicago, 1955), pp. 168–77.

Chapter 7: Postwar Years

Two works by John Kenneth Galbraith influenced the ideas that are expressed in this chapter: *The Affluent Society* (New York, 1963) provides much of the context; and "The Economics of the American Housewife," *Atlantic Monthly* (August 1973), pp. 78–83, sup-

Bibliographic Essays

plied many insights into the economic meaning of housework in an affluent society. David M. Potter, *People of Plenty, Economic Abundance and the American Character* (Chicago, 1954), also helped me to establish the frame within which I came to understand the postwar years. The two classic sociological studies of housewives—Helena Z. Lopata, *Occupation: Housewife* (London, 1971), and Ann Oakley, *The Sociology of Housework* (New York, 1974)—were extremely helpful, both in providing information and in suggesting modes of analysis. Many of the more restricted studies published in Sarah Fenstermaker Berk, ed., *Women and Household Labor* (Beverley Hills, Calif., 1980), extend and enlarge upon the investigations of Lopata and Oakley, as do these articles: Catherine White Berheide, Sarah Fenstermaker Berk, and Richard A. Berk, "Household Work in the Suburbs: The Job and Its Participants," *Pacific Sociological Review*, 19 (October 1976): 491–517; Christine Bose, "Technology and Changes in the Division of Labor in the American Home," *Womens Studies International* 2 (1979): 14–38; Heidi Hartmann, "Capitalism, Patriarchy and Job Segregation by Sex," *Signs: Journal of Women in Culture and Society* 1 (Spring 1976): 137–69; Martin Meissner, et al., "No Exit for Wives: Sexual Division of Labor and the Cumulation of Household Demands," *Canadian Review of Sociology and Anthropology* 12 (November 1975): 424–39; Joan Rothschild, "Technology, 'Women's Work,' and the Social Control of Women," in Margherita Rendel, ed., *Women, Politics and Social Development* (London, 1981); Charles N. Thrall, "Who Does What: Role Stereotypy, Children's Work and Continuity between Generations in the Household Division of Labor," *Human Relations* 31 (March 1978): 249–65; Charles N. Thrall, "The Conservative Use of Modern Household Technology," *Technology and Culture* 23 (April 1982): 175–94; Joann Vanek, "Household Technology and Social Status: Rising Living Standards and Status and Residence Differences," *Technology and Culture* 19 (July 1978): 361–75; and Joann Vanek, "Housewives and Workers," in Ann H. Stromberg and Shirley Harkness, eds., *Women Working: Theories and Facts in Perspective* (Palo Alto, Calif., 1978), pp. 202–30. Nona Glazer-Malbin provided a review of some of this literature in "Housework: A Review Essay," *Signs, Journal of Women in Culture and Society* 1 (Summer 1976):905–22.

Men's participation in household labor is addressed, in passing, in many of the preceding studies; but, for efforts to address the question directly, see William R. Beer, *Househusbands: Men and Housework in American Families* (New York, 1983); Martha Hill, "Measuring and Valuing Nonmarket Time Spent in Maintenance of Major Durables and Home Improvements" (unpublished paper, Survey Research Center, University of Michigan); Martha S. Hill and Thomas Juster, "Constraints and Complementarities in Time Use" (unpublished paper, Survey Research Center, University of Michigan); Mike McGrady, *The Kitchen Sink Papers: My Life as a Househusband* (New York, 1975); and Joseph Pleck, "Men's Family Work: Three Perspectives and Some New Data," *The Family Coordinator* 28 (1979): 481–88.

Studies of time spent in housework have become larger (that is, the number of people studied is greater) and more rigorous in the last twenty years than they were in previous decades; and we can, therefore, put even more faith than was once possible in their results. For a survey of the history of these studies, see Joann Vanek, "Keeping Busy: Time Spent in Housework, United States, 1920–1970" (unpublished Ph.D. dissertation, University of Michigan, 1973); and Vanek's article, derived from her dissertation, "Time Spent in Housework," *Scientific American* 231 (November 1974):116–20. For some of these extensive and rigorous studies, see, in roughly chronological order: James Morgan, Ismail Sirageldin, and Nancy Baerwaldt, *Productive Americans* (Ann Arbor, Mich., 1966): Alexander Szalai, et al., eds., *The Use of Time* (The Hague, 1972); Kathryn Walker and Margaret Woods, *Time Use: A Measure of Household Production of Family Goods and Services* (Washington, D.C., 1976); John P. Robinson, *How Americans Use Time: A Social-Psychological Analysis of Everyday Behavior* (New York, 1977); and Richard A. Berk and Sarah Fenstermaker Berk, *Labor and Leisure at Home: Content and Organization of the Household Day* (Beverley Hills, Calif., 1979).

Until 1970, the Census Bureau did not consistently collect data about the diffusion of household appliances; consequently I had to rely, as in the previous chapters, on studies done by market researchers; several of these studies provided insights into other matters as well. Listed in roughly chronological order, those upon which I could lay my hands (since most market research studies are proprietary) were Woman's Home Companion, *Family Food and Grocery Purchasing* (New York, 1941); Mary Davis Gillies, *What Women Want*

232

Bibliographic Essays

in *Their Kitchens of Tomorrow, A Report on the Kitchen of Tomorrow Contest Sponsored by McCall's Magazine* (New York, 1944); McFadden Publications, Inc., *The Household Appliance Market Today, Trends and Potentials* (New York, 1946); Social Research, Inc., *Chicagoland Women and Their Clothing* (Chicago, 1957); True Story Women's Group, *The New America* (New York, 1957); Audits and Surveys, Inc., *Look National Appliance Survey*, 2 vols. (New York, 1959); Lee Rainwater and Gerald Handel, *Status of the Working Class in Changing American Society* (Chicago, 1961); General Electric Company, *The Homemaking Habits of the Working Wife* (New York, 1962); Ernest Dichter, *Handbook of Consumer Motivations* (New York, 1964).

Community studies by sociologists and anthropologists, as well as social and economic investigations of working-class life (especially the lives of working-class women), have provided considerable grist for my particular mill. Listed in alphabetical order, the most helpful of these have been Bennett Berger, *Working Class Suburb* (Berkeley, Calif., 1960); David Caplovitz, *The Poor Pay More* (New York, 1963); Theodore Caplow, et al., *Middletown Families* (Minneapolis, 1982); John L. Fisher and Ann Fischer, "The New Englanders of Orchard Town, U.S.A.," in Beatrice Whiting, ed., *Six Cultures* (New York, 1963); Herbert J. Gans, *The Levittowners: Ways of Life and Politics in a New Suburban Community* (New York, 1967); Mirra Komarovsky, *Women in the Modern World* (New York, 1954); Mirra Komarovsky, *Blue Collar Marriage* (New York, 1962); Oscar Ornati, *Poverty Amid Affluence* (New York, 1956); Lee Rainwater, et al., *And the Poor Get Children* (Chicago, 1960); Lee Rainwater, *What Money Buys, Inequality and the Social Meanings of Income* (New York, 1974); Lee Rainwater, et al., *Workingman's Wife* (New York, 1959); Lillian Rubin, *Worlds of Pain: Life in the Working Class Family* (New York, 1977); J. R. Seeley, R. A. Sim, and E. W. Loosley, *Crestwood Heights: A Study of the Culture of Suburban Life* (New York, 1963).

Studies of working women are now legion; but for those who want to come to some understanding of the upsurge in married women's labor force participation since the end of the Second World War, the best sources are Juanita Kreps, *Sex in the Marketplace* (New York, 1970); Clarence D. Long, *The Labor Force under Changing Income and Employment* (Princeton, 1958); National Manpower Council, *Work in the Lives of Married Women* (New York, 1958); F.I. Nye and Lois Hoffman, eds., *The Employed Mother in America* (Chicago, 1963); and Valerie Kincaid Oppenheimer, *The Female Labor Force in the United States, Demographic and Economic Factors Governing Its Growth and Changing Composition*, Population Monograph Series 5 (Berkeley, Calif., 1970). Long and Oppenheimer are the two labor economists who struggled mightily to find some way to establish a relationship between increased levels of household technology and increased workforce participation of married women.

No historian has, to my knowledge, succeeded in understanding the ideology of the immediate postwar years better than Betty Friedan did in *The Feminine Mystique* (New York, 1963). Since I grew up in those years I did not have much difficulty in remembering the nuances of that particular ideology, but those who need to have their memories nudged (or who are too young to remember) might glance at Mortimer Hunt, *Her Infinite Variety* (New York, 1963); Ferdinand Lundberg and Marynia Farnham, *Modern Woman, The Lost Sex* (New York, 1947); Russell Lynes, *A Surfeit of Honey* (New York, 1953); Robert Stein, ed., *Why Young Mothers Feel Trapped: A Redbook Documentary* (New York, 1965); and Lynn White, *Educating Our Daughters* (New York, 1950).

Two very different books about homemakers kept me company while I was working on this chapter: Rae André, *Homemakers, The Forgotten Workers* (Chicago, 1981); and Rose E. Steidl and Esther Crew Bratton, *Work in the Home* (New York, 1968). In addition, I must thank the editors of the "Living" (Wednesday) and "Home" (Thursday) sections of *The New York Times* for providing me, week in and week out for the past few years, with proof of the powerful forces that lie behind the desire to expand the time spent in housework. I wish that I could say that I had learned something from the literature of what is called the "new home economics"—but I have not, since I must confess that I cannot understand it. Interested readers can cut their teeth on Theodore W. Schultz, *Economics of the Family: Marriage, Children and Human Capital* (Chicago, 1973). I did, however, learn something about the unwritten rules by which we organize our lives from Mary Douglas, *Purity and Danger: An Analysis of Concepts of Purity and Taboo* (London, 1966); and Mary Douglas and Baron Isherwood, *The World of Goods* (New York, 1978).

NOTES

The numbers in brackets following a short title refer to its original citation in that chapter. The dates in brackets refer to the original date of publication of a work that has since been reprinted.

Chapter 1. An Introduction: Housework and Its Tools

1. For a brief introduction to this literature, see Eli Zaretsky, *Capitalism, The Family and Personal Life* (New York, 1974); Margaret Benston, "The Political Economy of Women's Liberation," *Monthly Review* 21 (September 1969):13–27; Lise Vogel, "The Earthly Family," *Radical America* 7 (July 1973):9–50; Wally Seccombe, "The Housewife and Her Labor under Capitalism," *New Left Review* 83 (January 1974):3–24.

2. Recent historical studies of market labor include Harry Braverman, *Labor and Monopoly Capital: The Degradation of Work in the Twentieth Century* (New York, 1975); Herbert G. Gutman, *Work, Culture and Society in Industrializing America* (New York, 1976); Susan E. Hirsch, *Roots of the American Working Class* (Philadelphia, 1978); David Montgomery, *Workers' Control in America* (New York, 1979). For a sound introduction to the history of housework, see Susan Strasser, *Never Done: A History of American Housework* (New York, 1982).

Chapter 2. Housewifery: Household Work and Household Tools Under Pre-Industrial Conditions

1. Thomas Tusser [1577]. The verse comes from a poem by Tusser, "The Authours Dialogue between two Bachelors, of wiving and thriving by Affirmation and Objection," which Tusser used as the introduction to a work, "The points of Huswiferie," that he added to his earlier work, *Five Hundred Pointes of Good Husbandrie* [1573]. I have quoted it from the edition edited by W. Payne and Sidney Herrtage (London, 1878), p. 158.

2. On the development of the doctrine of separate spheres, see Carl Degler, *At Odds: Women and the Family in American History* (New York, 1980); Nancy Cott, *Bonds of Womanhood: "Women's Sphere" in New England, 1780–1835* (New Haven, 1977); Ann Douglas, *The Feminization of American Culture* (New York, 1978); Kathryn Kish Sklar, *Catherine Beecher: A Study in American Domesticity* (New Haven, 1973); Barbara Welter, *Dimity Convictions: American Women*

in the Nineteenth Century (Columbus, Ohio, 1976); and Susan Strasser, *Never Done: A History of American Housework* (New York, 1982), chap. 10.

3. Peter Kalm, *Travels in North America* [1753], translated from Swedish into English by John Reinhold Forster [1770], revised and edited by Adolph B. Benson [1937], and reissued in facsimile of the 1937 edition (New York, 1964), vol. I, p. 602.

4. Gervase Markham, *Country Contentments* [London, 1615], reissued in facsimile (New York, 1973). The recipe is given in book 2, "The English Huswife," pp. 47–48.

5. Rebecca and Edward Burlend, *A True Picture of Emigration* [London, 1848], edited by Milo Milton Quaife [1937] and reissued in facsimile of the 1937 edition (New York, 1968), pp. 91–92.

6. On the early history of domestic service, see Lucy Maynard Salmon, *Domestic Serivice* (New York, 1897). The topic is discussed in more detail in chapter 5.

7. Burlend, *True Picture* [5], p. 152

8. David T. Nelson, translator and editor, *The Diary of Elizabeth Koren, 1853–1855* (Northfield, Minn., 1955).

9. Burlend, *True Picture* [5], chap. 4.

10. J. Leander Bishop, *A History of American Manufactures from 1608 to 1860,* 3rd ed. [1868] (New York, 1966), chap. 17.

11. Gloria Main, *Tobacco Colony: Life in Early Maryland 1650–1720* (Princeton, N.J., 1982), chaps. 4–7, esp. pp. 150, 169, 170, and 176.

12. Burlend, *True Picture* [5], pp. 78–79.

13. Main, *Tobacco Colony* [11], chaps. 5–6.

14. The probate records on which this section is based come from the archives of Suffolk County located in Riverhead, New York. I am indebted to Nancy Marr, a graduate student at the State University of New York at Stony Brook, for supplying me with copies of these records.

15. Suffolk County, Surrogate's Court probate file no. 1836.

16. Suffolk County, Surrogate's Court probate file no. 2028.

17. Suffolk County, Surrogate's Court, probate file no. 1279.

Chapter 3. The Invention of Housework: The Early Stages of Industrialization

1. The assumption that housework became easier in the nineteenth century is implicit, for example, in Carl Degler, *At Odds: Women and the Family in America from the Revolution to the Present* (New York, 1980), especially chaps. 2 and 8; and explicit in Alice Kessler-Harris, *Out to Work: A History of Wage Earning Women in the United States* (New York, 1982), pp. 110–12. It also underlies many older and more specialized treatments, such as Elizabeth Mickle Bacon, "The Growth of Household Conveniences in the United States from 1865 to 1900" (Ph.D. dissertation, Radcliffe College, 1942). The demographic data comes from Ansley J. Coale and Melvin Zelnick, *New Estimates of Fertility and Population in the United States* (Princeton, 1963), pp. 34–36.

2. Entry for 26 November 1795 in the diary of Martha Moore Ballard, 1785–1812, in Charles Elventon Nash, ed., *The History of Augusta* (Augusta, Me., 1904), p. 348, as quoted in Nancy Cott, *Bonds of Womanhood* (New Haven, 1977), p. 19.

3. Letter, 6 February 1888, from Mary Hallock Foote to Helena Gilder, Mary Hallock Foote Papers, Stanford University Library, as quoted in Degler, *At Odds* [1], p. 54.

4. Harriet Beecher Stowe to Calvin Stowe, 23 May 1844, in Stowe Papers, Schlesinger Library, Radcliffe College.

5. Frances Trollope, *Domestic Manners of the Americans* [1832] edited by Donald Smalley (New York, 1949), pp. 117–18.

6. Gro Svendsen to her parents, 20 November 1862, in *Frontier Mother: The Letters of Gro Svendsen* (Northfield, Minn., 1950), p. 28.

7. Catherine Beecher, *A Treatise on Domestic Economy* (Boston, 1841), p. 18.

8. The best sources for information on the changing technologies of housework in the nineteenth century are Bacon, "Growth of Household Conveniences" [1]; Walter Buehr, *Home, Sweet Home, in the Nineteenth Century* (New York, 1965); Siegfried Giedion, *Mechanization Takes Command* (New York, 1948), parts VI and VII; and Susan Strasser, *Never Done: A History of American Housework* (New York, 1982).

9. On the transformation of flour milling in the nineteenth century, see John Storck and Walter Dorwin Teague, *Flour for Man's Bread: A History of Milling* (Minneapolis, 1952); and Charles Byron Kuhlmann, *The Development of the Flour Milling Industry in the United States* (New York, 1929).

10. Greville and Dorothy Bathe, *Oliver Evans: A Chronicle of Early American Engineering* [1936] (New York, 1972). The milling handbook is Oliver Evans, *The Young Mill Wright and Miller's Guide* [1795] (New York, 1972); Thomas Ellicott is listed as a subsidiary author in the table of contents but not on the title page.

11. Evans, *Young Mill Wright* [10], p. 247; Bathe and Bathe, *Oliver Evans* [10], p. 177.

12. This summary is based upon Storck and Teague, *Flour For Man's Bread* [9], chaps. 12 and 13; Kuhlmann, *The Development of Flour Milling* [9], chaps. 8–10; and George Rogers Taylor, *The Transportation Revolution* (New York, 1951), pp. 210 and 362. For a specific study of the decline in wheat production in New York after the opening of the Erie Canal, see Roberta B. Miller, "Transportation Innovation and Regional Development in 19th Century New York: The Case of the Erie Canal," in Joel Tarr, ed., *Retrospective Technology Assessment, 1976* (San Francisco, 1977), pp. 75–86.

13. Sylvester Graham, *Treatise on Bread and Breadmaking* (Boston, 1837).

14. Taylor, *Transportation Revolution* [12], p. 161.

15. Computed from the annual wholesale prices given in *Historical Statistics of the United States* (Washington, 1960), series E102, p. 124.

16. Storck and Teague, *Flour for Man's Bread* [9], pp. 194–95.

17. Data taken from the *Census of Manufactures of 1860* as cited in Taylor, *Transportation Revolution* [12], pp. 243–44.

18. Werner L. Janney and Asa Moore Janney, eds., *John Jay Janney's Virginia, An American Farm Lad's Life in the Early 19th Century* [1812–1907] (McLean, Va., 1978), p. 35. My thanks to Alice Ross for this citation.

19. Fanny Kellogg, ed., *Tryphena Ely White's Journal, 1805* (New York, 1904), entry for Tuesday, 20 July.

20. Verna Mae Slone, *What My Heart Wants to Tell* (Washington, D.C., 1979), pp. 4 and 14. Although Slone describes techniques used in Appalachia in the early twentieth century, I have used her description here because nothing quite as graphic is extant from the nineteenth century, and the process seems to have survived, intact, in Appalachia. For a nineteenth-century account, see Sarah Brewer-Bonebright, *Reminiscences of New Caste, Iowa, 1848* (Des Moines, Iowa, 1921), pp. 170–72.

21. Phoebe Goodell Judson, *A Pioneer's Search for an Ideal Home: A Book of Personal Memoirs* (Tacoma, Wash., 1966). The quote is taken from Judson's account, written around 1920, of how she made the bread while travelling West in 1853.

22. Elizabeth Buffum Chace and Lucy Buffum Lovell, *Two Quaker Sisters* (New York, 1937). The quote is from the recollections of Elizabeth Buffum Chace, written in the 1880s but not published until 1937.

23. Catherine E. Beecher and Harriet Beecher Stowe, *The American Woman's Home* (New York, 1869), pp. 170–74.

24. Charles Latrobe, *The Rambler in North America* (London, 1835), p.108

25. Susannah Carter, *The Frugal Housewife or Complete Woman Cook* (London and Boston, n.d.), p. 126.

26. The popularity of these cakes is discussed in Meryle Evans, "Whisking Into Cake Heaven," *Food and Wine* (August 1979) 44–48.

27. Beecher, *Treatise on Domestic Economy* [7], chap. 25; Beecher and Stowe, *American Woman's Home* [23], chap. 5.

28. My account of the history of the stove is based upon: Josephine H. Pierce, *Fire on the Hearth: The Evolution and Romance of the Heating Stove* (Springfield, Mass., 1951); Lawrence Wright, *Home Fires Burning, The History of Domestic Heating and Cooking* (London, 1964); Alison Ravetz, "The Victorian Coal Kitchen and its Detractors," *Victorian Studies* 11 (June 1968): 428–45; Eugene Ferguson, "An Historical Sketch of Central Heating" (unpublished paper prepared for the Carpenter's Company, Philadelphia, 1974); Ferguson, "Victorian Heating Systems and Kitchen Equipment" (unpublished paper delivered at the Victorian Society, Philadelphia, 1974); and Giedion, *Mechanization Takes Command* [8], pp. 527–45. The latter work is not as authoritative on this subject as historians have supposed.

29. On Franklin's stove, see "An Account of the New Invented Pennsylvanian Fire-Places" [1744], in Leonard W. Labaree, ed., *The Papers of Benjamin Franklin*, vol. II (New Haven, 1960), pp. 419–46. For Rumford's various stove designs, see "On the Construction of Kitchen Fire-Places and Kitchen Utensils," [1799–1800], in *The Collected Works of Count Rumford*, vol. III (Cambridge, Mass., 1969), pp. 55–384.

30. Albert S. Bolles, *Industrial History of the United States* (Norwich, Conn., 1879), p. 276.

31. Beecher and Stowe, *American Woman's Home* [23], p. 420.

32. John Gregory, *Industrial Resources of Wisconsin* (Milwaukee, 1855), p. 254, as cited in Edgar W. Martin, *The Standard of Living in 1860* (Chicago, 1942), p. 113.

33. Bolles, *Industrial History* [30], p. 276.

34. Edward Everett Hale, *A New England Boyhood* (Boston, 1900), p. 58.

35. This analysis of developments in the iron industry in the nineteenth century is based upon Peter Temin, *Iron and Steel in Nineteenth Century America* (Cambridge, Mass., 1964); as well as on scattered material in J. Leander Bishop, *A History of American Manufactures*, 3rd ed. [1868] (New York, 1966).

36. On Mott, see Bishop, *History of American Manufactures* [35], vol. II, p. 576.

37. Ibid., p. 577.

38. Temin, *Iron and Steel* [35], pp. 38–39.

39. Hagner Family Papers, Queensborough Public Library, Jamaica, New York; and Manuscripts Division, New York Public Library, respectively. Figures for wages and prices come from Taylor, *Transportation Revolution* [12], chap. 13.

40. On marketing strategies of stovemakers, see Bolles, *Industrial History* [30], pp. 277–78.

41. Diary of Mary Bennett, entry for 20 January 1868, Cornell University Archives, Regional History Collection. For a lengthy description of the trials of stove maintenance, see Juliet Corson, *Cooking School Textbook* (Boston, 1863), pp. 17–20.

42. The general improvement in American diets in the nineteenth century is discussed in Richard Cummings, *The American and His Food: A History of Food Habits in the United States* (Chicago, 1940), chapters 4–7.

43. Letter from Ellen Birdseye Wheaton to Charlotte Amelia Birdseye, 21 April 1850, in Donald Gordon, ed.,. *The Diary of Ellen Birdseye Wheaton* (Boston, 1923), p. 14.

Chapter 4. Twentieth-Century Changes in Household Technology

1. For examples of this conventional wisdom in sociology texts, see, for example, Ernest W. Burgess and Harvey J. Locke, *The Family* (New York, 1950); or, Paul B. Horton and Chester L. Hunt, *Sociology* (New York, 1964). For a recent Marxist history of the family that incorporates this same basic set of ideas, see Eli Zaretsky, *Capitalism, The Family, and Personal Life* (New York, 1977).

2. See, for example, Thorstein Veblen, *The Theory of the Leisure Class* (New York, 1899); Simon Patten, *The Reconstruction of Economic Theory* (Philadelphia, 1912); Hazel Kyrk, *A Theory of Consumption* (Boston, 1923); Robert and Helen Lynd, *Middletown: A Study in American Culture* (New York, 1929); and Margaret Gilpin Reid, *Economics of Household Production* (New York, 1934).

3. For criticisms arising from history of technology, see Ruth Schwartz Cowan, "The 'Industrial Revolution' in the Home; Household Technology and Social Change in the 20th Century," *Technology and Culture* 17 (January 1976):1–42; from social history, see Elizabeth H. Pleck, "Two Worlds in One: Work and Family," *Journal of Social History* 10 (1976):179–93. Within sociology itself the model has not gone unassailed: for example, see William J. Goode, *After Divorce* (New York, 1956), especially chap. 1.

4. For data on consumption of flour, see Richard Osborn Cummings, *The American and His Food: A History of Food Habits in the United States* (Chicago, 1940), appendix D. This book is the only general survey of the development of the several branches of the food industry in the United States.

5. The growth of the meat-packing industries is traced in various chapters of Oscar Edward Anderson, Jr., *Refrigeration in America: A History of a New Technology and its Impact* (Princeton, N.J., 1953); and R. A. Clemen, *The American Livestock and Meat Industry* (New York, 1923).

6. Information about the history of the canning industries can be found in Cummings, *The American and His Food* [4], passim; as well as in James H. Collins, *The Story of Canned Foods* (New York, 1924); and Charles Francis, *A History of Food and its Preservation* (Princeton, 1937).

7. Joe B. Frantz, *Gail Borden: Dairyman to a Nation* (Norman, Okla., 1951); Robert C. Alberts, *The Good Provider: H. J. Heinz and His 57 Varieties* (Boston, 1973); Cummings, *The American and His Food* [4], p. 185.

8. The figures come from Cummings, *The American and His Food* [4], p. 186.

9. Although it is not specifically intended to be a history of the trusts, their growth and the impact of federal "busting" activities is described in detail in Victor S. Clark, *A History of Manufactures in the United States* (Washington, D.C., 1929), especially the chapters devoted to each industry in volumes II and III.

10. *Historical Statistics of the United States* (Washington, 1960), series P216, p. 419.

11. This account is based on Claudia Kidwell and Margaret C. Christman, *Suiting Everyone: The Democratization of Clothing in America* (Washington, D.C., 1974).

12. The economist was Albert Bolles, *The Industrial History of the United States* (Norwich, Conn., 1879), p. 291. On the sale of clothing by mail-order companies, see Kidwell and Christman, *Suiting Everyone* [11], pp. 155–64.

13. Data from Jesse E. Pope, *The Clothing Industry in New York*, University of Missouri, Social Science Studies, no. 1 (Columbia, Mo., 1905), p. 10.

14. Kidwell and Christman, *Suiting Everyone* [11], pp. 108–10.

15. Analysis of the Sears Roebuck Catalogue, as well as other historical judgments in this paragraph, are based upon Kidwell and Christman, *Suiting Everyone* [11], especially pp. 135–51.

16. For example, Lydia Maria Child, *The American Frugal Housewife* (Boston, 1836), passim; or Catharine E. Beecher, *A Treatise on Domestic Economy* (Boston, 1841), especially chaps. 6, 7, 21, and 22.

17. On the development of the patent medicine industry, see James Harvey Young, *American Self-Dosage Medicines: An Historical Perspective* (Lawrence, Kan., 1974).

18. Fannie Merritt Farmer, *The Boston Cooking School Cookbook* (Boston, 1896).

19. Data from Richard Harrison Shyrock, "Nursing Emerges as a Profession: The American Experience," in Judith Walzer Leavitt and Ronald Numbers, eds., *Sickness and Health in America* (Madison, Wis., 1978), pp. 207–8.

20. This brief historical account is based upon Vern Bullough and Bonnie Bullough, *The Care of the Sick: The Emergence of Modern Nursing* (New York, 1978). Data on hospital beds comes from Rosemary Stevens, *American Medicine and the Public Interest* (New Haven, Conn., 1971), p. 145; and *Historical Statistics* [10], series B209–220, p. 35.

21. *Historical Statistics* [10], series D156, p. 75.

22. On the development of hospitals, see Stevens, *American Medicine* [20], pp. 1–74; and Morris Vogel, *The Invention of the Modern Hospital: Boston 1870–1930* (Chicago, 1980).

23. Vogel, *Invention of the Modern Hospital* [22], chaps. 3–6; also, David Rosner, "Business at the Bedside: Health Care in Brooklyn, 1890–1915," in Susan Reverby and David Rosner, eds., *Health Care in America: Essays in Social History* (Philadelphia, 1979), pp. 117–32.

24. *Historical Statistics* [10], series B209–220, p. 35.

25. *Medical Care for the American People,* Final Report of the Committee on the Costs of Medical Care (Chicago, 1932), fig. 1, p. 6.

26. On nineteenth-century patterns of shopping and transportation, see Daniel Boorstin, *The Americans: The Democratic Experience* (New York, 1973), chaps. 9–14.

27. On the development of the department store, see Ralph M. Hower, *History of Macy's of New York, 1859–1919* (New York, 1943); and Hrant Pasdermadjian, *The Department Store: Its Origins, Evolution and Economics* (London, 1954). On the relation of urban transportation development to shopping patterns, see Boorstin, *The Americans* [26], pp. 104–5.

28. On rural mail-order shopping, see Boris Emmet and John E. Jeuck, *Catalogues and Counters: A History of Sears, Roebuck and Company* (Chicago, 1950); and Wayne E. Fuller, *R.F.D., The Changing Face of Rural America* (Bloomington, Ind., 1964).

29. There is no single secondary source from which the judgments made in this paragraph derive; see the Bibliographical Essay for a list of the nineteenth- and twentieth-century diaries, letters and memoirs that led to my conclusions.

30. James J. Flink, *America Adopts the Automobile, 1895–1910* (Cambridge, Mass., 1970); John B. Rae, *The Road and the Car in American Life* (Cambridge, Mass., 1971); and Michael F. Berger, *The Devil Wagon in God's Country: The Automobile and Social Change in Rural America, 1893–1929 (Hamden, Conn., 1979).*

31. *Lynd and Lynd, Middletown* [2], p. 251.

32. On Ford and his impact, see James J. Flink, *The Car Culture* (Cambridge, Mass., 1975), especially chap 4; and Reynold M. Wik, *Henry Ford and Grass Roots America* (Ann Arbor, Mich., 1972).

33. Quoted, without attribution, in Flink, *Car Culture* [32], p. 140.

34. *Historical Statistics* [10], series A242, p. 15; and Q315, p. 462.

35. Lynd and Lynd, *Middletown* [2], pp. 252–54.

36. The poem comes from *Frank Leslie's Illustrated Weekly* in 1907, as cited in Rudolf E. Anderson, *The Story of the American Automobile* (Washington, D.C., 1950), p. 198. The "new girl" is described in Margaret Deland, "The Change in the Feminine Ideal," *Atlantic Monthly* 105 (1910):290–95.

37. Rom Markin, *The Supermarket: An Analysis of Growth, Development and Change* (Pullman, Wash., 1968), chap. 1; and M.M. Zimmerman, *The Supermarket: A Revolution in Distribution* (New York, 1955).

38. Stevens, *American Medicine* [20], p. 145.

39. There is no single history of water-supply systems in the United States, since most authors treat each part of the system separately (sewers and aqueducts, for example, separately from plumbing and bathroom fixtures). My account is based upon Nelson M. Blake, *Water for the Cities: A History of the Urban Water Supply Problem in the United States* (Syracuse, N. Y., 1956); Ellis L. Armstrong, et al., eds., *History of Public Works in the United States, 1776–1976* (Chicago, 1976), chaps. 8 and 12; Morris M. Cohen, *Sewers for a Growing America* (Amber, Pa., 1966); Lawrence Wright, *Clean and Decent: The Fascinating History of the Bathroom and the Water Closet* (New York, 1960); Elizabeth Mickle Bacon, "The Growth of Household Conveniences in the United States, 1860–1900" (unpublished dissertation, Radcliffe College, 1942), passim; Siegfried Giedion, *Mechanization Takes Command* (New York, 1948), part VII; Clark, *History of Manufactures* [9], various chapters in volumes II and III which consider "sanitary pottery" and "pipes and tubes"; *Historical Statistics* [10], series D327, p. 76.

40. For a description of this bathroom, see, for example, Helen M. Sprackling, "The Modern Bathroom," *Parent's Magazine* (February 1933): 25.

41. On patterns of diffusion of water supply and plumbing facilities, see Lynd and Lynd, *Middletown* [2], especially p. 97; Robert and Helen Lynd, *Middletown in Transition* (New York, 1937), pp. 557–58; Leila Houghteling, *The Income and Standard of Living of Unskilled Laborers in Chicago* (Chicago, 1927), especially p. 109; R. O. Eastman, Inc., *Zanesville, Ohio and Thirty-Six Other American Cities* (New York, 1927), passim; United States Department of Agriculture, *Farm Housing Survey* (Washington, D.C., 1934), passim. For postwar developments, see successive censuses of housing after 1940.

42. A partial view of the extent to which personal cleanliness, personal health, and

public health were linked can be derived from George Rosen, *Preventive Medicine in the United States, 1900–1975* (New York, 1975).

43. On the history of the manufactured and natural gas industries, see Louis Stotz and Alexander Jamison, *History of the Gas Industry* (New York, 1938); Harold Williamson and Arnold R. Daum, *The American Petroleum Industry: The Age of Illumination, 1859–1899* (Evanston, Ill., 1959), chap. 1; and Frederick Collins, *Consolidated Gas Company of New York: A History* (New York, 1934).

44. On the period in which the gas, electric, and petroleum industries competed against each other for lighting and heating business, see Williamson and Daum, *American Petroleum Industry* [43], chaps. 13, 20, and 25.

45. Harold F. Williamson, et al., *The American Petroleum Industry, 1899–1959: The Age of Energy* (Evanston, Ill., 1963), p. 39.

46. Jane Busch, "Cooking Competition: Technology on the Domestic Market,in the 1930s," *Technology and Culture* 24 (April 1983): 222–44.

47. "Our Market for Ranges—and Our Competition," *Electrical Merchandising* 43 (May 1930): 38.

48. This account of the development of the electric generating and manufacturing businesses is based on Harold Sharlin, *The Making of the Electrical Age* (New York, 1963); Harold C. Passer, *The Electrical Manufacturers, 1875–1900* (Cambridge, Mass., 1953); and T. C. Martin, *The Story of Electricity* (New York, 1922); and Thomas P. Hughes, "The Electrification of America: The System Builders, *Technology and Culture*, 20 (January 1979): 124–61.

49. On standardization and its effect on the price of electricity, see Passer, *Electrical Manufacturers* [48], pp. 276–348; and Frank Joseph Kottke, *Electrical Technology and the Public Interest* (Washington, D.C., 1944).

50. *Historical Statistics* [10], series S71, p. 510.

51. There is no adequate and accurate history of domestic applicances. The sources of information for the preceeding paragraph are listed in the Bibliographic Essays.

52. "Prices, and Cost and Standards of Living," *Monthly Labor Review* 61 (December 1945): 1220–21.

53. Williamson and Daum, *American Petroleum Industry* [43], and Williamson, et al., *American Petroleum Industry* [45], are the basic sources for the discussion that follows.

54. On the history of central heating devices, see Bacon, "Growth of Household Conveniences" [39], passim; Eugene Ferguson, "Victorian Heating Systems and Kitchen Equipment" (unpublished paper, delivered before the Victorian Society, Philadelphia, 1974); Eugene Ferguson, "An Historical Sketch of Central Heating, 1800–1860" (unpublished paper, Carpenters Company, Philadelphia, 1974); Williamson, et al., *American Petroleum Industry* [45], pp. 265 and 293; and Lawrence Wright, *Home Fires Burning: The History of Domestic Heating and Cooking* (London, 1964). For the twentieth century, the best sources of information are trade journals; for a list of these, see the Bibliographic Essays.

55. Lynd and Lynd, *Middletown* [2], p. 96.

56. Lynd and Lynd, *Middletown in Transition* [41], p. 563.

57. On the numerical preponderance of laundresses among household servants, see David M. Katzman, *Seven Days a Week: Women and Domestic Service in Industrializing America* (New York, 1978), pp. 46–47.

58. On the growth of commercial laundries in the twentieth century, see Heidi I. Hartmann, "Capitalism and Women's Work in the Home, 1900–1930" (unpublished Ph.D. dissertation, Yale University, 1974), chap. 6; and Fred DeArmond, *The Laundry Industry* (New York, 1950); see also chapter 5 in this book.

59. For documentation of the increased time spent in laundry work and of quantity of laundry done, see Maud Wilson, "Laundry Time Costs," *Journal of Home Economics* 25 (1930): 735–38; and Amy Hewes, "Electrical Appliances in the Home, *Social Forces* 2 (December 1930): 235–42.

60. These are my figures, computed from *Historical Statistics* [10], series A255 ("number of households"), p. 16, and series D84 ("private household workers"), p. 74.

Chapter 5. The Roads Not Taken: Alternative Social and Technical Approaches to Housework

1. Laurel Thatcher Ulrich, *Goodwives: Image and Reality in the Lives of Women in Northern New England, 1680–1780* (New York, 1982), has described the ways in which women took advantage of the existence of these craftsmen to improve their standard of living in the colonial period (pp. 24–30, 68–86).

2. Dolores Hayden, *The Grand Domestic Revolution: A History of Feminist Designs for American Homes, Neighborhoods, and Cities* (Cambridge, Mass., 1981), chap. 10 and appendix table A1.

3. Ibid., p. 206.

4. Ibid., p. 220.

5. On the history of commercial laundries, see Fred DeArmond, *The Laundry Industry* (New York, 1950); Heidi Irmgard Hartmann, "Capitalism and Women's Work in the Home, 1900–1930," (unpublished Ph.D. dissertation, Yale University, 1974), chap. 6; Jacob Swisher, "The Evolution of Washday," *Iowa Journal of History and Politics* 38 (1940): 3–49; and Siegfried Giedion, *Mechanization Takes Command* (New York, 1948), pp. 558–68.

6. Giedion, *Mechanization Takes Command* [5], p. 562.

7. Hartmann, "Capitalism and Women's Work" [5], table 19, p. 287.

8. Edna L. Clark, "Who Does the Laundry?" *Starchroom Laundry Journal* 35 (15 October 1928): 100–102; Mabel Harte and Geraldine Gorton, "What Shall We Teach Regarding Clothing and Laundry Problems?" *Journal of Home Economics* 18, (March 1926): 132–33.

9. Catherine Beecher and Harriet Beecher Stowe, *The American Woman's Home* (New York, 1869), p. 334.

10. Christine Frederick, *Household Engineering* (Chicago, 1950), p. 146.

11. Hartman, "Capitalism and Women's Work" [5], chap. 6; DeArmond, *Laundry Industry* [5], pp. 210–12.

12. Robert and Helen Lynd, *Middletown: A Study in American Culture* (New York, 1929), pp. 174–75.

13. The widespread phenomenon of middle-class boarding in the nineteenth century is discussed in Susan Strasser, *Never Done: A History of American Housework* (New York, 1982), chap. 8. On apartment hotels, see Hayden, *Grand Domestic Revolution* [2], pp. 72–77, 195–205.

14. Hayden, *Grand Domestic Revolution* [2], pp. 72–73.

15. "Over the Drafting Board: Opinions Official and Unofficial," *Architectural Record* 73 (January 1903): 89.

16. *Kansas City Star* (11 April 1919), p. 23; this item was generously supplied to the author by Professor Mark Rose.

17. "Over the Drafting Board" [15]," p. 89. See also the set of articles under the general title "Is Housekeeping a Failure?" in *North American Review* (February 1889).

18. Charlotte Perkins Gilman, "Why Cooperative Housekeeping Fails," *Harper's Bazaar* 41 (July 1907): 629.

19. See Giedion, *Mechanization Takes Command* [5], pp. 586–87.

20. This was true in the past as well as in the present. See Hartmann, "Capitalism and Women's Work" [5], p. 319, quoting E. H. Roberts, *The Efficiency of the Home Laundering Plant,* Agricultural Extension Paper Bulletin 248 (Agricultural Experiment Station, Pullman, Wash., 1931), and recalculating from Mrs. Ralph Borsodi, "Women and Machines," *Advertising and Selling* 16 (12 November 1930): 23, (26 November 1930): 22, (10 December 1930): 30. The same point is made in DeArmond, *Laundry Industry* [5], pp. 217–18, quoting a study by Anne Aiken, New York State College of Home Economics, Cornell University.

21. For information on these sects, see Arthur Bestor, *Backwoods Utopias* (Philadelphia, 1950); Charles Nordhoff, *The Communistic Societies of the United States* [1875] (New York, 1966); Dolores Hayden, *Seven American Utopias: The Architecture of Communitarian Socialism, 1790–1975* (Cambridge, Mass., 1976); and Dorothy W. Douglas and Katharine Du Pre Lumpkin, "Communistic Settlements," *Encyclopedia of the Social Sciences,* vol. IV (New York, 1931), pp. 95–102.

22. Nordhoff, *Communistic Societies* [21], p. 401.

23. From *The Phalanx* 1 (8 February 1844): 317–19.

24. The story of Melusina Fay Pierce is told in Hayden, *Grand Domestic Revolution* [2], chap. 4. See also Melusina Fay Pierce, *Cooperative Housekeeping: How Not to Do It and How to Do It, a Study in Sociology* (Boston, 1884).

25. Hayden, *Grand Domestic Revolution* [2], appendix tables A1 and A2.

26. Mary L. Bull, "The Chatfield Laundry after Six Years," *Journal of Home Economics* 11 (1919): 222–24.

27. Benjamin Andrews, *Economics of the Household: Its Administration and Finance*, rev. ed. (New York, 1938), p. 487.

28. Hayden, *Grand Domestic Revolution* [2], pp. 217–19.

29. For more about these charitable enterprises, see Andrews, *Economics of the Household* [27], pp. 333–35; Charlotte Sulley, "A Cooperative Kitchen That Is Meeting a Need in Its Community," *Journal of Home Economics* 7 (1915): 373–75; "Two Cooperative Ventures," *Journal of Home Economics* 8 (1916): 554; Ruth Van Deeman, "A Cooperative Laundry in Greenwich Village," *Journal of Home Economics* 15 (1923): 252–54; and I. L. Peters, *Agencies for the Sale of Cooked Food without a Profit*, (Washington, D.C., 1919).

30. Hayden, *Grand Domestic Revolution* [2], pp. 167–70.

31. Caroline Hunt, *The Life of Ellen Swallow Richards* (Boston, 1912), pp. 220–25.

32. Editorial, *Ladies' Home Journal* (May 1918), p. 30.

33. On the early history of domestic service in the United States, see Lucy Maynard Salmon, *Domestic Service* (New York, 1897).

34. Joseph A. Hill, *Women in Gainful Occupations, 1870–1920*, Census Monograph IX (Washington, D.C., 1929), pp. 3–4, 35–36.

35. David A. Katzman, *Seven Days a Week: Domestic Service in Industrializing America, 1870 to 1920* (New York, 1980), chap. 2.

36. Ibid., Table 2.6, p. 61.

37. Quoted in Salmon, *Domestic Service* [33], p. 35.

38. On runaway servants, see Edmond S. Morgan, *American Slavery, American Freedom* (New York, 1975), pp. 216–18.

39. Frances Trollope, *Domestic Manners of the Americans* [1832], Donald Smalley, ed. (New York, 1949), p. 52.

40. Orra Langhorne, "Domestic Science in the South," *Journal of Social Science* 34 (November 1901): 170.

41. Lynd and Lynd, *Middletown* [12], p. 170.

42. For a summary of these arguments, see Katzman, *Seven Days a Week* [35], pp. 229–32.

43. See, for example, Antoinette B. Hervey, "The Saints in My Kitchen," *Outlook* 100 (17 February 1912): 367.

44. See, for example, Helen Campbell, *Prisoners of Poverty: Women Wage Workers, Their Trades and Their Lives* (Boston, 1887); or *First Report of the Commission on Household Employment of the YWCA* (Los Angeles, 1915). For Trollope, *Domestic Manners* [39], p. 52.

45. As quoted in Salmon, *Domestic Service* [33], pp. 149–50.

46. On this kind of complaint from servants, see Katzman, *Seven Days a Week* [35], pp. 236–49.

47. Annual Report, Maine Bureau of Industrial and Labor Statistics (Augusta, 1910) as quoted in Katzman, *Seven Days a Week* [35], p. 242.

48. Frances A. Kellor, *Out of Work: A Study of Employment Agencies* (New York, 1904), p. 10.

49. Lillian Pettengill, *Toilers of the Home, A Record of a College Woman's Experience as a Domestic Servant* (New York, 1903), pp. 241–42.

50. U.S. Senate, *Reports of the Immigration Commission, Occupations of the First and Second Generations of Immigrants in the United States* (Washington, D.C., 1911), as cited in Katzman, *Seven Days a Week* [35], p. 70.

51. Quoted in Helen Cambell, "Why Is There Objection to Domestic Service?," *Good Housekeeping* 11 (27 September 1890): 255.

52. The account that follows is based upon Oscar Edward Anderson, Jr., *Refrigeration in America: A History of a New Technology and Its Impact* (Princeton, N.J., 1953).

53. These figures come from U.S. Census Bureau data as quoted in Anderson, *Refrigeration* [52], pp. 114–15.

54. See "Arnold H. Goss Ends His Life," *Electric Refrigeration News* 25 (26 October 1938): 1, 2, 11. In addition to this article, my account of the origin of the Kelvinator is based on Anderson, *Refrigeration* [52], p. 195; obituary of Nathaniel B. Wales, *New York Times* (18 November 1974); J. W. Beckman, "Copeland Tells Story of Household Refrigeration Development," *Air Conditioning, Heating and Refrigeration News* 6 (6 July 1932): 9–11; and Giedion, *Mechanization Takes Command* [5], p. 602.

55. Beckman, "Copeland Tells Story" [54].

56. Stevenson's report, "Domestic Refrigerating Machines," can be found, in its original typewritten form, in the Technical Data Library, General Electric Company, Schenectady, N. Y., Data File 1120. The original report was dated 17 August 1923, but many appendices were added in the ensuing five years, making a document that runs to several hundred pages. I was given access to it originally and will quote from it (citing it as *DRM–GE*) through the kindness of Dr. George Wise, Corporate Research and Development, General Electric Company, Schenectady. The pagination in various sections of the report is not sequential. The complete list of companies and the report on their products is *DRM–GE*, vol. III.

57. *Electric Domestic Refrigeration, 1924*, a report of the Electric Domestic Refrigeration Committee, National Electric Light Association (New York, 1924), p. 2, table I.

58. Letter, Francis C. Pratt to Gerard Swope, 17 August 1923, *DRM–GE* [56], p. 4.

59. Anderson, *Refrigeration* [52], chap. 11; "Electrolux Inventors Receive Franklin Award," *Gas Age* 70 (2 July 1932); "Industry Pioneer Number," *Air Conditioning, Heating and Refrigeration News* 19 (7 October 1936), passim.

60. See *Electric Domestic Refrigeration, 1924* [57], p. 2; and *The Facts About Gas Refrigeration Today*, American Gas Association (New York, 1933).

61. There is no scholarly history of General Electric; the best of the popular accounts is John Winthrop Hammond, *Men and Volts, The Story of General Electric* (Philadelphia, 1941), the copyright on which was held by G.E. See also David G. Loth, *Swope of G.E.* (New York, 1958). On the history of G.E.'s refrigerator, see *DRM–GE* [56], Report 2, General Survey, Historical Introduction, pp. 1–2; and Report 1, Summary and Conclusions, Audiffren, pp. 16–19, and appendices 21 and 22.

62. See Loth, *Swope* [61], pp. 116–18; and letter from Pratt to Swope, 17 August 1923, *DRM–GE* [56].

63. *DRM–GE, [56]*, Report 1, Summary and Conclusions, Reasons for Exploitation, p. 24.

64. *DRM–GE* [56], Report 1, Summary and Conclusions, Reasons for Exploitation, p. 17.

65. "Outline History of the General Electric Household Refrigerator," (typescript, Public Relations Dept. G.E., Schenectady, N. Y., 1970); "G.E. Announces New Refrigerator," *G.E. Monogram* (October 1925): 22; Ralph Roeder, "General Electric Refrigerators" (typescript, Public Relations Dept., G.E., Schenectady N.Y., n.d.); and T.K. Quinn, *Giant Business, Threat to Democracy, The Autobiography of an Insider* (New York, 1956), chap. 8. Quinn was in charge of the refrigerator division of G.E. during the late 1920s and the early 1930s.

66. "Door of All-Steel G.E. Refrigerator Slammed Shut 300,000 Times but Remains in Excellent Condition," *G.E. Monogram* (April 1929): 25. *G.E. Monogram*, was an in-house magazine for G.E. employees.

67. "June Bride Animated Display," *On the Top* 9 (June 1935): 23. *On the Top* was a newsmagazine of G.E.'s Specialty Appliance Department.

68. Both quotations are from "Three Women a Smash Hit," *On the Top* 9 (June 1935): 7.

69. For a summary of the refrigerators that were available in the late 1930s and their relative advantages and disadvantages, see John F. Wostrel and John G. Praetz, *Household Electric Refrigeration, Including Gas Absorption Systems* (New York, 1938). For the relative market share of each manufacturer, see Frank Joseph Kottke, *Electrical Technology and the Public Interest* (Washington, D.C., 1944), pp. 168–70.

70. *Sixteenth Census of the United States, Housing, 1940*, vol. II, *General Characteristics*, part I, *United States Summary* (Washington, D.C., 1943), p. 2.

71. *DRM–GE* [56], vol. III, appendices.

72. Ibid., especially appendices on "Common Sense" and "Kelvinator."

73. H. B. Hull, *Household Refrigeration,* 3rd ed. (Chicago, 1927), p. 321.

74. *DRM–GE* [56], vol. III, appendix on "Common Sense.

75. "Survey of Gas Refrigerators." *American Gas Journal* (2 April 1927), pp. 329–34.

76. This and subsequent summaries of the early history of Servel are based upon the following articles in the *New York Times:* 11 August 1925 (26:4); 22 December 1925 (28:2); 23 January 1926 (23:1); 17 March 1926 (32:2); 18 March 1926 (34:2); 15 October 1926 (34:2); 5 August 1927 (23:6); 3 January 1928 (36:2); 5 May 1928 (3:1); and 15 October 1929 (48:5); as well as upon the entries for Servel in *Moody's Manual of Investments* for 1928 and 1940.

77. The discussion that follows is based upon material in the *Stuart Otto Papers* (hereafter cited as SOP), Department of Manuscripts and University Archives, Cornell University (no. 2389; especially the typewritten documents, "Household Refrigeration by Gas," 26 June 1957 and "Memorandum *re* Gas Refrigeration Corporation," 19 June 1940.

78. Advertisers proof copy, *Gas-Age Record* [16 May 1925], *SOP* [77].

79. "Household Refrigeration by Gas," pp. 1–2, *SOP* [77].

80. Ibid., p. 2.

81. The judgments made in this paragraph are based upon statements made by Stuart Otto to various correspondents; see, for example, "Report to United American Bosch Co., Spring, 1934," typescript, *SOP* [77]. *The Facts About Gas Refrigeration Today* American Gas Association (New York, 1933), will give the reader some sense of the reluctance of gas utility companies to become actively involved in selling gas refrigerators.

82. On estimates of the sales of Servel, see H. B. Hull, *Household Refrigeration,* 4th ed. (Chicago, 1933); and Don Wright, "Gray Sees Bright Future for Gas Refrigerator," *Gas Age* 34 (March 1958): 84; and "When Everybody Loves a Competitor," *Business Week* (25 November 1950), p. 72.

83. On some of the different forms of washing machine, see Giedion, *Mechanization Takes Command* [5], pp. 562–70; as well as Edna B Snyder, *A Study of Washing Machines,* University of Nebraska, Agricultural Experiment Station Research Bulletin 56 (Lincoln, 1931). On the tactics of the Maytag Corporation, see U.S. Federal Trade Commission, "Kitchen Furnishings and Domestic Appliances," vol. III of the *Report on the House Furnishings Industry* (Washington, 1925); and "U.S. Supreme Court Hears Patent Suit Arguments," *New York Times,* 20 April 1939 (25:3).

84. On the advantages of the central vacuum cleaner over the portable forms, see M. S. Cooley, *Vacuum Cleaning Systems* (New York, 1913), chap. 1. On the sales techniques of the portable vacuum cleaner manufacturers, see Frank G. Hoover, *Fabulous Dustpan: The Story of the Hoover Company* (New York, 1955); and Earl Lifshey, *The Housewares Story: A History of the American Housewares Industry* (Chicago, 1973), chap. 8.

85. The information in this sentence is derived from promotional material distributed by each of the companies mentioned; I am grateful to Richard Grant for helping me acquire these materials. See also Lifshey, *Housewares Story* [84], passim.

86. On Durant, see Mel Gustin, *Wild Billy: William C. Durant, Founder of General Motors* (Detroit, 1963), p. 187. On Landers, Frary and Clark, "A History of Landers, Frary & Clark" (typescript) in *Dean S. Paden Collection* (no. 281), Baker Library, Harvard University. On Westinghouse, see "Westinghouse Electric," *Fortune* (February 1938), p. 45. On Maytag, see Jacob Swisher, "The Evolution of Washday," *Iowa Journal of History and Politics* 38 (1940):39.

87. My thanks to Riva Berleant-Schiller for suggesting the relevance of this rule in this context.

88. Dolores Hayden takes this position in *The Grand Domestic Revolution* [2], chap. 14; so does Eli Zaretsky, *Capitalism, The Family and Personal Life* (New York, 1976); and Strasser, *Never Done* [13].

89. Lois Banner, *Elizabeth Cady Stanton: A Radical for Women's Rights* (Boston, 1980), chap. 3.

90. *Anna Kelton Wiley Papers,* Library of Congress.

Chapter 6. Household Technology and Household Work between
1900 and 1940

1. John B. Leeds, *The Household Budget: With a Special Inquiry into the Amount and Value of Household Work* (Ph. D. dissertation, Columbia University, 1917, privately printed); the quoted material is on p. 35.
2. *Household Account Book of L. R. Dodge (1889–1946)*, Manuscripts Collection, Baker Library, Harvard University (no. 1262). I am grateful to David Schmitz for the superb work that he did in analyzing for me the contents of this account book.
3. Leeds, *Household Budget* [1], p. 36.
4. *Dodge Account Book* [2] (1910); Leeds, *Household Budget* [1], pp. 36, 137.
5. Leeds, *Household Budget* [1], p. 135; *Dodge Account Book* [2] (1905, 1915).
6. *Dodge Account Book* [2] (1934).
7. Information about the Dodge's expenditures can be found in the *Dodge Account Book* under the appropriate years. The questionnaire used by Leeds is on pp. 215–26 of *Household Budget* [1]; on central heating see p. 61; on gas and electricity pp. 39 and 81; the quotation about washing practices is on p. 80.
8. The quote comes from *Household Budget* [1] p. 35; information about the employment of household servants is in chap. 3.
9. For the amounts that the Dodges paid for laundry and for seasonal assistance, see *Dodge Account Book* [2], passim. For information about allocation of laundry and cleaning chores, see *Household Budget* [1], chap. 3.
10. Marion Woodbury, "Time Required for Housework in a Family of Five With Small Children," *Journal of Home Economics* 10 (1918):226–30.
11. Claudia Bushman, *A Good Poor Man's Wife: Being a Chronicle of Harriet Hanson Robinson and Her Family in Nineteenth Century New England* (Hanover, N.H., 1981) p. 112.
12. Leeds, *Household Budget* [1], p. 54.
13. Christine Frederick, *The New Housekeeping: Efficiency Studies in Home Management* (Garden City, N.Y., 1913), p. 86.
14. Rebecca Gradwohl, "Teamwork in the Family," *Journal of Home Economics* 14 (1922): 494.
15. *The Ladies' Home Journal* (January 1918), p. 26.
16. Leeds, *Household Budget* [1], p. 68; Woodbury, "Time Required for Housework," [10] p. 230.
17. For a summary of the literature on this issue, see James T. Patterson, *America's Struggle Against Poverty, 1900–1980* (Cambridge, Mass., 1981), chap. 1.
18. On higher birthrates among the urban and the rural poor at this time, see Warren S. Thompson and P. K. Whelpton, "The Population of the Nation," in *Recent Social Trends in the United States,* Report of the President's Research Committee on Social Trends (New York, 1935), pp. 40–46. On the frequent presence of boarders in the homes of the urban poor, see Laurence A. Glasco, "The Life Cycles and Household Structures of American Ethnic Groups," *Journal of Urban History* 1 (May 1975): 339–64; and John Modell and Tamara Hareven, "Urbanization and the Malleable Household: An Examination of Boarding and Lodging in American Families," *Journal of Marriage and the Family* 35 (1973):470–95.
19. Mabel Hyde Kittridge, "The Needs of the Immigrant," *Journal of Home Economics* 5 (1913):308.
20. Margaret F. Byington, *Homestead: The Households of a Mill Town* (New York, 1910), p. 53; Robert Coit Chapin, *The Standard of Living Among Workingmen's Families in New York City* (New York, 1909), p. 102.
21. Bruno Lasker, "Fagots and Furnaces," *Survey* 40 (June, 1918):368–69.

22. Louise Bolard More, *Wage-Earners' Budgets: A Study of Standards and Cost of Living in New York City* (New York, 1907), pp. 208–9.

23. Byington, *Homestead* [20], p. 87.

24. Annie L. Hansen, "Two Years as a Domestic Educator in Buffalo, New York," *Journal of Home Economics* 5 (1913):435.

25. Leeds, *Household Budget* [1], p. 57.

26. For national statistics, see Joseph A. Hill, *Women in Gainful Occupations, 1870–1920*, U.S. Bureau of the Census, Monograph 9 (Washington, D.C., 1929), pp. 75–76. For Fall River, see Mark Aldrich, "Determinants of Mortality among New England Cotton Mill Workers during the Progressive Era, *Journal of Economic History* 42 (December 1982):861. For Passaic, see *The Family Status of Breadwinning Women*, Bulletin 23 of the Women's Bureau, U.S. Department of Labor (Washington D.C., 1922), p. 1.

27. *Family Status of Breadwinning Women* [26], p. 43.

28. Aldrich, "Determinants of Mortality" [26], p. 861.

29. E. G. Stern, *My Mother and I* (New York, 1917), p. 110.

30. Thomas Bell, *Out of this Furnace* [1941] (Pittsburgh, 1976), pp. 135–37.

31. Robert S. Lynd and Helen Merrell Lynd, *Middletown: A Study in American Culture* (New York, 1929), p. 27.

32. R. O. Eastman, Inc., *Zanesville, Ohio and Thirty-Six Other American Communities* (New York, 1927), pp. 69–71.

33. For national statistics, see *Historical Statistics of the United States, From Colonial Times to 1957* (Washington, 1960), series A242, p. 15; series Q315, p. 462. For Muncie, Lynd and Lynd, *Middletown* [31] p. 253.

34. Robert S. Lynd and Helen Merrell Lynd, *Middletown in Transition: A Study in Cultural Conflicts* (New York, 1937), p. 559. The data came from the F.E.R.A. Real Property Inventory of Muncie.

35. Amy Hewes, "Electrical Appliances in the Home, *Social Forces* 2 (December 1930): 235–242.

36. Lynd and Lynd, *Middletown* [31], pp. 169–70.

37. Ibid., pp. 86–87.

38. *Time Costs of Homemaking, A Study of 1,500 Rural and Urban Households*, U.S. Department of Agriculture, Agricultural Research Administration, Bureau of Human Nutrition and Home Economics, (mimeographed, 1944), pp. 6–7. *Household Management and Kitchens*, Reports of the President's Conference on Home Building and Home Ownership, vol. IX (Washington, D.C., 1932), pp. 5, 75.

39. *Historical Statistics* [33], Series D457–463, p. 74.

40. Anne O'Hare McCormack, "The World in Nineteen Thirty Three," *Ladies' Home Journal* (January 1933), p. 12.

41. Margaret Culken Banning, "Love Flies Out of the Kitchen," *Ladies' Home Journal* (January 1933), p. 43.

42. The LaFrance advertisement appeared in the *Ladies' Home Journal* (February 1933), p. 52.

43. J. R. Bohner, quoted in *Electrical Merchandising* 48 (July 1932):36.

44. Paraphrased from an article, "Managing Our Children in Wartime," *Ladies' Home Journal* (February 1918), p. 49.

45. For documentation of these points and for illustrations of the change that occurred in the visual material in advertisements, see Ruth Schwartz Cowan, "Two Washes in the Morning and a Bridge Party at Night: The American Housewife Between the Wars," *Women's Studies* 3 (1976):147–72, and "The 'Industrial Revolution' in the Home: Household Technology and Social Change in the 20th Century," *Technology and Culture* 17 (1976):1–23

46. "Meals for April," *American Home* (April 1931), p. 66.

47. The time studies of the 1920s were summarized in *Household Management and Kitchens*, [38], chap. 1. The time-study literature has recently been reanalyzed in Joann Vanek, "Keeping Busy: Time Spent in Housework, United States, 1920–1970" (Ph.D. dissertation, University of Michigan, 1973), and "Time Spent in Housework," *Scientific American* 231 (November 1974):116–25.

48. The first study referred to is *Time Costs of Homemaking* [38]. For Leeds and Wood-

bury, see Leeds, Household Budget [1], p. 68; and Woodbury, "Time Required for Housework" [10], p. 230.

49. Data for 1915, 1925, and 1935 are from *Historical Statistics* [33], series B107, p. 25; for 1980, see *Statistical Abstracts of the United States*, 1981 (Washington, D.C. 1981), p. 73.

50. Remarks made by various housewives of the "business class," as quoted in Lynd and Lynd, *Middletown* [31], pp. 146–47.

51. This point about changing child-care practices in the years between the wars has been made in Geoffrey H. Steere, "Child Rearing Literature and Modernization Theory," *Family in History Newsletter* 7 (1974):8–12; and Martha Wolfenstein, "Fun Morality: An Analysis of Recent Childtraining Literature," in Margaret Mead and Martha Wolfenstein, eds., *Childhood in Contemporary Cultures* (Chicago, 1955), pp. 168–77.

52. The relative stability of prosperous households during the Depression was pointed out by Winona Morgan, *The Family Meets the Depression* (Minneapolis, 1939), a sociological study of 331 such families.

53. Emily Post, *Etiquette: The Blue Book of Social Usage*, 5th ed., revised (New York, 1937), p. 823.

54. Lynd and Lynd, Middletown [31], p. 84.

55. *Zanesville and Thirty-Six Other American Communities* [32], p. 91.

56. For 1929 data, Maurice Leven, Harold G. Moulton, and Clark Warburton, *America's Capacity to Consume* (Washington, D.C., 1934), p. 54. For the impact of the Depression, see National Resources Committee, *Consumer Incomes in the United States: Their Distribution in 1935–36* (Washington, D.C., 1938).

57. Lynd and Lynd, *Middletown* [31], p. 27.

58. *Zanesville and Thirty-Six Other American Cities* [32], p. 52.

59. Ibid., pp. 43, 55, and 91.

60. The data and interpretations in this paragraph are taken from George Rosen, *Preventive Medicine in the United States, 1900–1975* (New York, 1975), passim.

61. Lynd and Lynd, *Middletown* [31], p. 123, and appendix table X, p. 520.

62. On the 1920s, see Thompson and Whelpton, "Population of the Nation" [18]. On the 1930s, see Dorothy Dunbar Bromley, "Birth Control and the Depression," *Harper's* 69 (October 1934):563–68. Also, Irene B. Taueber and H. T. Eldridge, "Some Demographic Aspects of the Changing Role of Women," *Annals of American Academy of Political and Social Science* 251 (1947):24–34.

63. *Zanesville and Thirty Six Other American Cities* [32], pp. 68–69.

64. Martha Hagood, *Mothers of the South: Portraiture of the White Tenant Farm Woman* (Chapel Hill, North Carolina, 1939), p. 99. The national data comes from *Historical Statistics* [33], series S70–80, p. 510.

65. James West, *Plainville, U.S.A.* (New York, 1945), p. 31.

66. *Farm Housing Survey*, U.S. Department of Agriculture (Washington, D.C., 1934), passim.

67. Lynd and Lynd, *Middletown* [31], pp. 174–75.

68. On repossession and its impact during the Depression, see Winifred D. Wandersee, *Women's Work and Family Values, 1920–1940* (Cambridge, Mass., 1981), chap. 2.

69. The wide diffusion of women's magazines is discussed in Lynd and Lynd, *Middletown* [31], p. 239; and in William Lloyd Warner and Paul S. Lunt, *The Social Life of a Modern Community*, Yankee City Series, vol. 1 (New Haven, 1941), chap. 19.

70. This content analysis was undertaken in 1975 by Timothy Patterson, then a graduate student at the State University of New York at Stony Brook; it has not been published.

71. A. Michael McMahon, "An American Courtship: Psychologists and Advertising Theory in the Progressive Era," *American Studies* 13 (1972): 5–18.

72. Wandersee, *Women's Work* [68], chap. 4; Alice Kessler Harris, *Out to Work, A History of Wage Earning Women in the United States* (New York, 1982), chap. 8.

73. Lynd and Lynd, *Middletown* [31], p. 29.

74. Ibid., p. 168.

Chapter 7. Postwar Years

1. This description of the New York City minimum standard budget is from James T. Patterson, *America's Struggle Against Poverty, 1900–1980* (Cambridge, Mass., 1981), p. 86. The same point about the high standard of living that had been achieved by working-class families in the years after the Second World War is made in Lee Rainwater, *What Money Buys: Inequality and the Social Meanings of Income* (New York, 1974), p. 122.

2. Patterson, *Struggle Against Poverty* [1], pp. 79, 160.

3. Unless otherwise indicated, the data presented in this paragraph and the next is derived from: *16th Decennial Census, Housing, 1940*, vol. II: "General Characteristics," part I: "United States Summary" (Washington, D.C., 1943); *17 Decennial Census, Housing, 1950*, vol. I: "General Characteristics," part I: "United States Summary" (Washington, D.C., 1953); various volumes of *Statistical Abstracts of the United States*; and *Provisional Estimates of Social, Economic and Housing Characteristics, 1980 Census*, Supplementary Report (Washington, D.C. 1982).

4. "Prices, and Cost and Standards of Living," *Monthly Labor Review* 61 (December 1945): 1220–21. The decennial census did not begin reporting on ownership of household appliances other than refrigerators until 1970; hence, data for decades prior to that is often difficult to find, except as estimates based on production figures. These data, from 1941, are based on samples that were part of the Survey of Spending and Saving in Wartime, conducted by the Bureau of Human Nutrition and Home Economics, U.S. Department of Agriculture.

5. Quoted in Mirra Komarovsky, *Women in the Modern World* (New York, 1953), pp. 108–9.

6. Lee Rainwater, Richard P. Coleman, and Gerald Handel, *Workingman's Wife: Her Personality, World and Life Style* (New York, 1959), p. 27.

7. For detailed evidence on this point, see Joann Vanek, "Household Technology and Social Status: Rising Living Standards and Status and Residence Differences in Housework," *Technology and Culture* 19 (July 1978):361–75.

8. John P. Robinson, *How Americans Use Time: A Social-Psychological Analysis of Everyday Behavior* (New York, 1977), pp. 61–78. I have used Robinson's data here because the analysis is particularly useful and because the sample was particularly large and particularly well selected. Robinson's results are consistent with all time studies of housework that have been performed since the end of the Second World War.

9. John B. Leeds, *The Household Budget: With a Special Inquiry into the Amount and Value of Household Work* (Ph.D. dissertation, Columbia University, 1917, printed privately); "Time Costs of Homemaking, A Study of 1500 Rural and Urban Households," United States Department of Agriculture, Agricultural Research Administration, Bureau of Human Nutrition and Home Economics (mimeograph, 1944).

10. On men's roles in housework, see William R. Beer, *Househusbands: Men and Housework in American Families* (New York, 1983); Martha S. Hill and Thomas Juster, "Constraints and Complementarities in Time Use," Institute for Social Research Working Paper Series, Survey Research Center, Ann Arbor, Michigan, 1980; Kathryn Walker, "Time Spent by Husbands in Household Work," *Family Economics Review*, June 1970, pp. 8–11; and Richard Berk and Sarah Fenstermaker Berk, *Labor and Leisure at Home: Content and Organization of the Household Day* (Beverley Hills, Calif., 1979).

11. The specific figures cited in these sentences are from Robinson, *How Americans Use Time* [8], and are consistent with the findings of other studies cited in notes 8 and 10.

12. On this point, see Charles A. Thrall, "The Conservative Use of Modern Household Technology," *Technology and Culture*, 22 (1981):303–26. as well as Hill and Juster, "Constraints and Complementarities" [10], and Berk and Berk, *Labor and Leisure* [10], chaps. 3 and 8.

13. Thrall, "Conservative Use" [12], p. 215.

14. *Statistical Abstracts of the United States, 1981* (Washington, D.C., 1981), pp. 140, 388.

15. For samples of this literature, see Ferdinand Lundberg and Marynia F. Farnham, *Modern Woman: The Lost Sex* (New York, 1947); Agnes Meyer, "Woman Aren't Men," *Atlantic Monthly* 186 (August 1950):53–36; Lynn White, *Educating Our Daughters* (New York, 1950); and Evelyn Ellis, "Social Psychological Correlates of Upward Social Mobility among Unmarried Career Women," *American Sociological Review* 17 (October 1952):19–30. For contemporary critiques of this literature, see Mortimer Hunt, *Her Infinite Variety* (New York, 1962); and, of course, a year later, Betty Friedan, *The Feminine Mystique* (New York, 1963).

16. Betty Friedan, *The Feminine Mystique*, [1963] 10th anniversary ed. (New York, 1974), p. 53.

17. An example is Hearst Magazines, *The Influence of Women on Buying* (New York, 1954).

18. The classic work in this genre is W. F. Ogburn and M. F. Nimkoff, *Technology and the Changing Family* (New York, 1954); the summary in this paragraph is paraphrased from chapter 3 of this book.

19. The phrase comes from Hunt, *Her Infinite Variety* [15], chap. 7, sec. 2.

20. Friedan, *Feminine Mystique* [16], p. 236.

21. Kurt Vonnegut, *Player Piano* (New York, 1952), p. 98.

22. Mirra Komarovsky has reported on these differing reactions of working-class and middle-class men to their wives' employment, in *Blue Collar Marriage* (New York, 1962), chap. 3, and *Women in the Modern World* [5], chap. 4.

23. Two investigator who failed to find conclusive evidence for this relationship are: Valerie Kincaid Oppenheimer, *The Female Labor Force in the United States,* Population Monograph Series, no. 5 (Berkeley, 1970), pp. 9–15; and Clarence D. Long, *The Labor Force under Changing Income and Employment* (Princeton, 1958), pp. 120–23.

24. On the inverse relationship between husband's income and wife's employment, see Juanita Kreps, *Sex in the Marketplace: American Women at Work* (Baltimore, 1971), pp. 19–24. On economic goals of married women's employment, Myra H. Strober, "Wives' Labor Force Behavior and Family Consumption Patterns," *American Economic Review* 67 (February 1977): 410–17; and Lois W. Hoffman, "Why They Work," in F. I. Nye and Lois W. Hoffman, eds., *The Employed Mother in America* (Chicago, 1963), pp. 18–40.

25. John T. Robinson, Philip Converse, and Alexander Szalai, "Everyday Life in Twelve Countries," in Alexander Szalai et al., *The Use of Time: Daily Activities of Urban and Suburban Populations in Twelve Countries* (The Hague, 1972), p. 144.

Index

Index

Index

Index

Index

This new edition of
*More Work for Mother: The Ironies of Household
Technology from the Open Hearth to the Microwave*
was finished in 1989.

The new material was commissioned and edited by Robert M. Young
and produced by Martin Klopstock and Selina O'Grady
for Free Association Books.

It was printed on a Miller TP41
on to 80 g/m^2 vol. 17.5 Bookwove.